W9-CKM-582

Interpersonal Psychotherapy
for Depressed Adolescents

Interpersonal Psychotherapy for Depressed Adolescents

LAURA MUFSON, Ph.D.
DONNA MOREAU, M.D.
MYRNA M. WEISSMAN, Ph.D.
GERALD L. KLERMAN, M.D.

Foreword by David Shaffer, M.D.

THE GUILFORD PRESS
New York   London

© 1993 The Guilford Press
A Division of Guilford Publications, Inc.
72 Spring Street, New York, NY 10012

All rights reserved

No part of this book may be reproduced, stored in a retrieval system, or transmitted, in any form or by any means, electronic, mechanical, photocopying, microfilming, recording, or otherwise, without written permission from the Publisher.

Printed in the United States of America

This book is printed on acid-free paper.

Last digit is print number: 9 8 7 6 5 4 3 2 1

Portions of this book have appeared in "Interpersonal Psychotherapy for Adolescent Depression: Description of Modification and Preliminary Application" by D. Moreau, L. Mufson, M. M. Weissman, and G. L. Klerman (1991), *Journal of the American Academy of Child and Adolescent Psychiatry, 30,* 642–651; *Interpersonal Psychotherapy of Depression* by G. L. Klerman, M. M. Weissman, B. J. Rounsaville, and E. S. Chevron (1984), New York: Basic Books; and "Interpersonal Psychotherapy: Efficacy and Adaptations" by G. L. Klerman and M. M. Weissman (1992), in E. S. Paykel (Ed.), *Handbook of Affective Disorders* (2nd ed., pp. 501–510), New York: Guilford Press. Permission to include these portions has been obtained.

Library of Congress Cataloging in Publication Data

Interpersonal psychotherapy for depressed adolescents / Laura Mufson
    . . . [et al.]; foreword by David Shaffer.
        p.   cm.
    Includes bibliographical references and index.
    ISBN 0-89862-686-2
    1. Depression in adolescence—Treatment.   2. Adolescent
psychotherapy.   I. Mufson, Laura.
    [DNLM: 1. Psychotherapy—in adolescence.   2. Psychotherapy—
methods.   3. Depression—therapy.   4. Depression—in adolescence.
5. Interpersonal Relations.   WM 171 I618 1993]
RJ506.D4I58   1993
616.85'27'00835—dc20
DNLM/DLC
for Library of Congress   93-1429
                                                                            CIP

To Gerald L. Klerman, M.D.
Clinician, scientist, mentor, and friend

Foreword

It was the late Gerald Klerman's genius to recognize that much of the morbidity of depressive illness follows from its effect on relationships. Clinicians who see adolescent patients and their families will be very familiar with this. We all know depressed teenagers who take offense easily, imagine slights when none are intended, and snap unpredictably at what, to others, seem quite neutral comments. These teenagers' friends and family are, more often than not, puzzled, offended, and angry. They keep their distance and may even resort to ill-conceived remedies such as "tough love," unwittingly perpetuating a vicious cycle of interpersonal friction and distance. The negative symptoms of depression—social withdrawal, lethargy, and apathy—also impact on relationships. Parents come to see us complaining, "How is he going to manage for himself when he leaves home?" "She just doesn't seem to care"; "Why should we look after him when he doesn't do anything to help himself?" These complaints are not only directed to us but, more often than not, are voiced to the depressed teenager: "Stop hanging around all the time"; "Be like other kids—get out and meet some people"; "You'll never get on if you won't mix with other people!" The depressed adolescent, unable to voice his or her feelings, may only be further demoralized.

For adolescents, such relationship difficulties may be of greater moment than the emotional pain of depressed mood. The withdrawal of family and peer support and the difficulty they experience in expressing themselves and in making and sustaining new friendships are occurring at a time when most adolescents are broadening their social network and negotiating with their family to change rules and expectations. To add to these problems, teenagers' newfound capacity for introspection may result in their viewing social failure not as a feature of transient "illness," but as an immutable part of their personality, contributing to feelings of hopelessness and despair that, especially in the young, so often lead to suicidal behavior.

Klerman and his colleagues recognized the need to develop specific treatments for relationship difficulties experienced by depressed patients. Evidence was forthcoming that otherwise useful treatment did not necessarily improve associated relationship difficulties. Interpersonal psychotherapy (IPT) was developed to address this problem. The goal of IPT is to educate patients about their illness and its consequences for relationships; elicit and clarify the patients' own relationship difficulties; and, over the course of a relatively small number of sessions, help patients to develop and practice new communication skills and improve their ability to deal with interpersonal problems. Although it bears some similarity to cognitive–behavioral therapy—both are time-limited, structured, and highly specific in their goals—they are also very different. Cognitive–behavioral therapy is designed to address distortions of the thoughts, or "self-statements," that precede behavior, while IPT focuses on the style and effectiveness of interpersonal relationships. Of course, both are very different from psychodynamic psychotherapy, which is not time-limited and has much broader goals of personality change through the interpretation of subconscious conflicts.

The success and appeal of IPT have led to many adaptations of Gerald Klerman and Myrna Weissman's original model. Techniques have now been described for such conditions as the eating disorders, substance abuse, and even human immunodeficiency virus (HIV) infection. However, until the appearance of this book, no version of IPT has been available for use among adolescents. The need for this book is great: there has almost certainly been a large increase in the number of depressed adolescents who are being diagnosed, and the management of depression is a leading component of almost all adolescent mental illness practice. Furthermore, it seems that while psychopharmacologic treatment may—and this still remains an open question—result in mood improvement among depressed children and adolescents, it does little to affect impaired relationships with family and peers (Puig-Antich et al., 1985b).

Laura Mufson and her colleagues worked closely with Dr. Klerman before his tragic death to adapt this powerful treatment for adolescents. The result is IPT-A, the first form of IPT specifically designed for adolescents, now undergoing systematic study.

This volume is more than a simple "how to do it" book, although it does that with great clarity. It is comprehensive and therefore likely to be useful to professionals with very different levels of training and experience. The first sections summarize much of what we know about adolescent depression and its treatment. They include succinct and informative descriptions of other treatments and clear and complete summaries of the treatment evaluation literature. Indeed, the book is an excellent source of information on treatment efficacy research. The reader is then led systematically through a description of IPT-A and how it should be applied during the different stages of treatment. It is replete with examples that will ring true to clinicians. While reading these chapters, I found myself repeatedly saying, "I wish I had done that with. . . ." The book concludes with practical advice on how to handle some common problems that arise during the course of therapy.

In sum, this volume addresses both scholarly and practical issues related to a very promising treatment of a common disorder. I strongly recommend it to all clinicians who treat adolescents with depression.

DAVID SHAFFER, M.D.

Preface

This book is a description of the modifications of interpersonal psychotherapy (IPT) to make it a suitable treatment for the nonpsychotic depressed adolescent outpatient (IPT-A). IPT-A has been developed for the treatment of the nonpsychotic, nonsuicidal, depressed adolescent outpatient who is not engaging in daily drug abuse or antisocial activities of a violent nature. IPT-A is not designed to handle adolescents in crisis. An open trial study of IPT-A for the treatment of adolescents with a wide spectrum of affective disorders (major depression, dysthymic disorder, adjustment disorder with depressed mood, depressive disorder not otherwise specified) has been completed, and a controlled clinical trial for the treatment of adolescents with a major depression is currently underway. IPT-A is 12-week (brief) psychotherapy with weekly face-to-face sessions interspersed with telephone contacts. Treatment involves the depressed adolescent as well as the parents. The four problem areas initially developed in IPT for adults are applied to adolescents and include grief, interpersonal role disputes, role transitions, and interpersonal deficits. In addition, a fifth problem area for adolescents has been added, the single-parent family.

Part I of this book provides a comprehensive overview of adolescent depression, including epidemiology, diagnosis, assessment, clinical course, family history, psychotherapy, and psychopharmacology. The rationale for the adaptation of IPT to treat adolescent depression is presented in this section. Part II of this book is written for the clinician who is trained to conduct psychotherapy for adolescent disorders and is familiar with IPT as it was initially developed for adults. It is designed to follow a step-by-step description of IPT-A as it is conducted by an experienced clinician. Part III of the book addresses some of the special issues that arise when one is working with adolescents. The book chapters are organized as follows: an overview of adolescent depression, the application of interpersonal psychotherapy to the treatment of adolescent depression, and special issues in the treatment of adolescents. All chapters are illustrated with case vignettes and therapist scripts to illuminate the techniques of IPT for depressed adolescents (IPT-A).

While there is a pharmaceutical industry and support from the federal government for the development of new drugs, no such industry exists for the development of or even adaptation of new psychotherapies. When a new product is being developed, time is required to try out different approaches, different doses, usage with different populations, and timing of administration until the right product is achieved. It is a series of steps that may often include backward as well as forward movement in the progression toward the final product. The steps necessary to develop psychotherapies, such as working in a rich clinical setting and collaborating with other clinicians, rarely fit the model of the standard scientific protocol as currently conceived and typically supported. Therefore, the modification of IPT needed commitment as well as a patching together of funding.

We are especially grateful to the NARSAD Foundation and the commitment and vision of Connie Lieber for providing funds for new investigators and for projects that at first seemed risky. This work would not have been accomplished, certainly not in this time period, without the funding of a NARSAD Young Investigator Award to Laura Mufson, Ph.D. We are also grateful to the John D. and Catherine T. MacArthur Foundation and the leadership of David Kupfer, M.D., in the Psychobiology of Depression Network. Dr. Kupfer provided us bridge funds for small projects as they related to the development of IPT-A. The Anne Pollock Lederer Award to Myrna M. Weissman, Ph.D., for research relevant to depression in young adults came at just the right time to help us accelerate the development of the pilot open trial. All of this work now has the official sanction of the National Institute of Mental Health. Laura Mufson, Ph.D., received an NIMH FIRST award #1 R29 MH48715-01A1 to conduct the first controlled clinical trial of this new treatment. In addition, we thank NIMH #P50 MH43878-03 Center to Study Youth Depression, Anxiety, and Suicide for help in carrying out the open clinical trial. We are enormously grateful to this patchwork of supporters who have helped us get to this point in approximately 3 years.

We would also like to thank Dr. David Shaffer for his helpful comments on an earlier draft. Numerous others who assisted in the production of this book include Kathleen Pike, Ph.D., Janet Fairbanks, M.D., Chantal Follette, Anna Samoilov, and M. Therese Walsh, M.A. Of course, this book would not have been possible without the adolescents themselves who agreed to participate in this work in progress.

Laura Mufson thanks her family for stimulating her intellectual curiosity and for always encouraging her to seek out new and challenging experiences. She especially thanks Dan Mufson for his editorial acumen and her husband, Bennett Leifer, for his constant support, encouragement, and guidance throughout her career.

Donna Moreau would like to thank the writers Ascher/Straus for the privilege of being able to draw on a private bank of intelligence and wisdom that made it possible for her to navigate to the point of doing this work.

Most important, we would like to acknowledge the work of the late Gerald L. Klerman, M.D. Dr. Klerman was the originator of IPT and was enthusiastically involved in the modification of IPT for adolescents, the training of the first therapists, and the planning of the first trials.

His interest derived from two sources: first, a conviction that all treatments, including psychotherapy, should have a strong empirical base and that the first step in obtaining this base was the documentation of the treatment to be tested; and second, an observation made by him in the 1970s that increasingly younger-aged people were developing depression. He tested this observation formally in the 1980s in the NIMH Collaborative Study on the Psychobiology of Depression, a study he directed. The results were presented in a paper entitled "Birth-Cohort Trends in Rates of Major Depressive Disorder among Relatives of Patients with Affective Disorder" (Klerman et al., 1985). Given the developing data on the value of IPT in the treatment of depression, the large number of adolescents reporting depression, and the absence of data on other treatments from controlled clinical trials, the modification of IPT for depressed adolescents seemed a natural.

Although his illness sometimes delayed a meeting or sapped his energy, he scarcely missed a beat in pushing this project ahead and in inspiring our interest. He was intrigued and perplexed by the increasing rates of depression among the young and was convinced of the need for better treatments. Sitting on his desk was a manuscript outline drafted a few weeks before he died, entitled "Our Current Age of Youthful Melancholia."

Dr. Klerman's interest and energy in developing effective treatments and his high standards for clinical and research practice provided the backbone of our work. We are sorry he is not here to share with us the pleasure and enthusiasm we have in publishing this book, as we know he would. We hope that many depressed adolescents will benefit from this work, and it is our pleasure to carry on Dr. Klerman's work in the study of interpersonal psychotherapy for depressed adolescents.

LAURA MUFSON
DONNA MOREAU
MYRNA M. WEISSMAN (KLERMAN)

Contents

III
SPECIAL ISSUES IN
TREATING ADOLESCENTS

*Interpersonal Psychotherapy
for Depressed Adolescents*

· I ·

Overview

· 1 ·

The Origins and Development of Interpersonal Psychotherapy for Depression

Interpersonal psychotherapy (IPT) is a brief, time-limited psychotherapy that was initially developed in the late 1960s for the treatment of nonbipolar, nonpsychotic, depressed adult outpatients. The treatment is based on the premise that no matter what constitutes the underlying cause of depression, the depression is inextricably intertwined with the patient's interpersonal relationships. IPT's goals are (1) to decrease depressive symptomatology and (2) to improve interpersonal functioning by enhancing communication skills in significant relationships. IPT is a unique departure from other types of psychotherapeutic interventions because its focus is on current interpersonal conflicts, and it is one of the first therapeutic modalities to be operationalized in a treatment manual. IPT for depressed adolescents (IPT-A) is an innovative adaptation of a psychotherapeutic treatment that already has been shown to be effective in clinical trials. IPT can be administered after appropriate training by experienced psychiatrists, psychologists, and social workers. It can be used alone or with medication. This chapter describes the development, concepts, and evidence for efficacy of IPT in addition to the recent adaptations of IPT for other populations. By reviewing its history and development, the reader will gain a greater understanding of the conceptual framework that serves as the foundation for this adaptation.

3

BACKGROUND

Theoretical and Empirical Sources

IPT makes no assumptions about the etiology of depression. That is left for scientific investigation to fully identify and verify. However, IPT does assume that the development of clinical depression occurs in a social and interpersonal context and that the onset, response to treatment, and outcomes are influenced by the interpersonal relations between the depressed patient and significant others. This assumption is supported by the writings of Adolf Meyer and Harry Stack Sullivan as well as by more recent empirical investigation.

The ideas of Adolf Meyer, whose psychobiological approach to understanding psychiatric disorders places great emphasis on the patient's relationship to his or her environment (Meyer, 1957), form the theoretical base for IPT. Meyer viewed psychiatric disorders as an expression of the patient's attempt to adapt to his or her environment. An individual's response to environmental change is determined by prior experiences, particularly early experiences in the family and the individual's affiliation with various social groups. Harry Stack Sullivan, a colleague of Meyer's, wrote extensively about his own theories on interpersonal relationships and linked clinical psychiatry to the emerging social sciences (Sullivan, 1953).

The empirical basis for IPT includes studies associating stress and life events with the onset and clinical course of depression. Longitudinal studies demonstrating the social impairment of depressed women during the acute phase of their depressive episode as well as during their recovery highlighted the need for a treatment intervention that would directly address the persistent social problems of depressed adults. Studies by Brown and Harris (1978) that demonstrate the roles of intimacy and social supports as protection against depression in the face of adverse life stress supported the perceived importance of good social relations for emotional well-being. Specifically, studies by Pearlin and Lieberman (1979) show the impact of chronic social and interpersonal stress, particularly marital stress, on the onset of depression. Similarly, epidemiological data show a strong association between marital disputes and major depression (Weissman, 1987). The works of Bowlby (1969) and Henderson et al. (1978) emphasize the importance of attachment bonds and how the loss of social attachments can be associated with the onset of depression, a notion that is integral to the goals of IPT.

IPT has evolved over nearly 25 years of treatment and research experience with ambulatory depressed patients. The development of this modality began in 1968 as part of a clinical trial for depressed out-patients that intended to test approaches for preventing relapse follow-ing reduction of acute symptoms of depression with pharmacotherapy. By the mid-1960s, it was clear that the new antidepressants were effec-tive in reducing acute depressive symptoms. Sleep, appetite, and mood usually improved in 2 to 4 weeks. However, the relapse rate was high, and it was unclear both how long the medication regimen should con-tinue and whether there was any advantage to adding psychotherapy. The intent of standardizing the psychotherapy in a manual for the first clinical trial was to ensure a consistent approach among therapists. Our intent, however, was not to develop a new psychotherapy but, rather, to describe what we believed was reasonable and current practice with depressed patients.

Clinical Depression as Conceptualized in IPT

Clinical depression, within the IPT framework, is conceptualized as having three component processes. They are:

1. *Symptom formation,* involving the development of the depressive affect, signs, and symptoms, that may derive from psychobiolog-ical and/or psychodynamic mechanisms.
2. *Social functioning,* involving social interactions with other per-sons, that derives from learning based on childhood experiences, concurrent social reinforcement, and/or current personal efforts at mastery and competence as a result of the depression.
3. *Personality,* involving more enduring traits and behaviors—the handling of anger and guilt and overall self-esteem—that con-stitute the person's unique reactions and patterns of functioning and that may contribute to a predisposition to symptom develop-ment.

IPT, as it was originally developed, intervenes in the first two processes. Because of the brevity of the treatment, the low level of psychothera-peutic intensity, and its focus on the current depressive episode, IPT does not purport to have an impact on the enduring aspects of person-ality.

In fact, in IPT there is the intentional avoidance, during the treatment of the acute symptomatic episode, of issues related to person-ality functioning and character pathology. Our clinical experience sug-gests that more than minimum attention to issues of personality and character, especially in the symptomatic phase, will result in delay of recovery and prolongation of the depressive episode. Moreover, many behaviors during the acute illness that appear to be personality traits (such as dependency or irritability) resolve with the alleviation of symptoms.

We define IPT at three levels: strategies for approaching specific tasks, techniques used to accomplish these tasks, and therapeutic stance. IPT resembles other therapies in techniques and stance but not in strategies as they are applied to specific tasks. The therapeutic strategies of IPT are designed to help the patient master the interpersonal context of the depression. Strategies include education, clarification of feelings and expectations, development of communication skills, and role playing.

The strategies of IPT are applied to the three phases of treatment. During the first phase, the depression is diagnosed within a medical model and explained to the patient. The major problem associated with the onset of the depression is identified and an explicit treatment contract to work on this problem area is made with the patient. The topical content of the sessions is, therefore, not open-ended. When this phase is completed, the intermediate phase begins. It is here that work on the major, current, interpersonal problem areas is undertaken. Treating the depressed patient's problems in interpersonal relations proceeds by exploring the four problem areas commonly associated with the onset of depression—grief, role disputes, role transition, or interpersonal deficit. The middle phase of IPT focuses on the individual patient's particular interpersonal problem area as it relates to the onset of depression. During the termination phase, feelings about termination are discussed, progress is reviewed, and the remaining work is outlined. As in other brief treatments, the arrangements for termination are explicit, and one must adhere to them. To further understand the IPT structure, including techniques and stance as developed for adult depression, readers are referred to the book *Interpersonal Psychotherapy for Depression* (Klerman et al., 1984) for details.

IPT facilitates recovery from acute depression by relieving depressive symptoms and by helping the patient become more effective in dealing with current interpersonal problems that are associated with the onset of symptoms. Symptom relief begins with helping the patient understand that the vague and uncomfortable symptoms are part of a known syndrome, which responds to various treatments and has a good prognosis. Psychotropic drugs may be used in conjunction with IPT to alleviate symptoms more rapidly. The decision about medication is made primarily on the basis of symptom severity and not on the presence or absence of psychosocial explanations for the symptoms.

IPT COMPARED WITH OTHER PSYCHOTHERAPIES

Most therapies emphasize helping the patient to develop a sense of mastery and reduce social isolation. They may differ, however, in duration of treatment and as to whether the patient's problem is defined as lying in the distant past, the immediate past, or the present. IPT differs from other psychotherapies in its specified brief duration and its explicit attention to the current illness and related interpersonal context.

IPT deals with current, not past, interpersonal relationships, focusing on the patient's immediate social context just before and following the onset of the current depressive episode. Past depressive episodes, early family relationships, previous significant relationships, and friendship patterns are assessed in order to understand overall patterns in the patient's interpersonal relations. The psychotherapist does not frame the patient's current situation as a manifestation of internal conflict or as a recurrence of prior intrafamilial maladaptive patterns; rather, he or she explores the patient's current disorder in terms of interpersonal relations.

IPT and Psychodynamic Psychotherapy

Psychoanalytic theory, with it emphasis on the role of unconscious mental processes and the repetition of early traumatic childhood experiences, gave rise to psychodynamic psychotherapy, a common and general approach to psychotherapy. Symptoms and difficulties in social functioning are seen as derivatives of deeper, more fundamental unresolved conflicts and character problems. Adult difficulties are seen as the recapitulation of unresolved issues in childhood, and the reconstruction of intrafamilial interpersonal relationships during childhood and adolescence is undertaken. Psychodynamic psychotherapy has modified many of the therapeutic techniques of classical psychoanalysis for application to a variety of clinical conditions and personality difficulties. In psychodynamic psychotherapy, resolving the transference, which the patient develops in relation to the therapist, becomes the work of the psychotherapeutic process. Efforts are made to uncover unconscious mental processes—wishes, fantasies, defenses—through use of free-association techniques, dream analysis, exploration of fantasies, and defense analysis. According to the psychodynamic view, excess dependency characterizes the interpersonal relations of the depressed individual and has its origin in childhood. Depression is not regarded as a primary affect but, rather, as a derivative of hostility. Hostility and instinctual aggression are transformed by the activities of the superego and experienced as depression, guilt, and self-reproach. Psychodynamically oriented psychotherapy for depression aims to uncover these unconscious conflicts and to modify the rage and hostility so as to free the ego for more independent, autonomous functioning. This may require long periods of intensive therapy.

In contrast, the interpersonal approach to psychotherapy regards depressive affect as a normal state, a biologically based emotional response to the loss of an attachment bonding. This response is common to all mammals, primates, and humans, and has significant evolutionary value in the development of the species, particularly given the immature state with which the human infant is born and the need for a prolonged period of protection, nurturance, and succor. Thus, dependency upon the mothering parental figure is a normal aspect of childhood and infant development, and autonomy and independence emerge only gradually. Difficulties that arise in the struggle to achieve autonomy can result in a characteristic pattern of response that we identify as sadness or depression. IPT seeks resolution of the interpersonal difficulties that arise during this process and rapid reduction of the concomitant depressive symptoms through the acquisition of interpersonal skills and the promotion of social adjustment.

IPT and Cognitive–Behavioral Therapy

IPT and cognitive–behavioral therapy (CBT) share several external features. Both have been developed specifically for depression and are time-limited therapies. Both have manuals specifying the procedures and have undergone testing in a number of controlled, clinical trials. CBT is widely used for a variety of disorders and has a training program that facilitates clinical trials.

Beyond these features, the similarities between the two therapeutic modalities end. IPT and CBT differ both in theory and in procedure. CBT derives from the phenomenological school of psychology that assumes that the individual's view of self determines behavior. The depressed person has a triad of negative feelings about the self, the past, and the future. CBT for depression correspondingly assumes that the affective response in depression is determined by the way an individual structures his or her experience ideationally (Beck, 1976). As a result of an emergence of certain maladaptive cognitive themes, the depressed patient tends to regard him- or herself and the future in a negative way. Correction of negative concepts is expected to alleviate the depressive symptoms. For example, an extremely low self-concept can be treated by presenting a hierarchy of cognitive tasks and, through these tasks, demonstrating the invalidity of the patient's self-reproaches.

The CBT therapist clarifies how the patient views things, the bases for these views, their accuracies and consequences, and thereby challenges the negative self-image directly. The empirical testing of the cognitions is encouraged by the cognitive therapist through homework assignment, graded tasks, and clarifying assumptions. In contrast, IPT does not engage the patient in graded tasks or homework. Rather, it deals with the patient's negative self-images by attempting to understand their interpersonal context, improving interpersonal skills to result in more positive social interactions, or by viewing these negative self-images as part of the symptom picture, which will be alleviated as the interpersonal problems are resolved.

EFFICACY OF IPT FOR DEPRESSION

To standardize the treatment so that clinical trials could be undertaken, the concepts, techniques, and methods of IPT were specified and operationally described in a manual which has undergone a number of revisions and was published as a volume (Klerman et al., 1984). In addition, a training program for experienced psychotherapists of different disciplines providing the treatment for these clinical trials was developed (Weissman et al., 1982).

IPT has been evaluated in a number of studies for depression both as an acute and as a maintenance treatment. These controlled clinical trials provide the foundation for clinical practice utilizing IPT and for efforts to modify IPT for application to other clinical conditions. IPT has been tested alone and in comparison and in combination with tricyclics in six clinical trials with depressed patients, three of acute treatment (Elkin et al., 1989; Sloane et al., 1985; Weissman et al., 1979) and three of maintenance treatment (Klerman et al., 1974; Frank et al., 1990b; Reynolds & Imber, 1988; Weissman et al., 1974). Five completed studies have included a drug comparison group (Elkin et al., 1989; Klerman et al., 1974; Frank et al., 1990b; Reynolds & Imber, 1988; Sloane et al., 1985; Weissman et al., 1979), and four have included a combination of IPT and drugs (Klerman et al., 1974; Reynolds & Imber, 1988; Weissman et al., 1979; Kupfer et al., 1989).

Acute Treatment Studies

There have been two controlled trials of the use of IPT in the treatment of acute depressive episodes in adults. These are the New Haven–Boston Acute Treatment Study and the National Institute of Mental Health (NIMH) Collaborative Study.

New Haven–Boston Acute Treatment Study

The first study of IPT for the treatment of acute depression was initiated in 1973. It was a 16-week treatment study of 81 ambulatory depressed patients, both men and women, using IPT and amitriptyline each alone and in combination against a nonscheduled psychotherapy treatment (DiMascio et al., 1979; Weissman et al., 1979). IPT was administered weekly by experienced psychiatrists. This study demonstrated that both active treatments, IPT and the tricyclic, were more effective than the control treatment and that combined treatment was superior to either treatment.

In addition, a 1-year follow-up study provided evidence that the therapeutic benefit of IPT was sustained for many patients. Patients who had received IPT either alone or in combination with drugs were functioning better than patients who had received either drugs alone or the control treatment (Weissman et al., 1981). At the 1-year follow-up, there was no effect on symptom relapse or recurrence. A fraction of patients in all treatments relapsed, and additional treatment was required.

NIMH Collaborative Study

For ambulatory depressed patients, a multicenter, controlled, clinical trial of drugs and two psychotherapies—CBT and IPT—in the treatment of acute ambulatory depression was initiated by the NIMH (Elkin et al., 1989). Two hundred fifty outpatients were randomly assigned to four treatment conditions for 16 weeks: CBT, IPT, imipramine, and a placebo–clinical management combination. Extensive efforts were made in the selection and training of the psychotherapists. Of the 250 patients who entered treatment, 68% completed at least 15 weeks and 12 sessions of treatment. Overall, the findings showed that all active treatments were superior to placebo in the reduction of symptoms over a 16-week period. Other findings summarized were: The overall degree of improvement for all patients, regardless of treatment, was highly significant clinically; over half of the patients were symptom-free at the end of treatment.

More patients in the placebo–clinical management condition dropped out or were withdrawn, twice as many as for IPT, which had the lowest attrition rate. At the end of 12 weeks of treatment, the two psychotherapies and imipramine were equivalent in the reduction of depressive symptoms on many measures. Imipramine had a more rapid initial onset of action and more consistent differences from placebo than either of the two psychotherapies.

Although many of the patients who were less severely depressed at intake improved with all treatment conditions, including the placebo group, more severely depressed patients in the placebo group did poorly. For the less severely depressed group, there were no differences among the treatments. Forty-four percent of the sample were moderately depressed at intake. For the more severe group (Hamilton Rating Scale for Depression [HRSD] score of 20 or more at intake), patients in the IPT and the imipramine groups had better outcome scores than placebo group on the HRSD. Of the psychotherapies, only IPT was significantly superior to placebo for the severely depressed group; indeed for the severely depressed patients, IPT did as well as imipramine on some outcome measures. The statistical approach used in these analyses was controversial and reanalysis has been undertaken. Thus, more information on this study is still forthcoming.

IPT as Maintenance Treatment for Depression

With increased knowledge of the natural history and clinical course of depression, it became apparent that many patients had recurrences and relapses, and they required long-term treatment. There have been two randomized controlled trials evaluating the role of IPT as maintenance treatment. These are the New Haven–Boston Maintenance Treatment Study and the Pittsburgh Studies.

New Haven–Boston Maintenance Treatment Study

The first systematic study of IPT, begun in 1968, was of maintenance treatment (Klerman et al., 1974; Paykel et al., 1976) and by today's standards, it would be considered a continuation study. This first study of IPT was designed to determine how long treatment with tricyclic antidepressants should continue and what role, if any, psychotherapy had in maintenance treatment.

One hundred fifty acutely depressed outpatients who had responded to amitriptyline with symptom reduction were studied. Each patient had received 8 months of maintenance treatment with drugs alone, psychotherapy (IPT) alone, or a combination of both. The major findings were that maintenance drug treatment prevented relapse (Klerman et al., 1974) and the effect of IPT was on enhancing social functioning (Weissman et al., 1974). Moreover, the effects of psychotherapy were not apparent for 6 to 8 months. Because of the differential effects of the treatments, the combination of drugs and psychotherapy was found the most efficacious (Paykel et al., 1976; Klerman et al., 1974), and no negative interactions between drugs and psychotherapy were found.

Pittsburgh Study of Maintenance Treatment of Recurrent Depression

In the early 1980s, the University of Pittsburgh group designed and initiated a long-term clinical trial to determine the efficacy of drugs (imipramine) and/or IPT in the prevention of relapse for severe, recurrent depression (Frank et al., 1990b). The impetus for this study was the finding that there were a large number of patients with multiple recurrent episodes who were difficult to treat, had a high relapse rate, and were high utilizers of medical and social services. In this study patients with recurrent depression (at least two previous episodes of major depression) who had responded to imipramine plus interpersonal psychotherapy were randomly assigned to one of five treatments for 3 years of maintenance treatment: IPT alone, IPT and placebo, IPT and imipramine, clinical management and imipramine, clinical management and placebo. Contrary to previous experience, imipramine was administered in the highest doses (over 200 mg), and IPT was administered monthly, in the lowest dose ever used in clinical trials. The major findings were (1) a high rate of recurrence in 1 year for untreated control groups; (2) clinically meaningful and statistically significant prevention of relapse and recurrence by both imipramine and IPT; (3) a nonsignificant trend toward the value of combined treatment over either treatment alone; and (4) the value of high-dose imipramine (over 200 mg/day) in combination with the lowest dose of IPT ever used (monthly). Previously, considerably lower doses had been recommended. This long-term study, along with several others using drugs with and without psychotherapy, clearly established the value of maintenance treatment in the prevention of relapse and recurrence in major depression.

NEW APPLICATIONS OF IPT

Since IPT was developed, several new applications have appeared. IPT has been tested in a conjoint format for depressed patients with marital disputes (Foley et al., 1989); for patients in distress but not clinically depressed (interpersonal counseling; Klerman et al., 1987; Weissman & Klerman, 1988); for long-term maintenance treatment of recurrent depression (Frank et al., 1989, 1990b); for the elderly (Frank et al., 1988; Reynolds & Imber, 1988); for bipolar patients (Frank et al., 1990a); for the depressed medically ill in primary care (Schulberg et al., 1993); for opiate addicts (Rounsaville et al., 1983; Rounsaville & Kleber, 1985); for cocaine abusers (Carroll et al., 1992; Rounsaville et al., 1985); and for bulimia (Fairburn, 1988; Fairburn et al., 1991). IPT has been adapted for HIV-positive patients with depression (Markowitz et al., 1992); for depressed adolescents (Moreau et al., 1991); and for patients with dysthymia (Mason et al., 1993). Trials are under way or being planned for these populations. A modification of IPT for the acute treatment of depressed women with postpartum depression by M. O'Hara of the Department of Psychology at the University of Iowa and a modification of IPT for personality disorder by Laurie A. Gillies, Ph.D., of the Clarke Institute of Psychiatry in Toronto are both currently in early stages of development.

Conjoint IPT for Depressed Patients with Marital Disputes

Although the causal direction is unknown, clinical and epidemiologic studies have shown that marital disputes, separation, and divorce are strongly associated with the onset of depression (Rounsaville et al., 1979, 1980). When psychotherapy is prescribed, it is unclear whether the patient, the couple, or the entire family should be involved. Some evidence suggests that individual psychotherapy for depressed patients involved in marital disputes may promote premature separation or divorce (Gurman & Kniskern, 1978; Locke & Wallace, 1976).

Individual IPT was adapted to concentrate on the treatment of interpersonal marital disputes (IPT-CM). A treatment manual and a training program like those used in IPT were developed for IPT-CM in the initial phase of this study. Only patients who identified marital disputes as the major problem associated with the onset or exacerbation of their major depression were admitted into the pilot study. Eighteen patients were randomly assigned to IPT or IPT-CM and received 16 weekly therapy sessions. In IPT-CM, the spouse was required to participate in all psychotherapy sessions, whereas in IPT, the spouse did not meet with the therapist. At the end of treatment, patients in both groups expressed satisfaction in the reduction of depressive symptoms and social impairment from intake to termination of therapy. There was no significant difference between treatment groups in the degree of improvement in depressive symptoms and social functioning by end point (Foley et al., 1990).

However, Locke–Wallace Marital Adjustment Test scores (Locke & Wallace, 1976) at session 16 were significantly higher (indicative of better marital adjustment) for patients receiving IPT-CM than for patients receiving IPT. Scores on the Spanier Dyadic Adjustment Scale

(Spanier, 1976) also indicated greater improvement in marital function-ing for patients receiving IPT-CM than for patients receiving IPT. At session 16, patients receiving IPT-CM reported significantly higher lev-els in affectional expression (i.e., demonstrations of affection and sexual relations in the marriage) than patients receiving IPT.

These results need to be interpreted with caution, however, be-cause of the pilot nature of the study, the small size of the sample, the lack of a no-treatment control group, and the absence of a pharmaco-therapy or a combined pharmacotherapy–psychotherapy comparison group. If the study were repeated, we would recommend that medication be freely allowed or used as a comparison condition and that there be more effort to reduce the symptoms of depression before proceeding to undertake the marital issue. Perhaps a sequential design would be useful with initial treatment of medication to produce symptom reduction and with the psychotherapy being introduced as symptom reduction was proven effective.

Interpersonal Counseling for Stress and Distress in Primary Care

Previous investigations have documented high frequencies of anxiety, depression, and functional bodily complaints in patients in primary-care medical settings (Brodaty & Andrews, 1983; Goldberg, 1972; Hoeper et al., 1980). Although some of these patients have diagnosable psychiatric disorders, a large percentage have symptoms that do not meet estab-lished criteria for psychiatric disorders. A mental health research pro-gram formed in a large health maintenance organization in the greater Boston area found that "problems of living" and symptoms of anxiety and depression were among the main reasons for individual primary-care visits (Klerman et al., 1987). These clinical problems contributed heavi-ly to high utilization of ambulatory services.

A brief psychosocial intervention, interpersonal counseling (IPC), was modified from IPT to deal with patients' symptoms of distress and was administered by nurse practitioners working in a primary-care set-ting. IPC is comprised of a maximum of six half-hour counseling sessions in the primary-care office, which focus on the patient's current function-ing (Weissman & Klerman, 1988). Particular attention is given to recent changes in life events; sources of stress in the family, home, and workplace, to friendship patterns, and to on-going difficulties in inter-personal relations. IPC assumes that such events provide the inter-personal context in which bodily and emotional symptoms related to anxiety, depression, and distress occur. The treatment manual includes session-by-session instructions as to the purpose and methods for IPC, including "scripts" to ensure comparability of procedures among the nurse counselors.

Patients with scores of 6 or higher on Goldberg GHQ were selected for assignment either to an experimental group that offered IPC or to a comparison group that was followed naturalistically (Klerman et al., 1987). Sixty-four patients were compared with a subgroup of 64 sex-matched untreated subjects with similar elevations in GHQ scores. Compared with a group of untreated subjects with initial elevations in GHQ scores, patients receiving the IPC intervention showed greater reduction in symptom scores over an average interval of 3 months. Many IPC-treated patients reported relief of symptoms after only one or two sessions. This study provided preliminary evidence that early detection and outreach to distressed adults, followed by brief treatment with IPC can, in the short-term, reduce symptoms of distress as measured by the GHQ. The main effect seemed to occur in symptoms related to mood, especially in those forms of mild and moderate depression commonly seen in medical patients. However, IPC did not result in reduction of utilization of health care services. In fact, there was an increase in use of mental health services as patients began to clarify the psychological source of their symptoms. Definitive evaluation of IPC awaits further study. A trial of IPT in primary care for depressed, medically ill patients is now under way by Schulberg at the University of Pittsburgh.

Recurrent Late-Life Depression

The problems of administering medication in the elderly, particularly the anticholinergic effects, have led to an interest in psychotherapy in this age group. Sloane et al. (1985) completed a 6-week pilot trial of IPT compared with nortriptyline and placebo for acute treatment in depressed elderly patients. The Sloane group did not specifically modify their manual for the elderly. A more comprehensive study following the design of Kupfer and Frank's maintenance trial is under way at the University of Pittsburgh for recurrent late-life depression (IPT-LLM) (Reynolds & Imber, 1988). Moreover, IPT has been explicitly modified for this study to deal with the special issues of the elderly patient (Frank et al., 1988) with recurrent depression.

Depressed Patients at Risk for AIDS/HIV-Seropositive

Although considerable psychosocial stress is faced by patients who are seropositive for the human immunodeficiency virus (HIV) and many diverse interventions have been proposed (including CBT, aerobic exercise, relaxation training), clinical trials of psychological treatments are largely absent. Noting that individuals affected with HIV are at considerable risk for depression, investigators have argued that they may be candidates for IPT. Markowitz and colleagues are developing a manual to deal with the special issues of these patients and have completed a pilot open trial with 21 depressed subjects at risk for AIDS by virtue of being HIV-seropositive. The authors note that the discovery of HIV seropositivity is a calamitous life event with significant interpersonal and personal repercussions. The four problem areas identified in IPT for depressed patients, the investigators note, can easily describe the problems faced by HIV patients, and the "here-and-now" framework of IPT can help maintain a hopeful focus in the face of lethal infection. The therapist avoids encouraging depressive ruminations on the past, including self-blame for having contracted HIV. Based on an open trial with 21 HIV patients, all homosexual or bisexual, the investigators have described their experience in treating the patients in terms of the four problem areas of IPT (Markowitz et al., 1992).

Bipolar Patients

IPT has been adapted for use in a clinical trial with bipolar patients (IPT-BP) by Frank and associates (1990a) at the University of Pittsburgh. The goals of both IPT and IPT-BP are the management of both affective symptoms and interpersonal difficulties facing the patient. However, in contrast to IPT, the bipolar adaptation places considerably more emphasis on the management of symptoms. This emphasis persists throughout the maintenance treatment phase that has been planned. IPT-BP addresses somewhat different aspects of role transitions and role disputes and constantly explores the interaction between changes in the interpersonal realm and symptoms. Preventative strategies include exploration of sources of interpersonal distress, frequency and intensity of social interactions, and overstimulation, such as the timing and regularity of sleep, work, and other social rhythms. The goal is to regulate social rhythms in order to keep the patient's social triggers for disruption under control. Other than these modifications, the goals and strategies of IPT, including the four problem areas, have been kept intact. The Frank group currently has underway a maintenance clinical trial for bipolar patients fashioned after their study of persons with recurrent unipolar depression.

Bulimia Nervosa

Fairburn (1988) at Oxford University has adapted IPT for patients with bulimia nervosa. The modifications for bulimia are only for the first phase of treatment. The first four sessions are devoted to analysis of the interpersonal context of the development and maintenance of bulimia (Fairburn, 1988; Fairburn et al., 1991). A clinical trial comparing cognitive and behavioral treatments and IPT in 75 patients over an 18-week period was recently completed. Patients with bulimia in all treatments showed a decrease in the level of general psychopathology, frequency of overeating, and number of bulimic episodes. CBT was more effective in reducing frequency of self-induced vomiting, extreme dieting, and in modifying attitudes toward shape and weight. This study did not have a no-treatment control group because the authors argue that previous studies show that patients with bulimia do not improve on waiting lists. Additionally, the results reported above are based on a sample of completers, which could affect results. Data on a 1-year follow-up are forthcoming. A multicenter clinical trial comparing IPT and CBT for bulimia is being planned.

Methadone-Maintained Opiate Addicts

Based on the observation that methadone maintenance programs with and without loosely defined counseling services have shown a trend for counseling to be associated with better program retention or completion, Rounsaville and colleagues (Rounsaville et al., 1983; Rounsaville & Kleber, 1985) developed a clinical trial to evaluate short-term interpersonal psychotherapy as treatment for psychiatric disorders in opiate addicts who were also participating in a full-service methadone hydrochloride maintenance program. Patients were randomly assigned to treatment and were compared with low-contact monthly treatment. All patients continued in the usual methadone program.

The IPT consisted of a weekly, individual, short-term treatment. The IPT manual for depression with minor modifications was used for the opiate addicts. Seventy-two opiate addicts randomly assigned to one of the two groups participated in the study. However, recruitment was a serious problem, as only 5% of the eligible clients agreed to participate, and only around half of the participants completed the study treatment. The outcome was similar in the two groups. Both obtained significant clinical improvement. Only 38% of the patients completed IPT, and 54% completed the low-contact condition. The authors concluded that weekly IPT added to the usual drug rehabilitation program did not offer any further benefits to opiate addicts. The patients were already receiving relatively intensive treatment, at least one 90-minute group psychotherapy session per week, in addition to daily contacts for urine specimens and meeting with the program counselor as needed. Thus, the once-a-week individual treatment, in which talking was required, seemed to offer very little over and above the already existing intensive treatment. The authors also noted that IPT, which has a short-term focus on one or two limited problems, may be at variance with the framework of a methadone maintenance program, which is seen as comparatively long-term treatment. Most of the clients continued to be involved in the methadone program following termination of psychotherapy.

Cocaine Addicts

Rounsaville et al. (1985) also have revised IPT for application to cocaine abusers. The goals in the adaptation were reduction or cessation of cocaine use and development of more productive strategies for dealing with social and interpersonal problems associated with the onset and perpetuation of cocaine use. The therapist's stance and phases of treatment were not changed in the adaptation. The focus on depressive symptoms changed to a focus on reducing cocaine use.

Forty-two outpatients who met DSM-III criteria for cocaine abuse were randomly assigned to one of two forms of psychotherapy, either relapse prevention RPT (a structured behavioral approach) or IPT for 12 weeks. Overall, there were no significant differences between treatments in continuous weeks of abstinence or recovery. The trend was for greater efficacy of the behavioral approach when patients were stratified by initial severity of substance use. Among the more severe users, patients who received RPT as compared with IPT were significantly more likely to achieve abstinence and to be classified as recovered. The authors concluded that psychotherapy may be effective for many ambulatory cocaine abusers, but that severe abusers may require the greater structure and direction offered by a treatment emphasizing learning and rehearsal of specific strategies to interrupt and control cocaine abuse.

CONCLUSION

The most efficacious trials of IPT are for the depressed outpatient, both as an acute and as a maintenance treatment. The findings for conjoint marital treatment, for patients in primary care in distress, and for persons with bulimia are promising, but the results are still based on small samples, and a multisite collaborative study is being planned. The adaptation and testing of IPT for geriatric patients with recurrent depression, depressed adolescents (to be described in this volume), HIV-seropositive patients, and dysthymics are still under way. The findings on IPT as a treatment for drug abusers, either cocaine or opiate addicts, are largely negative, although further testing in select samples from other sites may be warranted.

Although the positive findings of the clinical trials of IPT in the NIMH Collaborative Study and other studies described are encouraging, there are limitations. All the studies of IPT, including those by our group and by the NIMH, were conducted on depressed outpatients, and it is, therefore, not known whether IPT would be effective on depressed inpatients. Moreover, these results should not be interpreted as implying that all forms of psychotherapy are effective for depression or, alternatively, that only IPT is effective. The development of psychotherapies that are time-limited and of brief duration specifically designed for depression represents a significant advance in psychotherapy research. It is hoped that further research will yield information on which types of therapies are most efficacious for specific depressive disorders and specific patient populations.

In regard to the findings for depression, we conclude that many, but not all, treatments may be effective for depression. The depressed patient's interests are best served by the availability and scientific testing of different psychological as well as pharmacological treatments to be used alone or in combination. Ultimately, clinical testing and experience will determine which is the best treatment for a particular patient.

·2·

Nature of Depression
in Adolescents

This chapter reviews the epidemiology, nature, and course of child and adolescent depression and discusses the psychosocial and interpersonal impairments associated with depression in adolescents. These acute and enduring impairments are the factors that make IPT-A a particularly suitable therapy for depressed adolescents. Although the book's main subject is the adolescent, it is important to review data on both children and adolescents to gain a developmental perspective on adolescent depression. Discussion focuses on the nature and prevalence of depressive symptoms and major depression in the adolescent. The influence of family history, biological factors, and comorbidity is also discussed in regard to the diagnostic complexities and treatment of adolescent depression.

NOT ALL ADOLESCENTS ARE DEPRESSED

Traditional psychoanalytic and psychological theory proposed that all adolescents have periods of depression because they experience conflicts both within themselves and with others as a normal stage of development commonly referred to as "adolescent turmoil." G. Stanley Hall (1904) was the first to give this concept a name—*Sturm und Drang*, or "storm and stress." He believed that normal adolescents experience wide mood swings and variable functioning but that these did not signify psychopathology. Rather, turbulence was part of normal adolescent development, mainly occurring in middle to late adolescence. Similarly, Eissler (1958) described the adolescent as a slave to his impulses and prone to antisocial behavior, anxiety, and depression. The notion of adolescent turmoil as a normal state received wide clinical support (Freud, 1958; Blos, 1961) until recently.

Longitudinal and epidemiologic studies have refuted the view that adolescent turmoil is normative (Offer, 1969; Offer et al., 1982; Rutter et al., 1976a). Offer (1969), in a longitudinal study of adolescents, defined adolescent turmoil as "a significant disruption in the psychic organization of the adolescent that leads to psychological disequilibrium and tumult, resulting in fluctuating and unpredictable behavior." Adolescents have periods of feeling lonely and isolated from peers and experience conflicts with family and teachers, but these periods do not persist for any significant length of time or severely impair functioning.

Conflicting views defining "normal" adolescence are based in large part on the population being studied. As expected, if clinical populations are studied, many disturbed adolescents are seen. Studies of community-based samples of adolescents find significantly less adolescent turmoil present than was previously thought to exist (Offer, 1969). Rutter et al. (1976a) in the Isle of Wight study found that some turmoil is a fact of adolescence but that its association with depression and its future predictive value for psychiatric problems has been overestimated by clinicians. They found that parent–child alienation, evidence of an impaired significant interpersonal relationship that is a model for future relationships, is a more common feature of adolescents showing psychiatric problems, whereas inner turmoil is quite prevalent in all adolescents.

An important research and clinical task is to differentiate between "normal adolescents" and those with psychiatric disturbances in need of attention. The studies of Offer (1969) and Rutter et al. (1976a) suggest that socially withdrawn adolescents with dramatic mood swings, cognitive distortions, and increasing conflicts with parents and peers are not necessarily typical adolescents but, rather, are more likely to be psychiatrically ill. Such disturbances are now recognized as abnormal. Although a majority of adolescents pass through adolescence without prolonged periods of dysfunction, there is a group for whom the age period is difficult to traverse. For many such adolescents, this represents the early manifestations of a psychiatric illness.

There are many psychiatric disorders that commonly present in adolescence. An affective disorder is one of the more frequent psychiatric disorders encountered in adolescence and is accompanied by significant psychosocial impairment, particularly in interpersonal relationships. It is, therefore, prudent to evaluate adolescents whose behaviors and feelings fall outside of the normal range, because early intervention may lead to beneficial treatment and reduction of the long-term psychosocial morbidity. To this end, the development of effective psychosocial therapies is crucial. IPT-A is such an intervention that is specifically aimed at treating the interpersonal problems that are associated with adolescent depression. The epidemiology, nature, and risk factors of adolescent depression lend support to the theoretical foundation for the adaptation of IPT for adolescents.

EPIDEMIOLOGY OF DEPRESSION

Depression was not recognized as a diagnostic entity in children until the mid-1970s. Prior to that time, research on childhood and adolescent depression was minimal and the epidemiology unknown. The paucity of such information on children and adolescents was even more remarkable when compared to the research being done on adult depression. Early studies relied on reports from parents and teachers about the child and rarely asked the children about themselves. The introduction of systematic diagnostic assessment of children and adolescents in the mid-1970s increased the practice of obtaining information from the child as well as other informants. More recently, children and adolescents have been shown to be reliable informants about their mental states (Orvaschel et al., 1981; Weissman et al., 1987c) and report more affective symptoms than their parents and teachers report about them (Angold et al., 1987).

Early epidemiologic studies focused on depressive symptoms, and more recent studies have reported on depressive disorders. There is great variability in reports of prevalence rates of childhood depression resulting from variable diagnostic criteria, multiple populations (clinical vs. normal populations), different methods to obtain information (self-report questionnaires vs. structured interviews), and varying informants (parents, teachers, and/or children). Another difficulty in comparing studies is that some researchers have identified their subjects based on their having several symptoms of depression, whereas others have made identification based on the subjects meeting criteria for the disorder according to the American Psychiatric Association's *Diagnostic and Statistical Manual of Mental Disorders* (DSM). Therefore, one must be careful how depression has been defined in the particular study. Depressive symptoms are common in prepubertal children, whereas depressive disorders are more commonly found in adolescents both in epidemiological samples and clinical populations (Angold, 1988 a,b; Fleming & Offord, 1990). The following sections review studies of depressive symptoms and depressive disorders in adolescents.

Depressive Symptoms

One of the earliest major studies of prevalence rates was Rutter's Isle of Wight study of children and the follow-up several years later of these same children when they were adolescents. Rutter et al. (1976b) found that among 2,303 children, ages 10–11 years, 13% expressed depressed mood and 9% were preoccupied with depressed topics at the initial interview. When reinterviewed at 14–15 years, 40% reported substantial feelings of misery and depression, 20% expressed feelings of self-deprecation, and 7–8% expressed suicidal feelings (Rutter et al., 1976b). Since Rutter's initial study, prevalence rates based on adolescent self-reports of depressive symptoms have ranged from 8.6% to 55.6% (see Table 2.1).

The significance and prognosis of such high rates of depressive symptoms in multiple studies of adolescents are not clear. Some researchers suggest that the high rates result from adolescents reporting far more transitory symptoms of depression than do adults. Schoenbach et al. (1983) suggested that transitory symptoms may be part of normal

TABLE 2.1. Prevalence of Depressive Symptoms

Study	n	Age (yr)	Informants[a]	Instrument[b]	% depression
Albert & Beck, 1975	63	11–15	C	BDI	36.5%
Rutter et al., 1976b	2,303	14–15	P, T, C	Questionnaire interview	45%
Leon et al., 1980	138	13–16	C	CDI	15%
Teri, 1982b	568	14–17	C	BDI	32%
Kandel & Davies, 1982	4,202	14–19	C	Questionnaire	15–18%
Schoenbach et al., 1983	383	12–15	C	CES-D	50%
Kaplan et al., 1984	385	11–18	C	BDI	8.6%
Siegel & Griffin, 1984	99	12–18	C	BDI	20.2%
Gibbs, 1985	116	14–18	C	BDI	23%
Chien & Chang, 1985	2,888	HS studts	C	CES-D	40%
Sullivan & Engin, 1986	103	15–16	C	BDI	32%
Wells et al., 1987	424	16–19	C	BDI	33%
Weinberg & Emslie, 1988	3,294	13–17	C	BDI	18.1%
Fleming et al., 1989	1,127	12–16	P, C	Checklist	35.9% (M) 52.4% (F)

[a]P = parents; T = teachers; C = child; M = males; F = females; HS studts = high school students.
[b]BDI = Beck Depression Inventory; CDI = Children's Depression Inventory; CES-D = Center for Epidemiological Studies Depression Scale.

development, whereas the more significant and persistent symptoms may be indicative of psychopathology.

Depressive Disorder

Studies using semistructured interviews and applying more rigorous diagnostic criteria to reported symptoms have yielded reduced but significant rates of depressive disorders in adolescents. In addition, the few follow-up studies on adolescents reporting depressive symptoms suggest continued or recurrent depression into adulthood. There are six reported studies on the prevalence rates of depressive disorders in adolescents and four other studies on children and adolescents (Fleming & Offord, 1990). The prevalence rates for current major depression range from 0.4%–5.7%, and 8.3% for lifetime rate of major depression (Fleming & Offord, 1990).

NATURE OF ADOLESCENT DEPRESSION

One problem encountered in the study of adolescent depression is whether the use of adult diagnostic criteria is appropriate. The DSM-III-R does not have a separate diagnostic category for depression in children and adolescents. The only modification for adolescents is a substitution of irritability for depressed mood and minor changes in duration of symptoms for the diagnosis of dysthymic disorder from 2 years to 1 year. These modifications did not derive from empirical research but, rather, were based on clinical intuition and experience (Angold, unpublished). Controversy remains (Spitzer et al., 1978; Puig-Antich, 1980), and many still feel that a separate diagnostic entity should be created to better represent the depressive phenomena in children and adolescents.

Studies that have compared depressed adolescents to depressed adults conclude that, despite minor variations attributable to developmental stages, the symptom profile is the same (Hudgens, 1974; Carlson & Strober, 1979; Inamdar et at., 1979; Friedman et al., 1983). Minor variations include adolescent reports of more hypersomnia, less terminal insomnia, and hyperphagia. They exhibit a more fluctuating course characterized by more interpersonal problems (Simeon, 1989) and also make more suicide attempts than depressed adults.

There is increasing recognition that depressive conditions meeting adult criteria do occur in children, however, there are questions as to whether some child and adolescent depressions are missed by not using developmentally adjusted criteria. The effects of developmental changes in cognition and emotional expression on the presentation of depression over time have yet to be fully delineated. From childhood to adolescence there appears to be a transition from predominantly vegetative symptoms to more inner psychological or cognitive ones. Adolescents, in comparison to children, are thought to begin to resemble adults in their depth of despair, sense of hopelessness, propensity for suicide and accompanying anxiety and agitation (Bemporad & Lee, 1988). Ryan et al. (1987) conclude from their review of studies that developmental changes across childhood and adolescence have only mild to moderate effects on the expression of a limited number of affective symptoms in children with major depression.

The question becomes: If there are differences in symptomatology between adults and children, which symptom aggregates are necessary and sufficient to diagnose depression in children and adolescents and which symptoms are not? There is uncertainty as to whether the child or adolescent is capable of having the cognitive components of depression such as self-blame, helplessness, and guilt that are frequently found in adults. Moreover, if the children and adolescents voice these cognitions, should they be interpreted in the same way as the nonverbal components of depression in adults (Kazdin et al., 1985)? Are too many inferences regarding the meaning of particular child behaviors or statements being made? There has been no research as yet to address whether indices of depression and specific criteria vary with age systematically and how these may change as the individual approaches adulthood.

We believe that until these matters are resolved there is much to be gained by using the adult framework to identify child and adolescent depression. Adolescents, like adults who are depressed, can have chronic and/or recurrent symptoms and experience significant psychosocial impairment, particularly in interpersonal relationships. The similarities to adult depression include negative self-cognitions, depressed mood, sleep and appetite disturbances, tearfulness, difficulty functioning at job or school due to poor concentration, and suicidal ideation (Kashani et al., 1989; Ryan et al., 1987). Differences include lack of pervasive anhedonia in the adolescents, more reactivity to external situations or stressors, irritability at times rather than depressed mood, and lack of similar drug response to tricyclic antidepressants (Mitchell et al., 1988; Carlson & Strober, 1979). Despite the differences between depressed adults and adolescents, it seems reasonable to approach the treatment of adolescents with therapies that have been shown to be effective with depressed adults. Clinical trials have demonstrated that IPT is an effective treatment for adult depression (see Chapter 1). The current adaptation (IPT-A) has included the psychosocial stages of development for adolescents as central elements in the treatment goals and strategies.

COURSE OF ADOLESCENT DEPRESSION

Clinical experience suggests that the course of adolescent depression may also differ from that of adult depression. It may be more likely for adolescents to have episodically intense periods of depression interspersed with periods of improved functioning (Angst et al., 1990). During these periods of improved functioning, adolescents may be more likely to drop out of treatment. Adolescents may prefer a treatment that is brief and deals with the current problem, preferring to return for treatment when needed, rather than being in treatment and in the patient role for a prolonged period of time. IPT-A is a brief, focused treatment that seems to appeal to many adolescents for these reasons.

Few studies have thoroughly examined the course of adolescent depression, and further study is needed. The few follow-up studies that do exist have indicated a generally poor prognosis with a high risk for future episodes of affective illness and chronic psychosocial problems (Garber et al., 1988; Keller et al., 1988). This clearly suggests the need for some type of psychotherapeutic intervention, but further clarification of the course of illness, recurrence and recovery rates, and associated impairment and comorbidity is needed to begin to design and implement treatment strategies. IPT-A is such a strategy based on current knowledge of the nature and course of adolescent depression, and tailored to meet the needs and impairments of depressed adolescents.

Kandel and Davies (1986), in their 9-year follow-up of a high school sample, found that depressive symptoms in adolescence were the most significant predictive factor for depressive symptoms in adulthood. Depressed adolescents were also at greater risk for significant psychosocial difficulties including less capacity for intimacy, higher rates of unemployment, higher rates of divorce, increased estrangement from parents and greater drug and alcohol use compared to nondepressed adolescents. Similar results have been reported by Poznanski et al. (1976) and Chess et al. (1983).

Kovacs et al. (1984) have published the largest follow-up study on depressed children to date. They reported on 65 children, ages 8 to 13 years, evaluated at intake and at 2-, 6-, and 12-month follow-up; semiannual interviews were conducted in later years. DSM-III diagnoses were based on semistructured interviews with the child and with the parent about the child, and they included diagnoses of dysthymic disorder, major depressive disorder, and/or adjustment disorder with depressed mood. The group reported that two-thirds of subjects with major depression and dysthymic disorder had a subsequent episode by the end of 5 years. One year after the onset of major depression, 41% still had not recovered, and 8% had not recovered at 2 years after onset. Kovacs et al. (1984) also found that in the children who did recover from their episode of major depression, 26% will have a new episode within a year after their recovery, and 40% will have a recurrence within 2 years after recovery from initial episode.

Keller et al. (1988) reported results from a 2-year follow-up on 38 nonreferred adolescents who had been diagnosed with a current or past major depression. The 38 adolescents were the depressed subset of 275 children from one of four groups: children of parents with depression; relatives of high-risk probands; acquaintances of high-risk probands; or a true probability sample recruited from an HMO group. The median age of onset for depression was 14 years. The probability of persistent depression after 1 year was 21% and after 2 years was 10%. Keller et al. (1988) believe that these rates parallel those rates of chronicity and recovery that occur in adult depression. Harrington et al. (1990) did a retrospective follow-up study on 52 subjects who had been seen in the hospital for depression 20–30 years previously. They found that patients' depression as adolescents often continued or reoccurred in adulthood suggesting a strong continuity of depressive symptoms for adolescents who were diagnosed as depressed according to adult criteria. They reported that depressed children were at greater risk of adult depression than nondepressed controls and that the risk of suicide attempts in adulthood was three times that of the control group.

Follow-up studies on hospitalized, depressed adolescents also report chronicity and recurrence of depression (Garber et al., 1988; Strober, 1985; Welner et al., 1979). Even more striking, Keller et al. (1991) suggest a significant pattern of underrecognition and undertreatment of adolescent depression both in clinically referred and nonreferred populations. This body of research strongly suggests that children and adolescents with a major depression are at significant risk for future episodes of depression both in late adolescence and young adulthood. Chronic and significant psychosocial impairment and interpersonal difficulties are associated with adolescent depression, and these difficulties persist into adulthood.

Whether IPT-A will be effective in reducing the long-term psychosocial impairments associated with depression first presenting in adolescence remains to be seen. Research on IPT-A employing longitudinal follow-up strategies to assess psychosocial functioning needs to be designed and implemented. The first step in this process has been an open clinical trial. A short-term follow-up of these adolescents is currently under way, as is a controlled clinical trial of IPT-A.

RISK FACTORS

Risk factors associated with depression include age, gender, socioeconomic factors, birth cohort, family relationships, and family history. These are briefly reviewed below with an emphasis on those risk factors that lend support to IPT-A as a potentially efficacious treatment and that are addressed in IPT-A.

Age

Prevalence rates of depressive symptoms and depressive disorders increase with age, marked by a sharp increase after puberty. Rates of depressive symptoms in children are approximately 9%, whereas by adolescence, the rates increase to 22% to 40% depending on the study (Rutter et al., 1976b; Kaplan et al., 1984). The increase in major depression from preadolescent to adolescent years is a consistent finding in the majority of studies (Ryan et al., 1986b; Offord et al., 1987). Prevalence rates of adolescent depression disorders vary from 1.3% to 8% (Kashani et al., 1987; Rutter et al., 1976b, Weissman et al., 1987a).

Gender Differences

The increase in rates of depression noted at puberty is accompanied by an acceleration in the rates in girls. (Kashani et al., 1987; Rutter et al., 1976b); whereas prepubertally the rates in boys and girls are about equal, by adolescence, the sex ratio approaches 2:1, which is almost equivalent to the gender difference found in adult depression. The Ontario Health Study (Fleming et al., 1989) reported depressed symptoms in 36.9% of boys compared to 55.6% of girls. Similarly, Kandel and Davies (1982) found a greater incidence of depressive symptoms in adolescent girls than boys. Kashani & Sherman (1988) also found that the adolescent girls in his study needed more psychological intervention than the boys.

Socioeconomic Factors

Low socioeconomic status (SES) has been associated with adult depressive symptoms (Cytryn et al., 1986) and, more recently, with depressive symptoms in children. Kaplan et al. (1984), in a study of high school students from diverse socioeconomic classes, found that lower SES adolescents had a higher total Beck Depression Inventory score than those adolescents from higher SES. Similarly, Siegel and Griffin (1984) found that the depressed adolescents tended to come from middle- or lower-class families, who also reported a higher incidence of divorce. Garrison et al. (1989), reporting on a survey of 677 public school students, found that depressive symptoms were associated with minority race and lower SES. These studies are consistent with adult studies' findings about the relationship between depressive symptoms and SES. However, whether there is the same association with the clinical disorder of major depression is not clear.

Changes in Rates of Depression

According to Klerman (1988) there have been two major changes in the epidemiology of depression since World War II: (1) an increase in rates of depression in more recently born generations and (2) a significant shift toward an earlier age of onset. Epidemiological studies show that the cohort born after World War II, termed the "baby boom" generation, has experienced a marked increase in rates of depression with an earlier age of onset, often in adolescence. In addition, within each birth cohort, rates of depression are highest in females. The reason for this increase is unclear, but it does not appear to be merely an artifact.

Family Relationships

Risk factors that have been associated with increased rates of depressive symptoms or major depression in adolescence include parental death and quality of the family relationships. Bowlby first presented the constructs of attachment theory based on clinical case material (Bowlby, 1980). Later studies have supported his early theories. According to Wells et al. (1985), parental loss through death is a well-documented risk factor for depression in adolescence. Reinherz et al. (1989) conducted a 10-year longitudinal study of a lower-middle-class community and found that 21% of the 15-year-olds reported high levels of depressive symptoms on the Children's Depression Inventory. Among the risk factors identified for these adolescents was the death of a parent, particularly for the girls. Although these and other studies have not demonstrated a robust link between early parental loss and later depression, this may be secondary to inadequate conceptualization of the association and resultant faulty methodology. Brown et al. (1986) have put forth an interactive model of depression related to early childhood loss that requires a current adverse event before there is "translation into an episode of depression."

In addition to early parental loss, the quality of family relationships in terms of warmth, cohesiveness, and punitiveness has been associated with childhood depression. Fendrich et al. (1990), in a study of children at risk for psychiatric illness by virtue of major depression in the parents, found that children reporting low family cohesion and affectionless control had higher rates of major depression than children reporting more cohesive and warmer family relations. Reinherz et al. (1989) also identified family cohesiveness as a mediator of high depressive symptomatology. There is evidence that parents of depressed children are often angry, punitive, detached, and belittling (Kashani et al., 1988), which may either increase the child's vulnerability to depression or exacerbate the course of an existing episode.

Family History of Depression

There is increasingly strong evidence that major depression runs in families and that being the child of a depressed parent places one at increased risk for the development of major depression (Weissman et al., 1984a, 1987a; Beardslee et al., 1983; Orvaschel, 1990; Hammen et al., 1990). There is evidence that the earlier the age of onset of depression in the child or adolescent the greater the familial loading in the relative (Weissman et al., 1987a). In addition, the rate of depression increases by age for the children regardless of proband group, thus confirming the period of late adolescence as an age period when many children become depressed even if there is no familial risk (Weissman et al., 1988; Beardslee et al., 1988). Numerous studies show a strong aggregation of affective disorders in the first-degree relatives of depressed probands including both adults and children (Gershon et al., 1982) and an increased risk of affective disorder among adult relatives of children with affective disorders (Puig-Antich, 1980). The few cross-fostering (Cadoret, 1978) and twin studies (Torgerson, 1986) suggest a genetic contribution for major depression and bipolar disorder.

Weissman et al. (1987a) found that children of depressed parents as compared to children of never mentally ill parents are at three-fold increased risk to develop school problems and suicidal behavior. Whether the risk results from a combination of genetic vulnerability, environmental stresses, and impaired parenting skills of the depressed parents is unclear. These effects are most likely influenced by the gender of the child and ill parent, the age of child at time of parent's illness, the nature of the relationship between child and depressed parent, the course and recovery of parental illness, and the psychiatric status of the other parent and other support figures (Weissman et al., 1984b; 1987a; Beardslee et al., 1983; Downey & Coyne, 1990). Weissman et al. (1987a) found an increase in overall prevalence of major depression, substance abuse, psychiatric treatment, poor social functioning, and school problems in children of depressed parents as compared with children of normal parents.

Risk Factors and IPT-A

IPT has been adapted to meet the developmental issues and needs of adolescents, particularly as they are effected by depression. IPT-A focuses on damaged interpersonal relationships, particularly those occurring within the family. Parents and siblings are brought into the treatment either for support of the adolescent or for direct intervention to change patterns in familial relations or to affect intrafamilial communications. Familial relationships are models for extrafamilial intimate relationships. Strategies for changing the adolescent's interpersonal relationships with family members can be extrapolated by the adolescent to relationships outside the family system. Given the increasing rates of adolescent depression, the development and implementation of IPT-A are occurring at an opportune time.

FACTORS ASSOCIATED WITH ADOLESCENT DEPRESSION

Biological variables, comorbidity, and impaired psychosocial functioning are factors associated with adolescent depression and, as such, are important to consider in the development of psychotherapeutic and psychopharmacological interventions. Although altered biological variables have no direct effect on psychotherapeutic strategies, they will be reviewed because they are an important component of adolescent depression and are on the cutting edge of adolescent depression research. Research into the biological basis of depression may help in establishing the continuity between childhood and adult depression, the genetics of depression, and the implementation of effective pharmacological treatments. In addition, there has been so much emphasis on "biochemical depression" that we believe it is important for clinicians to be familiar with the current state of knowledge in this area. The effects of a depressive episode for an adolescent are so far-reaching that any pharmacological intervention needs to include psychosocial strategies. If IPT-A is going to be a recommended treatment for a depressed adolescent, the clinician should be able to address generally the parents' and adolescent's questions regarding the biochemical basis of depression and to emphasize the necessity of a treatment intervention that deals with the accompanying psychosocial and interpersonal impairment.

Biological Studies of Depressed Children

Biological studies in adult depressives include 24-hour cortisol levels, dexamethasone suppression test (DST), polysomnography (sleep EEG), growth hormone secretion, thyroid stimulating hormone, and immune deficiency (Puig-Antich, 1987). Although none of these variables have yielded the foundation for a biological basis of depression, significant results have been reported. Specifically, the majority of adult depressives have elevated 24-hour cortisol levels (Carroll et al., 1976); fail to suppress on the DST (Carroll, 1982); have a low rate of growth hormone secretion in response to insulin (Sachar et al., 1971; Mueller et al., 1972); and have abnormal sleep graphs (Coble et al., 1980; Gillin et al., 1979; Kupfer, 1976; Kupfer & Foster, 1979; Vogel, et al. 1980). The data on adult depressives demonstrating decreased or blunted thyroid-stimulating hormone response to thyrotropin-releasing hormone stimulation (25%) (Loosen, 1985) and decreased immunologic response as measured by T and B cells resulting from cortisol nonsuppression following a DST are less convincing (Targum et al., 1990).

These investigations have been extended to children and adolescents with major depression. Although the studies are few, the results are markedly different from those found in adults (see Puig-Antich, 1987, for review). Data from biological studies on children and adolescents as compared to adult data are presented, because the results of these biological studies appear to be an interactive effect of age and abnormality. Ten to fifteen percent of depressed children have elevated 24-hour mean cortisol levels compared to 40–60% of depressed adults. The results of the DST in depressed children have been highly variable with some studies supporting hypersecretion and others refuting hypersecretion. Twenty-four-hour mean cortisol levels and results of the DST in depressed adolescents are similar to those found in adult depressives. The interactive effects of age and depression are hypothesized to affect cortisol secretion (Puig-Antich, 1987).

Whereas low levels of growth hormone are secreted during sleep of adult depressives, depressed children secrete high levels of growth hormone during sleep compared to nondepressed psychiatric and normal controls (Puig-Antich, 1987). There is no difference in growth hormone secretion during sleep between depressed and nondepressed adolescents. Insulin tolerance test (ITT) causes insulin-induced hypoglycemia which in turn causes release of growth hormone. This effect is mediated by age and estrogens. Depressed children respond to ITT in a similar fashion to postmenopausal adult depressives. It is hypothesized that growth hormone response to ITT is abnormal secondary to depression during puberty and postmenopause.

The abnormal results from sleep graphs demonstrated in adult depressives have not been found in depressed children and have been found unreliably in depressed adolescents. Interestingly, the abnormal results are not demonstrable in depressed adults in their early 20s either. Puig-Antich et al. (1982), in sleep studies of depressed children and adolescents, found that sleep disturbances only emerge in later adolescence. Again, there seems to be an interaction between depression and age such that the abnormality does not appear until later in the lifespan when a disorder is present (Puig-Antich, 1987).

Comorbidity

Comorbidity is the occurrence of more than one psychiatric disorder at the same time. It commonly occurs in children and adolescents who are depressed. Disorders that have been found to be associated with major depression in adolescence include attention deficit disorder (Biederman et al., 1987), anxiety disorders (Kovacs et al., 1989; Alessi et al., 1987; Bernstein & Garfinkel, 1986), conduct disorders (Alessi & Robbins, 1984; Marriage et al., 1986; Kovacs et al., 1988), and eating disorders (Swift et al., 1986). Ryan et al. (1987) found that mild conduct problems were present in 25% of adolescents but were disruptive in only 11% of the adolescents. They found that comorbidity with anxiety disorders and conduct disorder were found to be more frequent in prepubertal children than adolescents with depression. Geller et al. (1985) found an association between separation anxiety and major depression in prepubertal children and an association between antisocial behavior and depression in adolescent boys. Levy and Deykin (1989) found that when major depression was present in adolescents, the rate of suicidal ideation or behavior was markedly higher for both males and females, even in an untreated sample. Still, half the students who admitted to having made a suicide attempt did not meet diagnostic criteria for major depression at any time. Kovacs et al. (1988) found some indications that older age at onset of depression is associated with the presence of comorbid conduct disorder. The conduct disorder appeared to develop mostly as a complication of major depression. It was only primary for one-third of the cases (Kovacs et al., 1988), however, depression comorbid with conduct disorder was associated with greater impairment in functioning. Researchers consistently find that among children and adolescents with a major affective disorder, about one-third also have a comorbid diagnosis of conduct disorder or a similar behavior problem (Carlson & Cantwell, 1980; Puig-Antich, 1982; Kashani et al., 1987). In addition, two-thirds of adolescent school refusers meet criteria for affective disorder (see Harrington, 1989). The interactive effects of comorbid disorders on impairment in functioning and long-term course of the disorders are still not clear.

Psychosocial Functioning

There is little question that major depression has an adverse effect on a child's academic performance, family and peer relationships, may increase alcohol and drug use, and may lead to suicide attempts. In a study of prepubertal depressives, Puig-Antich et al. (1985a) found that mother–child relationships were markedly impaired in prepubertal children with a current diagnosis of major depression as compared with psychiatric and other disorders and normal controls. They found that the mother's pattern of low warmth, high irritability, and withdrawal were apparent not only in the marital relationship, but in the parenting style as well. These children with major depression also were less able to maintain a special or best friendship and less able to make and maintain peer relationships. They found that the specific age and sex of the children showed no association with psychosocial functioning. In another study of prepubertal children after they had sustained recovery from their index episode, Puig-Antich et al. (1985b) found that whereas their school functioning had improved, they still suffered impairment in the familial and peer relationships. Thus, although their depressions had resolved, they were left with interpersonal deficits.

Additionally, the social or interpersonal problems associated with depression often linger, even though the acute depressive symptoms may have resolved. Moreover, depressive symptoms are often chronic or recurrent. The aspects of psychosocial functioning that are most impaired during the depressive episode seemed either to take longer to resolve or to resolve only partially (Puig-Antich et al., 1985a). Similarly, Kandel and Davies (1986) found that adolescent dysphoric symptoms are associated with later difficulties in social functioning such as increased school dropout, greater estrangement in personal relationships with parents and significant others, and more engagement in illegal activities. Garber et al. (1988) also found that depressed adolescents had significant adjustment difficulties in social activities, family relationships, and significant partner relationships. Altman and Gotlib (1988) in a study of the social behavior of depressed children found that depressed children experienced themselves as less socially competent. Several longitudinal studies of depressed adolescents have followed the adolescents into early adult life. Although the studies have limitations, their findings suggest that self-ratings of depression in the adolescent community predict similar problems in early adulthood and that depressed adolescent patients are at high risk for subsequent major affective disturbance (Harrington et al., 1990). In their study of adult outcomes of depressed children, Harrington et al. (1990) conclude that depressive conditions in young people show substantial continuity with depression in adult life.

IPT-A and Associated Factors of Depression

Although IPT-A does not purport to treat conduct disorder or anxiety disorders, these disorders often accompany depressive disorders, and many of the symptoms that comprise these disorders also are associated with depressive disorders. By treating the depression with IPT-A, these secondary symptoms may resolve. When they do not, further treatment may be appropriately recommended. Further study of IPT-A is necessary to determine whether or not IPT-A is effective in ameliorating conduct and anxiety symptoms associated with depression. Previous research on pharmacological treatment of depression has demonstrated that although the depressive mood may respond to medication, the psychosocial and interpersonal problems persist. IPT-A was designed with this in mind, and it attempts to address these associated symptoms and impairments.

CONCLUSION

We can conclude that major depression does occur in adolescents, and when it does there tends to be recurrence and chronicity. Moreover, there are significant psychosocial impairments that occur in the acute stages, continue after recovery, and persist into adulthood. These psychosocial impairments are either of an interpersonal type or lead to interpersonal difficulties. Adolescents who are members of families with a history of affective disorders and whose families experience interpersonal problems are at significant risk for depression themselves. These facts call for a psychosocial psychotherapeutic intervention to treat adolescent depression, no matter what the biological substrate and genetics of depression may be. IPT-A has been found to be effective in isolated cases and in an open clinical trial, and it awaits the results of further investigations. As we discuss in the next chapter, the scientific basis for treatment of depressed children and adolescents is scant.

· 3 ·

Current Treatments for
Adolescent Depression

The scientific research on treatment of depressed adolescents is sparse, and the results from available studies are disappointing. Numerous studies have demonstrated the efficacy of pharmacotherapy and short-term psychotherapies, alone and in combination, for acute and maintenance treatment of adults with major depression (see Weissman et al., 1987b, for review). Psychopharmacology studies of depression in children and adolescents have been unable to establish efficacy as has been done in adult depression. In addition, there are no published treatment studies of any individual psychotherapy in the treatment of childhood or adolescent depression that have employed minimum scientific standards (i.e., diagnostically homogeneous samples, specified treatment, random assignment to experimental and control groups). This chapter reviews the few clinical trials of treatment with depressed adolescents and also reviews other treatments that are widely used clinically, but have not been tested empirically.

PHARMACOTHERAPY

Numerous studies on the use of tricyclic antidepressants (TCAs) in children were published between the 1970s and 1980s (see Garfinkle, 1986, for comprehensive review). All of these studies were open clinical trials, and many studied children with disorders other than depression. The studies suggest the efficacy of imipramine for the treatment of depression in prepubertal children, but do not support its efficacy in adolescents (Ryan et al., 1986a; Strober et al., 1990). All of these studies, however, have methodological problems that leave open the question of whether or not antidepressants are efficacious for the treat-

36

ment of childhood depression. Most did not use specified diagnostic criteria or systematic assessment of diagnoses, used low doses of medication, or did not report on length of treatment (Moreau, 1990). The overall positive response rate of 75% reported in these open clinical trials (Puig-Antich & Weston, 1983) was an impetus for further studies using a more rigorous research design.

The few controlled clinical trials of pharmacotherapy in depressed adolescents have not demonstrated efficacy either. It is unclear whether this is because of methodological problems such as small sample size, diagnostic variability, or the biological uniqueness of adolescents (see Campbell & Spencer, 1988, for review). More recent studies on depressed adolescents have attempted to address early methodological deficiencies by using structured diagnostic interviews yielding DSM-III diagnoses; however, results from these studies fail to demonstrate statistically significant differences in response between antidepressant medication and placebo (Geller et al., 1990; Kramer & Feiguine, 1981; Ryan et al., 1986a; Strober et al., 1990). Nonetheless, there are several ongoing studies of pharmacological therapy for adolescent depression to investigate further the efficacy of medication (Ryan, 1990). Larger samples of depressed adolescents need to be included in well-designed studies testing the efficacy of pharmacotherapy and psychotherapy, each alone, and then in combination.

The TCAs most often studied include nortriptyline, imipramine (Tofranil), desipramine (Norpramine), and, more recently, the serotonergic agent fluoxetine (Prozac). Lithium carbonate has demonstrated efficacy for the treatment of bipolar disorder (Campbell & Spencer, 1988). Because it is a well-established treatment, we do not review the research background on its use except where it has been used to augment antidepressant medication. Rather, we focus on the open clinical trials using strict diagnostic criteria and the medication/placebo and double-blind studies of the antidepressant medications tested in depressed children and adolescents. There are six published studies in children—four double-blind studies (Kashani et al., 1980, 1984; Puig-Antich et al., 1987; Geller et al., 1989) and two placebo versus medication (Petti & Unis, 1981; Preskorn et al., 1987)—and nine studies in adolescents—three double-blind studies (Geller et al., 1990; Kramer & Feiguine, 1981; Simeon et al., 1990), four open clinical trials (Strober et al., 1990; Ryan et al., 1986a, 1988b; Ryan, 1990), as well as two studies using lithium augmentation (Ryan et al., 1988a; Strober et al., 1990).

Kashani et al. (1980) and Petti and Unis (1981) reported on one child each, the former using amitriptyline in a double-blind placebo design and the latter using imipramine versus placebo. Kashani's subject became hypomanic necessitating a dose reduction. Petti and Unis

(1981) reported marked improvement with no reported side effects. Kashani et al. (1984) reported on nine prepubertal depressed children who were randomly assigned to either amitriptyline or placebo after a 3- to 4-week baseline hospital evaluation for a 4-week trial and were then switched to the other. Depression scores decreased with both drug and placebo, but there was a greater nonsignificant decrease with the drug. ($p = .09$).

Puig-Antich et al. (1987) reported on 38 depressed prepubertal children who were given imipramine after a 2-week evaluation in a double-blind placebo control design. Placebo and drug response rate were similar (68% vs. 56%). However, in a complementary study in which 30 of the 38 subjects were tested for total serum drug level, combined levels of imipramine and desipramine predicted a positive response to the drug. Preskorn et al. (1987) reported that antidepressant medication was superior to placebo in children who did not suppress on the dexamethasone suppression test. Further study is needed to determine whether plasma levels or subtypes of depressive disorders predict a positive response to medication in depressed children. Geller et al. (1989) reported on 50 depressed children who entered a 2-week single-blind placebo washout period followed by an 8-week random assignment, double-blind placebo controlled period. They found no significant differences in response between placebo or fixed level of nortriptyline.

Imipramine was given to 34 depressed adolescent inpatients in an open-label trial (Ryan et al., 1986) at doses titrated to 5 mg/kg per day as tolerated for 6 weeks. At the end of the trial, only 44% of the patients demonstrated diminution in depressive symptoms, and most remained symptomatic. Plasma levels of drugs (combined imipramine and desipramine) did not correspond to improvement. Strober et al. (1990) reported on a similar study using imipramine at doses of 5 mg/kg per day for 6 weeks in 34 inpatient depressed adolescents with similar results. They reported that although serum levels did not correlate with improvement, all responders had levels greater than 180 ng/ml. Ryan (1990) tried to distinguish placebo responders from medication responders in a study of 14 children and adolescents given nortriptyline ($n = 9$), imipramine ($n = 3$), or amitriptyline ($n = 2$). They used a technique proposed by Quitkin et al. (cited in Ryan, 1990) in which it is hypothesized that responders have a pattern characterized by an initial lag in improvement followed by sustained improvement, and placebo responders demonstrate an immediate improvement followed by a variable course. They concluded that Quitkin's hypothesis (Ryan, 1990) was not supported in depressed adolescents.

Kramer and Feiguine (1981), Geller et al. (1990), and Simeon et al. (1990) reported on a total of 81 depressed adolescents treated with antidepressants in a double-blind design. Kramer and Feiguine (1981) gave amitriptyline or placebo to 20 depressed adolescent inpatients after a 2-day evaluation and reported that drug was no more effective than placebo after 6 weeks. Geller et al. (1990) randomly assigned 31 subjects to the nortriptyline or placebo 8-week trial after a 2-week single-blind placebo wash-out phase and reported that the study had been terminated early because there was only one subject who had actively responded to drug. Twenty-one subjects improved during the placebo wash-out phase and were not assigned to the double-blind phase of the study. Simeon et al. (1990) assigned 40 subjects, 30 of whom completed the study, to a double-blind study of fluoxetine versus placebo. Although fluoxetine was more efficacious than placebo on all clinical measures except sleep, the differences were not statistically significant.

In an open clinical trial (determined by retrospective chart review), monoamine oxidase inhibitors (MAOIs) either alone or in combination were used to treat 23 depressed adolescents who failed to respond to a 6-week course of TCAs (Ryan et al., 1988b). Poor dietary compliance was a problem in the study, and the authors stated that the risks of complications from dietary indiscretion outweigh the possible benefits of the medication in impulsive unreliable adolescents or adolescents who use drugs or alcohol. Unstable families were also considered a contraindication to the use of MAOIs.

Taking all the studies together, a total of 186 depressed adolescents have been enrolled in medication trials, including 105 in open trials and 81 in double-blind design. The results thus far do not support the efficacy of antidepressant medication for the treatment of adolescent depression. However, there are a number of studies under way or in the planning phase, and further information should be forthcoming.

Two additional studies reported on the efficacy of TCAs augmented with lithium for the treatment of depressed adolescents who failed to respond to TCAs alone. In an open treatment study of 14 depressed adolescents, 43% responded to the augmented treatment (Ryan et al., 1988a). The adolescents had a trial of either amitryptyline, desipramine, or nortriptyline at adequate doses for a minimum of 6 weeks in most cases and exhibited only a partial response at best to the drug. There were no differences in baseline status or lithium level between responders and nonresponders. In the other study, only one adolescent showed improvement with the addition of lithium (Strober et al., 1990). Here again, further work is needed to determine whether lithium augmentation can play an effective role in the pharmacological treatment of adolescent depression.

The poor response of depressed adolescents to the various antidepressant medications and combinations of medications that are efficacious in adult depressives poses a significant theoretical dilemma: if it is postulated that adolescent depression is the analog of adult depression why do the depressed adolescents fail to respond? Several theories have been proposed to explain the poor response of depressed adolescents to antidepressant medication. These include type of medication, hormonal differences between adolescents and adults, inclusion of adolescents who will become bipolar or who are depressive phenocopies, dosage problems, and plasma levels (Ryan, 1990). In addition, it must be considered (1) whether there is a subgroup of depressed adolescents whose symptoms resolve more rapidly than do the symptoms of adults, (2) whether the time-limited symptomatology represents early manifestation of the adult disorder or whether it is a different disorder yet to be delineated, and (3) whether the duration of symptoms for a diagnosis of major depression in adolescents should be greater than 2 to 6 weeks. The answers to these questions await further study. In the meantime, it is standard clinical practice to treat depressed adolescents whose symptoms are persistent, impairing, and unremitting with the antidepressant medications demonstrated to be efficacious in adult depressives.

PSYCHOSOCIAL TREATMENTS

In clinical practice, depressed adolescents frequently receive the psychotherapies that are efficacious in the treatment of adults (Hersen & Van Hasselt, 1987). A number of thoughtful papers by leading clinicians have described their clinical experience and theoretical perspectives on psychotherapy for the depressed adolescent (Bemporad, 1988; Cytryn & McKnew, 1985; Kestenbaum & Kron, 1987; Liebowitz & Kernberg, 1988; Nissen, 1986). In contrast to the small number of treatments that have been tested empirically in depressed adolescents, numerous ones are used clinically. These treatments include: psychodynamic psychotherapy/psychoanalysis, cognitive–behavioral psychotherapy, behavior therapy, family therapy, and group therapy. The goal of all these treatments is to alleviate the psychological symptoms and improve functioning. Techniques consist of psychological interventions, whose goals are to alter the behavior, thoughts, or attitudes of the patient that are felt to be contributing to the problems. Specifically, the short-term goal is to relieve suffering from dysphoric symptoms. The long-term goal of treatment is to limit the functional impairment from the symptoms, (such as poor interpersonal relationships, family conflict, school refusal) and to prevent chronicity and recurrence of the depressive episodes.

Although there are no published studies meeting all accepted scientific criteria for clinical trials, there have been several studies that have examined the efficacy of psychotherapy for the treatment of depression in adolescents: Reynolds and Coats (1986), cognitive–behavioral therapy; Robbins et al. (1989), interpersonal psychotherapy; and Lewinsohn et al. (1990), Coping with Depression group psychotherapy. Clinical studies have demonstrated the feasibility of conducting controlled clinical trials with depressed adolescents and the possible efficacy of group psychotherapy based on trials in the population. However, there has not been one controlled trial with random assignment, DSM-III diagnoses, and individual psychotherapy for this population.

Cognitive Therapy

The defining characteristics of cognitive treatment are that it is directive, structured, often time-limited, and emphasizes changing cognitions that are associated with behavioral events and problem-solving skills (Kovacs, 1979; Matson, 1989). The underlying construct is that a person's cognitions determine how a person feels (Emery et al., 1983). There are various modifications of the general cognitive tenets developed by Aaron Beck.

Beck hypothesizes a three-part cognitive model of depression: negative view of self, the world, and the future (Beck et al., 1979). He postulates that a person reacts to stress by activating this set of dysfunctional beliefs. These negative cognitions can be a result of faulty thought processes such as overgeneralization, personalization, absolute dichotomous thinking, and selective abstraction (Beck, 1967). As a result of these cognitive processes, the person approaches life by minimizing the positive aspects and accentuating the negative aspects, resulting in depressive cognitions. The treatment focuses on correcting those misattributions and misperceptions through structured tasks in and out of sessions. Beck believes that the individual learns to master problems and situations by reevaluating and correcting his or her thinking (Beck et al., 1979).

The goals of cognitive therapy are (1) to obtain symptom relief and (2) to uncover beliefs that lead to depression and subject these beliefs to reality testing (Emery et al., 1983). The techniques used to accomplish these goals include monitoring the negative cognitions, helping the patient to make the connections between and among cognition, affect, and behavior, and learning to identify and alter dysfunctional beliefs (Beck et al., 1979). Emery et al. (1983) in their use of cognitive therapy with depressed children and adolescents found it helpful to work with the parents as well as the adolescents to restructure the parents' expectations for their children that result in decreased self-esteem. The goal of therapy is to decrease the reinforcement of the adolescent's dysfunctional cognitions. Cognitive therapy differs from psychodynamic treatment in that the therapist does not make interpretations of unconscious factors. It differs from IPT-A in its focus on dysfunctional belief systems, whereas IPT-A would focus on dysfunctional interpersonal communication processes.

Another model of cognitive therapy is based on Seligman's model of learned helplessness that was derived from animal experimentation (Seligman & Maier, 1967). Seligman found that there were many correlations between behavior of learned helplessness and that of depression. He concluded that both were characterized by impaired motivation, impaired cognition, lowered self-esteem, aggression or assertive deficit, appetite disturbance, and physiological deficits (Petti, 1983). Seligman's model proposes that repeated experience with failure results in a sense of helplessness and hopelessness that the situation can not change, a sense that in turn results in depressive cognitions (Seligman & Maier, 1967). Treatment focuses on these feelings of helplessness and hopelessness by attempting to structure some success experiences to dissipate the negative feelings and create a sense of hopefulness and mastery. Specific strategies include assistance in changing expectations for unpleasant events and relinquishing unattainable goals, acquisition of social or problem-solving skills, and changing attribution style (Petti, 1983).

There have been many clinical trials with depressed adults assessing the efficacy of cognitive therapy based on Beck's model (Kovacs et al., 1981; Murphy et al., 1984; Rush et al., 1977). Clinical reports on the efficacy of cognitive therapy and cognitive–behavioral therapy with depressed adolescents range from single case reports to clinical trials of a group format. Wilkes and Rush (1988) have suggested methods for adapting cognitive therapy for the treatment of nonpsychotic depressed adolescents and have proposed a treatment model of cognitive therapy for this age group. This work is under further development, and a manual is being prepared. We await the initiation of clinical trials and data from this work.

Reynolds and Coats (1986) reported on a clinical trial comparing cognitive–behavioral therapy, relaxation training, and wait-list control for the treatment of depressive symptoms in 30 adolescents. Treatment was conducted in 10 small group meetings of 50 minutes each over 5 weeks. The findings indicated the superiority of the two active treatments in the reduction of depressive symptoms when compared to wait-list control, with no differences between the two active treatments. This study, however, used depressive symptoms, not diagnosis, as the entrance criteria, so it is not generalizable to treatment of adolescents with major depression disorder.

Behavioral Approaches

Although there are behavioral elements in cognitive therapy, there is another treatment modality that more strictly focuses on the behavior of the individual as the root of the depression. One of the major behavioral models of depression is that of the loss of positive reinforcement. Lewinsohn et al. (1969) found that depressed individuals appeared to lack access to sufficient schedules of positive reinforcement that are a result of either the complete absence of reinforcement or the individual's inability to access them because of lack of appropriate skills. The low rate of positive reinforcement for one's behavior can lead to depression. In turn, the depressive affect being displayed further decreases the individual's chances of receiving positive reinforcement for his or her behavior thereby exacerbating or increasing the depression. Lewinsohn's treatment for depression has focused on teaching adolescents the skills necessary to obtain the needed positive reinforcement to break the depressive feedback cycle.

A behavioral psychoeducational approach for coping with depression, with modifications for adolescents, has been developed by Clarke and Lewinsohn (1989). A group format also has been completed and was used by Lewinsohn et al. (1990). Lewinsohn et al. (1990) have conducted a clinical trial with 54 depressed adolescents comparing two different presentations of the Coping with Depression Course for adolescents with a wait-list control. The adolescents were diagnosed using the Kiddie–Schedule for Affective Disorders and Schizophrenia for School-Age Children—Epidemiologic Version and met Research Diagnostic Criteria for major, minor, or intermittent depression. Subjects in the active treatment groups either received group therapy with no treatment provided for their parents or received group therapy with treatment provided for their parents. The results showed that the patients in the two active treatments improved significantly more on the depressive measures than the wait-list group. There were no significant differences between the two active treatments. There was, however, a trend for greater improvement in the patients whose parents also participated in the treatment, in comparison to the group whose parents did not participate. This study is the largest and best to date.

There has been an absence of formal use and/or testing in clinical trials of more strictly behavioral techniques with adolescents who have been diagnosed as depressed. The techniques have been used with depressive symptoms associated with other psychiatric disorders (Petti, 1983). The results of the use of behavioral techniques with adolescents are usually published in the form of case reports. Adolescents have been reported to respond to techniques focusing on self-control and social interactions (Petti, 1983). Self-monitoring behavior is often seen as an effective means to change. Some specific behavioral techniques that have been used in treatment of depressive symptoms and illustrated in case reports include modelling appropriate behavior, behavioral rehearsal, information giving, skills training, and homework regarding particular behaviors to be conducted outside the sessions (Petti, 1983).

Interpersonal Approach

Recently, the findings of clinical trials with adults stimulated the notion of whether an interpersonal type of therapy would be an effective treatment for depressed adolescents. Robbins and associates (1989), in a pilot treatment strategy for 38 adolescents hospitalized with major depression, conducted an open trial of psychotherapy that they described as similar to IPT. They noted that 47% of the patients responded with a reduction of symptoms when treated with the psychotherapy alone. The nonresponders were then treated with a combined tricyclic antidepressant and psychotherapy, and 92% responded. Dexamethasone nonsuppression and melancholic subtype were associated with failure to respond to psychotherapy alone. Interpretation of the results of this study are confounded by the fact that there appears to be a 50% placebo response rate in depressed adolescents regardless of type of treatment (i.e., medication or nonspecific psychotherapeutic intervention alone). Also, it is not possible to know whether responders in the second stage of the study improved because of medication, psychotherapy, or combined treatment.

Robbins et al. (1989) conducted this study without modifying the manual specifically for depressed adolescents; thus the procedures for the treatment are not defined. To further study the efficacy of interpersonal psychotherapy with depressed adolescents, our standardization of interpersonal psychotherapy for depressed adolescents, outlined in this book, is necessary. Fourteen depressed adolescents have been treated in an open clinical trial of IPT-A using the standardized treatment manual (Mufson et al., 1992). Further studies will need to address the issues of placebo response and differentiating positive responses among medication, IPT, and combined treatment. A controlled clinical trial (in progress at this time) will be the first step toward clarifying these issues.

Psychodynamic Psychotherapy

Psychodynamic psychotherapy is commonly used to treat depressed adolescents. The principles derive from psychoanalytic theories. In the most simple terms, they are based on the premise that symptoms of distress are a result of unconscious conflicts. These symptoms can be addressed and decreased through such interventions as confrontation, clarification, and interpretation (Liebowitz & Kernberg, 1988). Within the psychodynamic psychotherapy framework, there are several types of psychodynamic psychotherapy: child psychoanalysis, expressive or exploratory child psychotherapy, supportive psychotherapy, and expressive supportive child psychotherapy. The specific application and goals of each of these therapies are described in Liebowitz and Kernberg's excellent review of psychodynamic psychotherapies for children.

Psychodynamic theory understands depression as resulting from changes in the sense of self caused by a loss of relationships or achievements or constructs that were used to support a self-image or identity (Bemporad, 1988). The adolescent is particularly vulnerable to depression because the developmental task of adolescence is to change and solidify one's identity. Consequently, the adolescent may become vulnerable to losses that may occur in this process. These vulnerabilities in character are believed to be a result of early childhood experiences that will not only shape adolescence but will affect adult personality and coping skills as well. Psychodynamic psychotherapists believe that psychological improvement will result from intrapsychic, characterological change.

The roles of the therapist are to help the adolescent identify distortions about the self and one's relationships, place them in the historical context of the relationship or situation, and help the adolescent have more realistic expectations and goals for relationships and self-concept. Symptom relief is achieved by bringing into conscious awareness the unconscious conflicts and memories that the adolescent may have hidden from him- or herself. There are many techniques and concepts specific to psychodynamic psychotherapy (Offenkrantz et al., 1982). IPT-A differs from psychodynamic psychotherapy with adolescents in its time-limited framework, its focus on current interpersonal issues rather than intrapsychic ones, and the more directive stance of the therapist in the actual therapy sessions.

Some of the problems that are encountered in psychodynamic psychotherapy with depressed adolescents are a result of the cognitive maturity of adolescents. Interpretations of the symbolic nature may be difficult for some adolescents to understand and may be frightening and alienating if not preceded by clarification and confrontation (Liebowitz & Kernberg, 1988). Other adolescents may respond by intellectualizing their problems to the omission of emotions. Another aspect of the treatment that may be less appealing to adolescents is that the treatment is not time-limited meaning that, upon entering treatment, the adolescent does not know the length of treatment. There is no manual standardizing the treatment, and therapists believe the treatment varies significantly with the nature of the specific patient–therapist alliance. To date there have been no controlled clinical trials of psychodynamic psychotherapy with depressed adolescents.

Family Therapy

Family therapists conceptualize depression as occurring within the family system. People are a product of their social context or family system, and the individual cannot be understood in isolation of some understanding of the larger context (Nichols, 1984). Logically therefore, the most effective way to treat the individual's problem is to affect his or her family interactions. Disequilibrium among the family members, improper alliances, or communication difficulties can result in the creation of an identified patient who manifests the family's problems in his or her depression. Therefore, the therapist addresses the adolescent's depression by addressing the pathology in the family system. There is no one specific model of a dysfunctional family that has been linked to depression in children and adolescents. Specific issues typically addressed in family therapy that can be applied to depression as well as other psychiatric disorders include the concept of boundaries between family members, enmeshment of family members, and the importance of role relations in families. Family therapy is usually a brief, action-oriented approach whose goal is to resolve the symptoms by changing the family members' behavior in the present (Nichols, 1984).

Within the family therapy modality, there are several different types of treatment ranging from systems family therapy (Haley, 1976), structural family therapy (Minuchin, 1974), to contextual family therapy (Boszormenyi-Nagy & Krasner, 1986). These treatments differ in types of techniques and focus of treatment ranging from communication and interpersonal problem-solving skills (systems therapy), reframing interactions, altering boundaries, and family hierarchy (structural therapy), to the use of paradoxical techniques such as prescribing the symptom that the therapist and patient are actually trying to eliminate. The guiding principle is that the most significant influence on an individual's behavior lies in the family relationships, the responses of the family system to the individual, and vice versa. There have been several studies on the efficacy of family therapy for the treatment of family dysfunction and other disorders, but the studies have not been specifically for the treatment of adolescent depression.

Group Psychotherapy

One of the main goals of group therapy, for almost any psychiatric problem, is to put the adolescent in contact with peers who have similar difficulties, who can provide support for each other, and who can provide each other with opportunities to practice new skills for interpersonal relationships. The specific goals of group therapy can include (1) enabling the individual to perceive similarity of one's needs with others, (2) generating alternative solutions to particular conflicts, (3) learning more effective social skills, and (4) increasing awareness of others' need and feelings (Corey, 1981). Many groups for depressed adolescents are specifically social-skills training groups. In such a group the focus of treatment is on identifying and practicing social skills that may alleviate conflict in relationships with family and friends. Within the group session, members will often role play different communication skills such as clarification of the problem, eliciting another person's point of view, and expression of their own feelings. Other groups may be less structured. Adolescents in these groups may use the sessions to discuss the problems they are having with family and friends, to learn whether or not their situation differs from many other adolescents, and together to generate solutions and gain confirmation of their feelings in the situation. Another significant aspect of these groups is that many of them are time-limited with set goals and programs to accomplish within that time. The social skills groups differ from IPT-A because the group format precludes more intensive focus on the individual adolescent's specific interpersonal problem and provides fewer opportunities to follow through each adolescent's particular interpersonal issue to successful resolution. As discussed above, there have been clinical trials of a structured type of cognitive–behavioral group for depressed adolescents (Lewinsohn et al., 1990; Reynolds & Coats, 1986) in addition to social-skills groups that have demonstrated some efficacy (Fine et al., 1989, 1991).

CONCLUSION

There is both a clinical need for effective psychotherapeutic interventions with depressed adolescents and a scientific imperative to establish efficacy among the multitude of currently available therapies. Keller et al. (1991), in an epidemiologic study, found a significantly low rate of treatment in adolescents and children with major depression. Recognition and treatment of depression in adolescents would likely increase if an effort were made to investigate and document effective treatments for the population.

IPT-A differs from the previously reviewed therapies in a number of ways. It differs from psychodynamic psychotherapy in that it is time-limited, and the transference is neither encouraged nor interpreted. Intrapsychic change and characterological change are not goals of IPT-A as they are in psychodynamic psychotherapy. The goal of cognitive therapy is to change the patient's way of thinking, whereas the goal of IPT-A is to change how the patient relates to his or her social and interpersonal environment by effecting change in communication and patterns of reactions and responses. IPT-A emphasizes interpersonal relationships as they effect and are effected by depression.

Despite the scarcity of controlled clinical trials of treatments for depressed adolescents, a myriad of therapeutic techniques are widely used with them. The treatments need to be assessed further regarding their efficacy with adolescents. Given the involvement of exogenous factors in adolescent depression, psychosocial treatments are likely to have their place as effective treatments either alone or in combination with pharmacological treatment. The next section will delineate the major principles of interpersonal psychotherapy formulated to address those interpersonal issues we believe play a significant role in the maintenance of depression and where we believe therapeutic interventions should be aimed.

·II·

*Application of
Interpersonal Psychotherapy
for Depressed Adolescents*

·4·

The Initial Phase: Assessment and Diagnosis of Depression

IPT-A is designed for use with adolescents ages 12–18 years old who have an acute-onset major depression. Adolescents are suitable for the treatment if they are suffering from a DSM-III-R major depression, are of normal intelligence, and are not actively suicidal. Depressed adolescents with psychotic symptoms or primary diagnoses of manic depression, substance abuse, anxiety disorders, or conduct disorders have not been treated with IPT-A. The two main goals of IPT-A are (1) to decrease the depressive symptoms and (2) to improve the interpersonal problems associated with the onset of the depressive episode. The initial visits (1 through 4) are devoted to diagnosing the depression, obtaining an interpersonal inventory, identifying one or more problem areas, and negotiating the therapeutic contract. During this phase of IPT-A the therapist should accomplish eight tasks:

1. Diagnose the depressive disorder according to current diagnostic systems.
2. Assess patient suitability for this particular type of treatment.
3. Conduct an interpersonal inventory (review of significant relationships) and relate the depression to the interpersonal context.
4. Identify the interpersonal difficulties in one or more principal problem areas.
5. Explain the theory and goals of interpersonal therapy.
6. Make a treatment contract with the patient and parent.
7. Explain the patient's and parent's expected role in the treatment.
8. Begin treating the depression.

This chapter focuses on the diagnostic assessment process (steps 1 and 2). The interpersonal inventory and identification of problem areas (steps 3 and 4) will be detailed in Chapter 5, and establishing the therapeutic contract (steps 5–7) will be detailed in Chapter 6. Treating the depression takes place from the first session to the final session.

DIAGNOSING THE DEPRESSION

The goal of diagnostic assessment for IPT-A is twofold: (1) to make a clinical diagnosis meeting current diagnostic criteria and (2) to ascertain the adolescent's level of psychosocial functioning and pinpoint areas of interpersonal problems. To this end, all available sources of information should be tapped including the adolescent, the parents and other family members, teachers and other school personnel, and other caretakers such as pediatricians and clergy. The importance of obtaining as much information as possible from people who see the patient in various roles and circumstances should be explained to the adolescent and the parents who, it is hoped, will provide consent to speak to the other important people in the adolescent's life. Without this permission, the therapist is not at liberty to speak to anyone other than the patient and parents.

Diagnostic procedures include clinical interviews with the adolescent and the parents about the adolescent and interviews with other key figures in the adolescent's life. Psychological testing can also be a useful addition to diagnosis, particularly if there is a question of a learning disability complicating a depression. Medical tests for physical illness such as thyroid disease, diabetes, liver, or kidney disease may be performed to rule out the possibility of organic illness causing depression or mood swings. Psychobiological variables have no place in clinical diagnosing, although this is an area of active research that may be fruitful for diagnosis and treatment in the future. In addition, there are a variety of instruments that may be used to assist the clinician in making a psychiatric diagnosis of adolescent psychopathology and monitoring response to treatment. Different instruments are targeted for the adolescents, the parents, and teachers.

Many methods of assessment have been designed to improve diagnostic accuracy and reliability. These tools range from structured and semistructured interviews to symptom scales and self-report inventories. Although most of these instruments have been designed for research purposes, they can also be helpful to the general clinician. A comprehensive guide to these instruments can be found in Rutter et al. (1988). Instruments useful for the clinician are reviewed briefly here.

Research has demonstrated the use of assessment instruments to improve psychiatric diagnosis of children and adolescents. Although the instruments were designed for research, many of them can also be beneficial when used in general clinical practice. The instruments afford the clinician the opportunity to have guidelines for a systematic review of disorders, to obtain information systematically from a variety of sources, to be able to compare the quality and/or nature of the information obtained from the sources, and to monitor closely changes in the adolescents' psychological state. However, they are not a substitute for clinical acumen and are most effective in a clinical situation when skillfully woven into the assessment and therapeutic process whose foundation is the relationship between patient and clinician.

Sources of Information

There are several important issues to consider in the assessment process that include the nature of the information being obtained from various sources and the informant from whom the information is being obtained. The IPT-A therapist is interested in obtaining information about current and past depressive symptoms, history of current depression including possible precipitant, type and course of previous psychiatric illness, psychosocial history and current psychosocial functioning, and family and medical history. One of the primary steps in diagnosing children and assessing their functioning is to obtain information about the presence and severity of specific symptoms (Kazdin et al., 1983). When obtaining this information, the therapist always keeps in mind the interpersonal context of the depression (see Chapter 5).

Research has demonstrated considerable discrepancies between parents' and children's reports on the degree and nature of children's psychopathology. Researchers have found that parents, teachers, and children report different types of symptoms or problems (Kazdin et al., 1983; Edelbrock et al., 1986). Discrepancies between parent and child reports are consistently found using a variety of assessment instruments including symptom scales and diagnostic interviews and using a variety of diagnostic criteria (Moretti et al., 1985; Lobovits & Handal, 1985; Leon et al., 1980; Kashani et al., 1985). Parents and children may use different criteria of severity for determining when a behavior is worth mentioning, and as observers they may be unable to perceive what is problematic for their child. In addition, they may have different areas of concern that are reflected in their responses (Kashani et al., 1985). Angold et al. (1987) found that parents are relatively unlikely to report symptoms which their children do not report, but children often report symptoms that their parents do not report. This is particularly true in the area of reports on suicidality, ideation or attempts (Velez & Cohen, 1988; Walker et al., 1989).

Depressive symptoms can often be silent or misinterpreted. Some parents or teachers might consider the adolescent's silence and isolation as a "phase" or just a slight exacerbation of how the adolescent usually is. The social withdrawal may be so intense that the adolescent is basically ignored, particularly, if there are other adolescents or events that immediately capture and demand the attention of the adults. Irritability or anger may be the first symptom that the adolescent presents with, and if time is not devoted to talking to the adolescent to see if there is significant depression, the adolescent can be labelled simply as a problem that needs to be dealt with in a disciplinary manner.

Therefore, it is important for the clinician to interview the parents about their child, but the more accurate information is likely to be obtained from the adolescent. Angold (1988b) concludes that there appears to be a pattern of low sensitivity and high specificity for parental reports of children's depressive symptoms. Particularly with adolescents, it seems important to interview the patient directly for an accurate and complete picture of his or her internal emotional state. For a full picture of the child's psychopathology, it appears prudent, however, to obtain information from as many sources as possible including parents and teachers.

The clinician's ability to obtain and synthesize information is key to making an accurate assessment and diagnosis. The astute clinician will often reinterview someone with new information obtained from another informant. Discrepancies should be addressed directly with each informant in an attempt to clarify the point in question. The clinician needs to keep an open mind at all points of treatment, and to be able to integrate new information and reformulate diagnostic assessments accordingly.

Types of Interviews

There are several types of clinical interviews used to make a diagnosis. These include unstructured, semistructured, and structured diagnostic interviews. Unstructured interviews are those conducted by clinicians that do not follow specific questions or have particular response options. It is assumed that the clinician has knowledge and experience in the area of adolescent psychiatry. This is typically the type of interview that is used by the clinician when the patient presents him- or herself to the office for an evaluation for treatment. The information gathered and the method for obtaining the information are a function of the clinician and his or her training. A semistructured interview is designed with specific questions that are to be asked by the interviewer. The interview still relies on the clinician's judgment and familiarity with principles of psychopathology in the decisions about whether or how to probe for more information to make the diagnosis (Eldelbrock & Costello, 1988). Two commonly used semistructured interviews are the Interview Schedule for Children (ISC) (Kovacs, 1982) and the Schedule for Affective Disorders and Schizophrenia, childhood version (K-SADS) (Chambers et al., 1985).

A structured interview is characterized by being highly structured, employing direct questions, providing specific codes for recording responses, and minimizing the need for clinical judgment regarding whether or not to probe for more information. The structured interview can be administered by a lay interviewer, since it requires less training, clinical judgment and inference than the semistructured or unstructured interview (Edelbrock & Costello, 1988). Examples of a structured interview include the Diagnostic Interview Schedule for Children (DISC, version 2.3) (Fisher et al., 1992) and the Diagnostic Interview for Children and Adolescents (DICA) (Herjanic & Reich, 1982). Structured interviews are believed to permit diagnostic assessment according to systematic and specific criteria for psychiatric diagnosis and to standardize methods for eliciting symptoms concerning a range of symptoms and behaviors (Gutterman et al., 1987). Herjanic and Reich (1982) believe that the structured interview maximizes the reliability of the information being obtained. Interviews also may vary as to the time frame they assess, ranging from assessment of functioning in the past week to lifetime diagnoses. For a complete review of interviews see Rutter et al. (1988).

For the purposes of our study on interpersonal psychotherapy for the treatment of depressed adolescents we selected the K-SADS. There are several versions of the K-SADS including the present episode version and the epidemiologic–lifetime version. Many of the reliability studies have been conducted with the K-SADS-P (present) version administered to children ages 6–17 years. The assessment of symptoms and diagnoses of depressive syndromes was found to have acceptable reliability as were the three depressive diagnoses (Chambers et al., 1985). Parent–child agreement on depressive symptoms was moderate, and raters were instructed to give greater weight to the child's report for diagnostic summary. Other studies using the K-SADS-E (epidemiologic) version have found agreement about depressive symptoms between parents and children to be significant, but low (Angold et al., 1987). Chambers et al. (1985) concluded that child and adolescent depression and its symptoms could be assessed with sufficient reliability by the K-SADS to generate valid diagnoses.

We believe the semistructured interview can also be helpful for the general clinician assessment. Although it is designed with specific questions to be asked, it still relies on the clinician's judgment to know when to pursue further questioning or to change the probe questions to obtain more detailed information. Its format provides the clinician with a systematic guide for assessing all DSM-III-R diagnoses ensuring a complete assessment.

Self-Report Instruments

Clinicians and researchers also use self-report instruments in addition to the clinical interview to assess depression. Some of the most commonly used self-report instruments to assess depression in children and adolescents include the Beck Depression Inventory (BDI), Children's Depression Inventory (CDI), and the Center for Epidemiological Studies Depression Scale (CES-D). For the purposes of our work in interpersonal psychotherapy, we chose to administer the BDI. The BDI was designed to assess a level of symptom severity rather than to generate a diagnosis (Kashani et al., 1990). Teri (1982a) administered the BDI to an adolescent sample and found it to be reliable with the population. Kashani et al. (1990) used the BDI with a sample of clinic-referred adolescents and concluded that the BDI efficiently and accurately identified and differentiated depressed from nondepressed adolescents. In a sample of psychiatrically hospitalized adolescents, BDI scores were found to correlate highly with a global rating of depression made by direct clinical examination (Strober et al., 1981). The BDI cutoff score of 16 and above for moderate and severe depression permits correct classification of 81% of a depressed adolescent inpatient sample (Strober et al., 1981). In another study, including both an inpatient sample and a school sample, the BDI proved to be a sufficiently accurate screening measure for major depression in adolescents (Barrera et al., 1988). The CDI is an adaptation of the BDI for school-aged children up to 13 years old (Kovacs, 1985). Given the age range of our subject population and the positive findings of its use with adolescents, we used the BDI to obtain a self-report of the adolescent's depressive symptoms.

In clinical practice, the self-report instruments may be used in a variety of ways. While they are used to establish a baseline of symptomatology as part of the assessment, they can also be used periodically throughout the treatment as a way of monitoring the adolescent's progress or lack of progress. They can serve as a monitor of remaining symptoms, either illustrating progress or indicating a need for change in treatment because of a lack of improvement. They are self-administered and take very little time to complete. Not only can the self-report instrument help the clinician get an idea of the treatment's effects, but it can help the adolescent track his or her symptoms, and the changes in functioning often become a topic of discussion during the session. The ratings can be helpful in leading to a discussion on how life events and feelings can have an impact on day-to-day functioning.

Clinician-Rated Instruments

Another type of measure that is used to assess adolescent depression is the clinician-rated instrument. The clinician rates the patient on a scale of items based on a clinical interview and observations of the patient. A frequently used clinician-rated symptom scale is the Hamilton Rating Scale for Depression (HRSD). The scale is oriented toward the behavioral and somatic features of depression. It has been found to distinguish clearly among three groups of subjects with a progressive increase in severity score of depressive symptomatology. Given the strong research record of the HRSD (Robbins et al., 1985), the authors used it in their study of depressed adolescents in order to be able to compare the adolescent's self-report with an independent evaluation of symptomatology. This might also be helpful for the clinician who might want to compare his or her own perception of the adolescent's psychological distress with the adolescent's perception. The discrepancies would serve as a useful topic of discussion regarding how the adolescent feels inside versus what he or she conveys to others and how this affects the responses he or she elicits from other people.

CONDUCTING THE FIRST AND SECOND SESSIONS

During the first session, the therapist asks the patient about reasons for seeking treatment, the recent history of the depression, specific symptoms of depression and associated psychosocial functioning such as suicidality, drug abuse, and antisocial behavior. This also is the time to evaluate the need for medication. A recent comprehensive physical examination should be required for all patients in order to rule out organic causes of the depression, such as hypothyroidism and side effects of medications, such as steroid treatment or birth control pills.

In addition, the therapist should review past depressive episodes, the presence of any past manic or hypomanic episodes, environmental or interpersonal precipitant, and previous treatment or methods of resolution. Social, academic, and/or family consequences of the depression should also be explored. Suicidal intent must be carefully assessed because it may be a contraindication to outpatient treatment (see Chapter

13). All of this information should be obtained by the end of the second session so the therapist can begin to make a determination about treatment recommendations and whether IPT-A is a suitable treatment modality.

An important component of the first two sessions is to educate the patient and parent about the depressive condition. The education process includes review of symptoms and methods of treatment as well as reassurance and guidance in managing symptoms. The initial guidance is important in fostering a sense that one has already begun working on the problem, a sense that contributes to the patient's commitment to the treatment and engagement in the therapeutic relationship.

Parent Involvement in the Initial Session

Parents should be interviewed in the initial session. The therapist may meet with the parents and adolescent for part of the time and then with the adolescent alone. A comprehensive history of the adolescent's symptoms including type, duration, and social functioning should be obtained from both parent and adolescent. The parent should be similarly educated about depression and possible treatments, including a discussion of whether there is a need for medication. Parents should be given information about how to manage the adolescent's depressive symptoms such as encouraging the child to do as much as possible, identifying warning signs of worsening of the condition, and planning strategies to deal with an emergency, such as increasing suicidal ideation or a suicide attempt. The therapist should inform the parents that they may be asked to participate in future sessions if it seems as though it might be helpful in addressing a problem related to the depression. There are circumstances in which the parent may refuse to be involved in the treatment or the adolescent may refuse to have the parent be involved. This is discussed in the section on special issues in the treatment of adolescents.

REVIEW OF SYMPTOMS

The detailed review of the patient's symptoms has four purposes: (1) to assist the therapist in correct diagnosis; (2) to show the patient that his or her symptoms are part of a known syndrome that is understood and that can be effectively treated; (3) to place the symptoms in their interpersonal context and identify the specific problem area; and (4) to illustrate for the patient the active nature of his or her own role and the therapist's role in the treatment. At the conclusion of the review, the patient should know that the depression symptoms are time-limited, reflective of a disorder that can be treated successfully, and that he or she will be able to function better with treatment.

The review of symptoms enables the therapist to make a DSM-III-R diagnosis of major depression (see Table 4.1), and to diagnose all comorbid disorders using DSM-III-R criteria. To this end, the following symptoms as outlined in the K-SADS (Puig-Antich et al., 1980) should be probed.

Depressed Mood. Has there ever been a time when you felt sad, down, empty, moody, like crying, unhappy, or you had a bad or unhappy feeling inside most of the time? How long during the day did it last? A long time or short time? How long—the whole morning? All afternoon? From waking up in the morning until lunch? Less? More? Is it worse in the morning or later in the day?

Anhedonia. Has there ever been a time when you just couldn't have as much fun as usual? Or were having much less fun than your friends? How long did it last? Did you enjoy anything at that time? Has there been a time when you felt bored most of the time? When was that? Do you know why you were feeling that way? Could you have changed it? Could you have found anything to do that was fun? Was there anything you enjoyed or you felt like doing at that time?

Separation Issues. Do these sad feelings happen only when you are away from your (major attachment figure) or your family? What was going on in your life when you felt that way or before you felt that way? Had anything happened that upset you? Was something bothering you?

Grief Reaction. Had someone you were very close to just died or moved away or had you just had a pet die? Is the way you feel different from when someone close to you had died? (A pet?)

Lack of Reactivity. When you are sad, and when something good happens, do you feel better?

Appetite and Weight. Have you lost your appetite or lost weight? How much? Are you hungrier than usual or have you gained weight? How much?

Initial Insomnia. Do you have trouble sleeping? What is your usual bedtime and awakening time? Do you have trouble falling asleep? How long does it take? What keeps you awake? What thoughts do you have when you get into bed?

Middle Insomnia. Do you wake up during the night and then can't go back to sleep right away?

Terminal Insomnia. Do you wake up before you have to? Do you feel rested upon awakening? How much too early do you wake up?

Hypersomnia. Do you sleep more than usual for you? How much more? Do you take naps during the day?

Agitation. Do you have trouble sitting still or are you walking back and forth?

Retardation. Do you talk or move more slowly than usual?

Fatigue. Are you very tired or do you have less energy than usual?

Diurnal Variation. Do you feel worse in the morning or afternoon? Significantly worse or just a little bit worse?

Depersonalization. Do you ever feel like you are outside of yourself watching yourself do things and say things but not feeling part of it?

Paranoid Symptoms. Have you felt as though people are talking about you? That strangers are talking about you? Do you worry that someone or a group is trying to hurt you? Who? What are they trying to do? Why would they want to hurt you?

Obsessive and Compulsive Symptoms. Do you ever have thoughts that keep coming into your mind that seem to come from nowhere and intrude upon your thinking? Are they the same thoughts each time? Are there things you have to keep doing and redoing even though you know it is not necessary? Such as checking that you have locked the door or washing your hands repeatedly?

Excessive Guilt. Do you feel guilty (bad) about things that happened a long time ago? Do you blame yourself for things that aren't your fault? Do you think you should be punished more than you are? Do you feel that you aren't a good person or do you feel worthless?

Concentration Difficulty. Do you have difficulty paying attention or keeping your mind on your schoolwork? Have your grades gone down? Do you have to make a much bigger effort than before just to keep up? Do you feel like your thoughts are slowed down?

Suicidal Ideation or Behavior. Do you think about death a lot? Do you think about killing yourself? Do you have a plan? Did you ever try to kill yourself? (See Chapter 14.)

Sexual Symptoms. Ask if sexually active. If so, continue with questions. If not, go to next area. Has your interest in boys/girls changed recently? Have you had less sexual interest than usual? Are you interested in the same or opposite sex? Are you sexually active? If so, are you using birth control? Difficulty becoming excited? Sexual relations less often? Difficulty in obtaining an erection (boys) or reaching a climax?

Helplessness. Do you feel unable to change the situation? Do you feel like you don't know what to do to feel differently?

Hopelessness. Do you feel that the situation will never be different? Do feel that there is little chance that you will feel better in the future?

Somatic Symptoms. Are you experiencing any physical aches and pains? Headaches? Stomachaches? Joint pains? Trouble going to the bathroom? Frequency of urination? Jaw pain? Neck aches?

Hallucinations. Do you hear voices when no one is around and

TABLE 4.1. Criteria for Major Depressive Episode as Defined by DSM-III-R

A. At least five of the following symptoms have been present during the same two-week period and represent a change from previous functioning: at least one of the symptoms is either (1) depressed mood, or (2) loss of interest or pleasure. (Do not include symptoms that are clearly due to a physical condition, mood-congruent delusions or hallucinations, incoherence, or marked loosening of associations.)

(1) depressed mood (or can be irritable mood in children and adolescents) most of the day, nearly every day, as indicated either by subjective account or observation by others
(2) markedly diminished interest or pleasure in all, or almost all, activities most of the day, nearly every day (as indicated either by subjective account or observation by others of apathy most of the time)
(3) significant weight loss or weight gain when not dieting (e.g., more than 5% of body weight in a month), or decrease or increase in appetite nearly every day (in children, consider failure to make expected weight gains)
(4) insomnia or hypersomnia nearly every day
(5) psychomotor agitation or retardation nearly every day (observable by others, not merely subjective feelings of restlessness or being slowed down)
(6) fatigue or loss of energy nearly every day
(7) feelings of worthlessness or excessive or inappropriate guilt (which may be delusional) nearly every day (not merely self-reproach or guilt about being sick)
(8) diminished ability to think or concentrate, or indecisiveness, nearly every day (either by subjective account or as observed by others)
(9) recurrent thoughts of death (not just fear of dying), recurrent suicidal ideation without a specific plan, or a suicide attempt or a specific plan for committing suicide

B. (1) It cannot be established that an organic factor initiated and maintained the disturbance
(2) The disturbance is not a normal reaction to the death of a loved one (Uncomplicated Bereavement)

For Melancholic Type:

The presence of at least five of the following:

(1) loss of interest or pleasure in all, or almost all, activities
(2) lack of reactivity to usually pleasurable stimuli (does not feel much better, even temporarily, when something good happens)
(3) depression regularly worse in the morning
(4) early morning awakening (at least two hours before usual time of awakening)
(5) psychomotor retardation or agitation (not merely subjective complaints)
(6) significant anorexia or weight loss (e.g., more than 5% of body weight in a month)
(7) no significant personality disturbance before first Major Depressive Episode
(8) one or more previous Major Depressive Episodes followed by complete, or nearly complete, recovery
(9) previous good response to specific and adequate somatic antidepressant therapy, e.g., tricyclics, ECT, MAOI, lithium

Note. Reprinted by permission from American Psychiatric Association (1987, pp. 222–224). See DSM-III-R for other depression diagnoses.

that no one can hear but you? What do those voices say? Do they speak to you or just call your name? Do you ever see things that no one can see but you?

The adolescents should be encouraged to describe the depression symptoms using their own language or set of beliefs. For example, some patients will see their experience in religious terms: "God is punishing me for not being a better daughter." Others will blame the problem on someone else—a mother for not listening to them, or a friend for not being understanding and tolerant of their behavior. The therapist will have the opportunity to explore these beliefs further and put them in the appropriate context for treatment later in the evaluation process.

Depression in adolescents also can be complicated by a conduct disorder, by an anxiety disorder including panic disorder, or by a substance-use disorder. There should be a review of symptoms for these disorders, as outlined in the K-SADS (Puig-Antich et al., 1980). (See Tables 4.2 and 4.3.)

The reader is referred to DSM-III-R for symptom review for the

TABLE 4.2. Conduct Disorder

Determine if pre- or postdates depression.

1. Have you ever stolen valuables from outside the home while no one was looking or no one was there?
2. Have you ever forged checks?
3. Have you ever forged your parents signature on school reports?
4. Have you ever run away from home overnight? When? Why?
5. Have you ever been expelled from school for over a week or suspended several times? For what?
6. Are you often absent from school? How often? What are you doing when you don't go to school?
7. Do you often get into trouble for breaking a lot of rules at home? At school? Are you obedient?
8. Do you often tell lies? About what?
9. Do you steal money? From whom, parents? From others? For what purpose?
10. Have you ever set fires? What did you set fire to?
11. Have you ever mugged or assaulted other people? Have you ever forced someone to engage in sexual activity with you?
12. Have you ever been physically cruel to animals?
13. Have you ever hurt someone badly on purpose? Have you ever broken into houses in order to steal? Have you ever stolen valuables from outside the home in a way that involved violence like armed robbery (gun, knife), purse snatching, extortion?

TABLE 4.3. Substance Use Disorder

Determine if pre- or postdates depression.
Substances include cannabis, amphetamines, cocaine,
barbiturates, opioids, hallucinogens, PCP, alcohol.

1. Have you ever taken any drugs to feel better or to get high—marijuana, narcotics, LSD, or things like these (barbiturates, uppers, downers, etc.)?
2. Have you ever used anything else to get high, lose weight, or stay awake?

(Suggested probes for each substance when applicable)

3. Did you ever use (substance)? Did you use it daily or regularly for as long as one month? How much did you use? How often? When was that?
4. Did you ever try to stop or cut down on your use? Did you ever stay high all day? How often? Did you ever have a bad or scary time when you were high? What happened? How many times did that happen? When?
5. Did you ever have problems with your friends, at school, or at home because of using (substance)? Did you get into fights, lose friends, or get into trouble?
6. Did you find that you had to use more and more (substance) to get high or that you didn't get as high when you used your usual amount?
7. How did it make you feel?
8. Did you experience withdrawal symptoms (cite examples for substance), when you stopped using (substance)?

---

anxiety disorders and learning disabilities. The adolescents should be assessed for the presence of these disorders as well.

Comorbidity with any of these disorders can result in multiple missed appointments, failure to focus on the tasks of therapy, or various life crises including legal complications. The therapist must make a clinical decision whether IPT-A can be an effective therapeutic approach, taking the adolescent diagnosis and severity of symptoms into consideration.

IDENTIFYING THE SYMPTOMS AS DEPRESSION

If the patient is in fact diagnosed with a depressive disorder, the first task should be to tell the patient explicitly that his or her symptoms indicate the presence of a specific disorder. The therapist can review each of the symptoms with the patient. If the physical exam results are negative, the therapist can inform and reassure the patient that the somatic symptoms are due to the depression rather than physical illness. It is important to reassure the patient that there is no serious physical illness, that the adolescent is not "going crazy," and that the psychological problems can be effectively treated.

The therapist should convey the diagnosis to the patient clearly by saying:

> *The sad, unhappy feelings you're having are causing you to have problems with your friends and family. These feelings and problems we call "symptoms" and define as depression. Your sad feelings make you want to stay by yourself and not want to go out with your friends anymore. You don't like to return phone calls and are irritable when your mother asks you to participate in household chores or family activities. She, in turn, doesn't understand what you're feeling and it seems as if she's always yelling at you. You're not able to complete your homework because you can't keep your mind on your work. You get angry with your teacher for expecting too much of you, but you also feel bad because you can't keep up with the rest of the class. You don't think the teacher likes you as much as she does the rest of the kids in your class. At night you get into bed and can't fall asleep because you're thinking of all the things you didn't accomplish during the day. You wake up in the middle of the night with a bad feeling in the pit of your stomach and can't fall back asleep. You've even stopped enjoying going out with your freinds after school for a slice of pizza. Food just doesn't taste good anymore. Your friends seem to be avoiding you and aren't inviting you out anymore. All of these interactions only make you feel worse about yourself, but you can't seem to do anything about it. You feel hopeless and don't see the point to going on with your life. These problems are all part of the clinical picture of depression.*

This discussion may be held jointly with parent(s) and child or with each of them separately.

The second task is to impart some general information about the course of depression and its treatment. For example:

> *Depression commonly occurs in children and adolescents as well as in adults. Depressed adolescents have problems in their relationships [cite specific examples for each adolescent] and these problems may be the only manifestation of the depression seen by the family. It is believed to be more common in girls than boys. Approximately 2–5% of adolescents may have a depressive disorder at any one time. Even though you feel badly now, depressions do respond to treatment. There is more than one way to treat depression, so that if the first approach does not work, there are other approaches to try. Most adolescents with depression recover rapidly with treatment. As a result of treatment you will likely feel better,*

your symptoms will decrease, and you will be able to function more normally at school and at home. Psychotherapy is one of the standard treatments for depression and has been proven effective in several studies. Therapy hopefully will help you understand what has been making you depressed and help you find ways to resolve the problems.

DETERMINING AN ADOLESCENT'S SUITABILITY FOR IPT-A

An integral part of the assessment process is determining an adolescent's suitability for IPT-A. This determination is not only based on diagnoses, both inclusive and exclusive disorders, it also includes assessing whether IPT-A is a reasonable treatment modality to recommend to the adolescent and adolescent's family.

Based on our clinical experience, the following characteristics of an adolescent make IPT-A a good treatment choice: the adolescent's ability to establish a therapeutic relationship with the therapist and a willingness to work in a one-to-one therapeutic relationship in a time-limited therapy; agreement between the adolescent and therapist that there is at least one interpersonal problem area that the adolescent is willing to focus on during the course of therapy; a family who supports the therapy or at least will not prematurely terminate the adolescent's treatment. The therapist can gauge the adolescent's ability to relate to the therapist during the assessment process by the adolescent's willingness to come to sessions and to be honest and open with the therapist about his or her feelings. An adolescent who is eager to discuss feelings and problems and is willing to explore with the therapist connections among feelings, events, and relationships is a particularly good candidate for IPT-A. IPT-A is probably most effective with adolescents who have had an acute onset of depressive symptoms and by history have not had severe interpersonal problems with friends or family. In such cases, there is often an identifiable precipitant to the depression, and the depression has resulted in interpersonal problems. However, IPT-A can also be helpful to adolescents with longstanding interpersonal problems; the goals for improvement, however, may need to be more circumscribed.

SUMMARY

By the end of the first two sessions, the therapist will have accomplished the tasks of diagnosing all DSM-IIIR disorders and determining whether IPT-A is a potentially effective treatment method for a particular adolescent. Comorbid diagnoses, family structure and relationships, and individual characteristics of the adolescent as determined by clinical history, diagnostic assessment tools, medical examination, and the emerging therapeutic relationship form the basis of the therapist's recommendation for IPT-A. The work of the therapy has already begun by this time. The adolescent and his or her parents have been given a diagnosis for the adolescent's problems. They have been educated about the depressive disorder, and the adolescent's symptoms have been related to the depressive disorder. It is now time for the therapist to obtain an interpersonal inventory and identify one or more problem areas.

·5·

The Interpersonal Context
of Depression

Following completion of the assessment for depression and suitability for
IPT-A, the therapist should turn the focus to understanding the interpersonal context of the depression, particularly the event that may have
precipitated the depressive episode, the reasons for seeking treatment
now, and what has been going on in significant relationships that may
be associated with the onset of symptoms. These are the tasks of sessions
3 and 4. This work culminates in the identification of one or more
problem areas as the focus of treatment.

THE INTERPERSONAL INVENTORY

It is necessary for the therapist to conduct a detailed review of the
patient's significant relationships both current and past to obtain a
complete picture of the nature of the patient's social relationships and
interpersonal functioning. A detailed review, called an interpersonal
inventory, is carried out during the initial phase of the treatment in
sessions 3 and 4. Although the majority of the interpersonal inventory
is conducted in these initial sessions, it may be updated as treatment
progresses and more information is gathered. The therapist should ask
the adolescent about the significant people in the adolescent's life including family, friends, and teachers.

> I would like to talk to you about the important people in your life, people
> like your mother and father, sisters and brothers, best friend, girlfriend
> or boyfriend, other close friends. Has your depression affected your
> relationship with the people you are closest to? How? Do you think you

have problems in your relationships with people? What are those problems? Are you able to feel close to people or is it hard for you to confide in people? Who in your family do you feel closest to, can you confide in, and go to for help? What makes that relationship so special for you? Who in your family don't you feel close to? What is the problem in your relationship with this person? What would you like to change about that relationship? Who outside of your family do you feel especially close to? What is it about that relationship that makes you feel close to that person? Do you have friends that you are not close to? What prevents you from feeling close to that person? Are there other people you are close with, like a teacher or a clergy person or a relative or a family friend? Of all the people we've been talking about, to whom do you feel closest? What would you like to change about yourself to help you have better relationships with the people in your life?

Generally, the therapist attempts to obtain this information from a parent and teachers, as well as from the adolescent. In discussions with them, information can be gathered about the patient's relationships with significant others, such as grandparents, boy- or girlfriend, and anyone else. The information should include:

1. The person's interactions with the patient, including how frequently they saw each other, what they did together and so forth.
2. The terms of the relationship or expectations for the relationship, whether or not these were fulfilled, revised, and their perceived effect on the outcome of the relationship. Is the relationship ongoing? If not, did it end positively or negatively?
3. A discussion of the positive and negative aspects of the relationship with specific examples of both sides of the relationship.
4. What changes the patient might want to make in the relationship and how to try and implement these changes either in him- or herself or the other party.
5. How the depression has affected their relationship with the adolescent and how it has affected the adolescent's other relationships.

These questions can help the parent or teacher gain perspective on how depression can affect a person's relationship and may help the adult place recurrent problems in the relationship in the context of a depressive episode that can be expected to resolve. Information supplied by people significant in the adolescent's life is used to supplement the information obtained directly from the adolescent. Clinical judgment applied by the therapist is used to correct distortions and misperceptions on the adolescent's part.

The therapist's primary interest in conducting the interpersonal review is to identify those interpersonal issues most relevant to the onset of the patient's depression. The therapist wants to identify any conflicts or interpersonal difficulties as well as identify potential areas for change. The therapist's goal is to identify a primary problem area. The identified problem may be difficulty with a relationship that has become exacerbated by a chronic depression or it may be an event involving an important person in the adolescent's life that has become problematic for the patient.

LIFE EVENTS ASSOCIATED WITH THE DEPRESSION

Diagnosis of major depression according to DSM-III-R criteria does not require the identification of a precipitant; however, through discussion one is often identified. Adolescents initially are not always aware of such an event, but often one can be elicited. The therapist should probe for (1) changes in family structure, (2) changes in school, (3) any moves, (4) death, illness, accident, or trauma, and (5) onset of sexuality and sexual relationships. Through discussion of stressful events, the therapist can learn a great deal about the adolescent's interpersonal functioning. Does the adolescent seek support in a healthy fashion, or does the adolescent provoke and alienate the people he or she can depend on the most? Does the adolescent deal directly with the people he or she is closest to, or do feelings emerge in misdirected and ill-conceived actions that are self-defeating and self-destructive? Does the adolescent socially and emotionally withdraw, increasing the depression, when feeling hurt and disappointed by a close relationship? What the therapist learns from such an exploration may not have been immediately apparent to the adolescent or not be something the adolescent was capable of articulating. The therapist can begin this exploration of interpersonal events by asking the patient to talk about recent events or changes in his or her life and interpersonal relationships.

> *What had been going on in your life around the time you began to feel depressed? At school? At home? How were you getting along with your parents? Siblings? Friends? Teachers? Have there been any changes in the relationships?*

To establish a time frame and sequence of events relating a possible precipitant to the depression, the therapist might say:

You told me before that you began to feel depressed one month ago. That seems to be around the same time you broke up with your boyfriend. Did you begin to get sad around the time you broke up with your boyfriend?

By establishing this time frame, the therapist is also facilitating the connection between the depression symptoms and an interpersonal circumstance or event. This connection is a necessary precursor to identification of the targeted problem area.

IDENTIFICATION OF MAJOR PROBLEM AREAS

Well-defined problem areas help the therapist formulate a strategy to improve interpersonal functioning within the context of the problem area. Typically, it is best for short-term treatment to focus on one problem area, but there are occasions when two problem areas may be identified. In such a case, it may be helpful to prioritize the problem areas in terms of which one to focus on initially. The five problem areas do not purport to cover all the underlying dynamics of a depressive disorder. Instead, they serve to help focus the treatment on a specific circumstance of interpersonal functioning that has potential for change and improvement and that may in turn generalize to other situations. The problem areas form the basis of establishing realistic goals for a brief treatment and may be identified as:

1. Grief caused by death, separation, illness in parents.
2. Interpersonal disputes with friends, teachers, parents, siblings.
3. Role transitions such as changing schools (elementary to junior high or junior high to high school), entering puberty, becoming sexually active, birth of another sibling, becoming a parent.
4. Interpersonal deficits such as difficulty initiating and maintaining relationships, communicating about feelings.
5. Single-parent family situations resulting from parental divorce, incarceration, death. (This problem area has been added specifically for the treatment of depressed adolescents.)

There are circumstances in which the therapist and patient do not agree on the identified problem area and/or relevant interpersonal issues, or the patient and the psychotherapist may disagree about the appropriate focus. The disagreement may result from a patient's denial of a particular problem's relationship to the depression or a minimization of the conflict. There are several options for the therapist in such a situation: (1) postpone identifying the specific problem area and goals until the patient gains a better understanding of the issue; (2) begin with very general goals and increase the focus as the therapist gains an understanding of the patient's difficulties; or (3) agree to address the patient's concerns first with the idea that you will address your areas of concern afterwards; or (4) acknowledge the patient may be right and accept that the therapist will need to revise the treatment plan.

It is important in these sessions to be more open-ended when talking with the adolescent in order to enable the individual to describe the experiences in his or her own words and to feel that he or she is being listened to and heard. The initial goal is to assist the adolescent in identifying the significant relationships, particularly the ones in which there are conflicts or difficulties. Once the key relationships are identified, therapist and patient can more specifically address the actual difficulties, the potential to make changes in the relationships, and possible strategies to facilitate these changes. It is important to help the patient see the connections the therapist makes between situations, feelings, and functioning. These connections should be made explicit so that the focus of future sessions is clear. For example, the therapist might say:

> *It seems from our discussions that you have been having conflicts with your parents. It is possible that these problems may be related to your feelings of depression, since these feelings emerged at the same time. Sometimes depression can make problems seem too large to handle. This is because you are depressed, not because you can't change the situation. As you feel better, you may find alternative ways to handle the situation. Over the next few weeks, we will meet once a week to talk about these problematic situations, and we will try to generate alternative ways to cope with the situation. At this time, medication does not appear necessary to relieve you of your symptoms, but it may be considered in the future if your symptoms continue.*

Patients may react to this type of interpersonal exploration in various ways. Hopefully, the patient will agree with your assessment. However, four typical negative reactions include:

1. Denial of the psychological basis of his or her problems and attribution of symptoms to a physical illness.
2. Unwillingness to acknowledge the possible connection among symptoms, functioning and stressful life events.
3. Denial of the presence of symptoms altogether or belief that he or she has control over the symptoms, such as not going to school.

4. Blaming external circumstances or people stating that "if only my parents or my teachers were different I would be fine," rather than assuming some responsibility for the problem.

If the adolescent's attitude persists in any of the manners described above and the adolescent refuses to engage in the treatment, it may be helpful to involve the parents in the treatment. Joint sessions should be held with the adolescent and parent to discuss each one's point of view in order to help the adolescent look at the problem from another perspective. The therapist's role at this time is not to argue with the patient or parent, or to try and change anyone's mind. Rather, the therapist should acknowledge the patient's experience of the symptoms, acknowledge the patient's view of how it affects his or her functioning, and discuss how treatment may be beneficial. If the patient continues to disagree with the therapist's assessment of the situation, the therapist should try and engage the patient to come to the session next week, so the therapist can again try and understand what is being experienced and how the therapist may be helpful.

I can understand that feeling sad a lot, having trouble sleeping, having frequent headaches and stomachaches are unpleasant and uncomfortable. I know you want to find out what is causing them, and I want to help you try do that over the next few weeks. Let's see how you are doing next week and discuss your concerns further, then.

It can often be helpful to review with the patient where you agree with the perceptions and where you may differ:

It seems we both agree that you are feeling sad almost every day, that you are having trouble sleeping, that you have lost your appetite, and that you don't feel like being with your friends the way you did previously. However, we have different views on what may be causing all these feelings for you. I suggested to you that the fights you are getting into with your mother about staying alone in your room, listening to music with the lights off, are related to your depression. Since you appear to disagree with that, I think we should continue to talk over the next few weeks and try to understand further what has been happening to you recently.

If the therapist and patient are still unable to find common goals, then IPT-A may not be the appropriate treatment for this patient or at this particular time, and the patient should be referred for another form of treatment. It can be very frustrating for patients to feel that the therapist doesn't agree or understand their point of view. This frustration may be manifested in acting-out behavior toward the therapy by not keeping appointments, arriving late, or stopping treatment. (The handling of such special problems is discussed in Chapter 15.)

CONNECTING DEPRESSIVE SYMPTOMS TO PROBLEM AREAS

When conducting the assessment of depressive symptoms and educating patients about depression, it is important for the therapist to stress, from the beginning, the relationship between the depression and interpersonal functioning. Although patients may be aware of the role of relationships in their problems, they still may be more inclined to see the problem as inherent in themselves, independent of the other person in the relationship, or blame the other person for causing them to feel bad. As a result, they perceive themselves as a failure or as somehow inadequate. The problems in their interpersonal relationships may not be readily apparent to them, or they may be so withdrawn from relationships that the opportunities to see hope for change are no longer there. Therefore, making the connection between the relationships and their depression is even more difficult for them. In such cases, it is the role of the therapist to help patients begin to make the connection through direct explanation:

> The specific causes of depression are unknown but include environmental and biological influences. Nonetheless, depression is commonly associated with difficulties in relationships, including problems with parents, friends, siblings, and teachers. It is not always clear which occur first, the problems in the relationship or the depression, because the depression can cause interpersonal difficulties, exacerbate interpersonal difficulties, or be the outcome of interpersonal difficulties. Problems in relationships with significant people can cause depressed feelings. Similarly, a person experiencing a depression may have difficulty thinking of appropriate coping skills for the problem. In this treatment we will try to understand your expectations for your relationships and yourself, and help you to fulfill the realistic ones and to cope with the unrealistic ones.

Following an explanation of the relationship between depression and interpersonal problems, the therapist should specifically explain his or her perception of the patient's particular interpersonal situation to the patient in the context of the depression. The constantly changing nature of interpersonal relationships should be stressed. Patients should be asked how they feel, if they would like the relationship to change, and what would have to change for them to feel better. Often, the patient reports wanting to feel understood.

SUMMARY

By the end of session 3, the therapist will obtain a comprehensive interpersonal inventory and will begin formulating an interpersonal assessment that lends itself to identifying one or more problem areas. During session 4 the therapist will present the adolescent with this assessment, and therapist and adolescent will agree on one primary problem area as the focus of treatment. The depressive symptoms and depressive disorder will then be placed in an interpersonal context. The next task will be establishing the treatment contract.

·6·

Setting the Treatment Contract

Setting the treatment contract involves outlining the adolescent's and parents' roles in the treatment, identifying treatment goals, clarifying expectations for treatment, and outlining the "nuts and bolts" of treatment. The main goals of IPT are improvement of interpersonal relationships and a decrease of the depressive symptoms. Patients usually experience a relief of symptoms such as return of appetite, improved sleep patterns, and more interest in their daily activities during the course of treatment. Both the improvement in interpersonal functioning and reduction of symptoms are equally important achievements and most frequently will occur together. Therapist and patient should set goals that are likely to be attainable within the brief treatment so that the patient can feel the goals were achieved and can have a sense of progress throughout the treatment.

GIVING THE ADOLESCENT A LIMITED "SICK ROLE"

By session 4, the therapist will have completed a symptom review, given the adolescent a diagnosis, educated the adolescent and parents about depression, and placed the adolescent's depression in an interpersonal context. The next task is to educate the adolescent about being a patient. The adolescent is given a limited "sick role." The purpose of the sick role is to allow patients some relief from performing their usual social role and to receive some special care in a time-limited way while they recover. The adolescent is encouraged to think of him- or herself as "in treatment." The parents and therapist should be alert to the adolescent tendency to withdraw socially as part of the depressive syndrome and to experience symptoms such as fatigue that are used to justify avoidance of social and school activities. The adolescent should be encouraged to maintain the usual social roles in the family, at school, and with friends. The parent is advised to be supportive and to encourage the adolescent to engage in as many normal activities as possible, although it is recognized that the adolescent may have difficulty performing up to par. The assignment of the "sick role" and psychoeducation can help family members to respond more positively toward the adolescent. It is important to discuss the "sick role" with the adolescent's parents stressing the need to be supportive and not punitive with their child. The psychotherapist might say something like:

> Your child does not feel like participating in many of her usual activities. She doesn't want to eat dinner with the family anymore and won't help out with the household chores. She won't watch television with the rest of the family but, rather, stays in her room alone in the evening and isn't even doing her homework. Every time you try to talk to her she gets angry with you and screams at you to leave her alone. This apathy and lethargy are symptoms of depression, not oppositional behavior. It is important for you to encourage your child, without getting angry, to do as many of her usual activities as possible while treatment is going on.

To the adolescent the psychotherapist might say:

> You may not feel like going out with your friends or doing your school-work, but it is important that you try and maintain as many of your usual activities as possible. It is part of what will make you feel better. Over the next month together, we will be working hard toward the goal of you feeling better. We expect that you will participate in your usual activities, like playing basketball and going to the movies with your friends, and that with treatment you will begin to feel much more energized. As time goes on and we begin to understand and cope with the problems around your becoming depressed, we have every reason to believe that you will feel better than ever.

The therapist should make it clear to the adolescent that the treatment is going to be a collaborative effort between the adolescent and the therapist. Emphasizing that they are a "team" decreases the adolescent's sense of isolation with the depression. It is essential to describe the recovery process to the adolescent so that the "sick role" is understood as time-limited. Discussion of recovery emphasizes the adolescent's participation in the treatment as necessary to facilitate improvement in functioning. The adolescent needs to be educated that therapy will involve work by the adolescent as well as the therapist to understand the conflict precipitating the depression and to find ways to resolve it. The theme of recovery should be an integral part of the treatment.

STEPS TOWARD RECOVERY

It is often helpful to identify different steps toward achieving the overall goal of recovery so that along the way the patient can realize several smaller achievements or signs of progress and change. For example, the therapist might tell the adolescent that over the next several weeks he or she will have more enthusiasm and energy to participate in usual activities as he or she gains a clearer perspective on the problems in his or her interpersonal relationships. The next step will be for the adolescent to try to make changes in those relationships so that they are more mutually satisfying. The therapist and adolescent will explore practical ways of making these changes. Throughout the work of the therapy the adolescent can expect to feel progressively less and less depressed as he or she resumes previous activities and perhaps becomes involved in new activities and relationships. This discussion should be very specific to an individual adolescent, keeping in mind what is realistic for the adolescent and what aspects of the adolescent and his or her circumstances may impose limitations on what can be achieved.

The therapist can use the therapy session to provide feedback to the patient. This may include assessments of the psychotherapist's general understanding of the patient's particular difficulty within the interpersonal problem area and of the associated impairment in functioning. Many patients, experiencing psychiatric symptoms for the first time, may underestimate the impact of the problem on day-to-day functioning as well as the more chronic impairment associated with it.

> *Case Example.* A 12-year-old girl was brought in by her mother for treatment with a depression of moderate severity. She was failing math; was fighting with her mother, who took no interest in her schoolwork or friends; and was not returning phone calls from friends. In addition, her father suffered from Alzheimer's disease and was taken care of by her mother and a full-time home attendant. In the course of the initial interview, it became clear that the girl was attempting to minimize the importance and repercussions of her father's illness and their impact on her life, denying that there were any problems to be worked out. She was reluctant to admit social isolation from peers and increasing conflict with her mother and sister.
>
> In establishing the treatment contract, the therapist explained to the patient that she was dealing with many more difficulties than did

most 12-year-olds. The therapist explained that her depression was in part precipitated by stressful life events of living with a father with Alzheimer's disease, feeling different and isolated from peers because of her father's illness, and feeling neglected by her mother who had become preoccupied with caring for her ill husband. The therapist identified the patient's problem area as role transitions. She was having difficulty making the transition from being a daughter in an intact family to being a daughter without a functional father and with a mother burdened by the care of her ill father. The therapist stated to her that these resulting difficulties were problems that could be alleviated. Although we cannot cure the patient's father, we can help her to find more satisfactory ways to deal with both her changing role in the family and her feelings surrounding her father's illness and its disruption of her home and family relationships.

THE THERAPEUTIC RELATIONSHIP

After discussion of the therapist's perception of the interpersonal problem and agreement on the focus of the treatment, discussion should turn to the practical aspects of the therapy. The therapist should educate the patient regarding expectations for involvement of family members, length of sessions, frequency of sessions, fee, management of missed or canceled sessions, the use of the telephone, and so forth. The culmination of this is a specific treatment contract. The points to be made in the contract include the following.

The Importance of Honesty

I would like you to feel comfortable with me and trust me, but I realize that it takes time to build these feelings. We've been working together for 4 weeks, and in that time I feel we have started to do that. I hope that as we get to know each other better you will be able to be open with me about all that you are feeling and thinking because in that way I can be of the most help to you. If you ever feel that you can't tell me what you're feeling, let's try to talk about that.

The Confidentiality Limits of the Interactions

What we talk about is confidential between the two of us, and I won't tell your parents unless I am concerned that your behavior poses a danger to yourself or others. If I feel the need to discuss things with your parents, I will tell you first before I do so. I will give you the opportunity to discuss it with me, and if I agree with your reasons for not telling them, I won't tell them. But if I don't agree, I will tell them, but we can discuss the manner in which I do so.

The Interpersonal Context of the Intervention

We have already agreed that your depression is affected by your relationships and, in turn, negatively affects those relationships. Over the next few weeks, we will continue to explore your depression in relation to possible stressors and/or conflicts in your daily life and relationships.

The Brief Nature of the Psychotherapy

We will meet once a week for 12 weeks for about 45 minutes each session, to talk about what is happening in your relationships and how the relationship difficulties might be related to your depression. Together we will try to find ways in which you can change your relationships and feel better.

Telephone Contact

During the first 4 weeks of treatment, I will call in-between sessions to check on how you are feeling. If at any time you feel the need to talk to me in-between the sessions, please call. It also is important that you phone if you cannot make an appointment so that we can reschedule and at least make some contact by phone. There may be times when you call that I can't talk to you, but I will arrange a mutually convenient time for us to talk.

The Problem Area

From what you tell me, your depression began with the onset of your father's illness and your mother's withdrawal from you to take care of him. I'd like to talk about the areas you seem to describe as related to your depression. One is the kind of transition you've had to make from being a child to being someone who can take care of herself more. A second issue is how to make friends when it is not easy for them to come and visit you and how you explain to them what it is like at your house. A third problem seems to be how you handle your feelings toward your father: your sadness at his sickness, your anger at the burden he's become and his disruption of the house, and your anger at your mother for her preoccupation with your father so she cannot take care of you as she did before. There may be other problems you would like to add.

It is important that the parents be apprised of the parameters of the therapy. They need to be told about frequency and length of sessions, fee, missed sessions, and length of treatment. The issue of confidentiality needs to be addressed with the parents as well so that they do not have expectations that the therapist will tell them what goes on in sessions. For example, the therapist might say to the parents:

> *We have found that the best way for treatment to work is if the child feels a confidentiality of his or her discussions with the therapist. You need to trust me and my judgment that I will tell you about an issue if I feel it is important. You should feel able to talk to me freely about your child, but I may not be able to share as much with you. I will keep you informed in general about your child's progress. If I feel your child's behavior poses a danger to him- or herself or others, I certainly will inform you and discuss the situation with you.*

TEACHING PATIENTS THEIR ROLE IN IPT-A

After identifying the patient's problem area and exploring the patient's goal for the problematic relationship, the therapist should explain to the patient the general techniques of the therapy. The patient actively participates in the treatment. Patients should understand that the focus of the sessions will be on difficulties that are occurring in the present not the past. During sessions the patient should discuss the previous week's events or feelings that might be related to how the patient is currently feeling.

During the initial sessions, the IPT-A therapist is active and directive in conducting the review of symptoms, obtaining an interpersonal history, delineating treatment goals and making the treatment contract. The therapist will be comparatively less directive and active in the middle phase of the therapy. It is necessary prior to beginning the middle phase of treatment to stress to the patient that he or she is responsible for selecting the topic of discussion for the ensuing sessions. The adolescent should be informed that the therapist will be less active than initially but will be there to ensure that the identified problem area is addressed. The therapist should explain to the patient that although the therapist will not ask as many questions as initially, this is not because of a lack of interest or involvement. Rather, the therapist would like the adolescent to have the freedom to bring up the topics and feelings that are most on his or her mind. To prepare the patients for the middle phase of treatment the therapist might say:

In the past few sessions we have discussed your depressive symptoms, and your significant relationships, and have agreed on a problem area of focus. In the sessions to come, we will be focusing on events and feelings related to this problem area. Your job will be to talk about these events and how your feelings may be affecting your relationships with others. We will discuss these situations in relation to the specific goals for change that we have identified. As we discuss these issues, other situations, feelings, or issues may come up that seem related to the problem area. You should feel free to discuss these topics as well, so that we can explore their relationship to the depression. It will be very important for you to talk about feelings as well as about the event itself. You are most in touch with your significant relationships and what is affecting you, so it is your role to monitor your feelings and select those topics for discussion that are most connected to feeling better. There are no right or wrong topics for discussion as long as they relate to your feelings. Therefore it is also important to share ideas or feelings that seem confusing or embarrassing to you. This includes being free to discuss feelings about the therapy itself, me, and/or our relationship.

This discussion is considered part of the negotiation of the treatment contract, as it outlines the therapist's expectations for the patient's behavior in the session and acknowledges the patient's expectations for the therapist. This negotiation experience can be a good model of how to conduct such interpersonal negotiations within the context of other relationships.

TEACHING PARENTS THEIR ROLE IN IPT-A

The parents will be an integral part of the initial session as the therapist will discuss with them the adolescent's depressive symptoms and need for treatment. As issues emerge, parents will need to be brought in again to be counselled regarding necessary changes at home or in school. The therapist will need to be educative and instructive to the parent. Ideally, one should give the parent the role of collaborative therapist, the one carrying on the work at home. For example, one might tell them:

I will be talking to your child once a week, identifying specific problem areas and discussing them. You are there with your child all the time, so your input will be as important as what I do. I want you to keep me informed as to how you see your child doing, any new problems that appear, and anything else you notice about your child. Don't be upset that I cannot tell you everything. I will not withhold information about any situation of danger to your child. In our experience, it is helpful for the adolescent to feel that the therapist's office is a safe place to talk and to facilitate trust in the therapist. Still, I will keep you up to date on your child's general progress. In addition, I may suggest changes at home based on my sessions with your child.

Some parents may be experiencing psychological difficulties of their own or may have need for greater guidance in handling their child than the IPT-A therapist can address. In such cases, it is useful to consider referring the parent(s) to another therapist for either a psychiatric evaluation or parent counseling.

CONTACT WITH SCHOOL AND EDUCATORS

The therapist should establish an alliance with both the parents and, in many cases, with the school system. Prior to assuming a role in relation to the school system, the therapist should discuss school involvement with the parent and obtain parental consent to discuss certain aspects of therapy with the school. The therapist can assume the patient-advocate role with the educational system, educating teachers about the effects of a depressive episode on school functioning. If school refusal is associated with the depression, it is important for the therapist to work out an appropriate plan with the school for making the child feel comfortable to return. This may include such things as reducing the course load, assigning one teacher to look out for the adolescent, and helping the school to temporarily revise expectations for the adolescent's performance while he or she recovers from the depression. The school should be encouraged to contact the therapist if any changes in the student are noticed and believed relevant to the treatment.

SUMMARY

This will complete the initial stage of therapy, the assessment phase. However, the therapy has already begun. The limited "sick role" assigned to the patient has been explained to the adolescent and the adolescent's parents. Expectations for the adolescent and the adolescent's parents have been clarified, and the adolescent's role in the therapeutic process has been outlined. The therapist has established a relationship with the school if that is indicated. The therapy is now ready to move into the middle phase of treatment. The middle phase will be discussed in depth in the chapter that follows, and in the chapters on each of the specific problem areas.

·7·

The Middle Phase

BEGINNING THE MIDDLE PHASE

Following agreement on the treatment contract and the identified problem area, the middle phase of treatment begins. Typically this occurs by session 5 and continues through session 8. The middle sessions focus on the problem area identified in the initial sessions. This means clarification of the problem, identification of effective strategies to attack the problem, and implementation of interventions to bring about resolution of the problem, alleviation of the symptoms, and improvement in interpersonal functioning. During the initial sessions, the therapist is involved in assessing symptomatology as it relates to interpersonal relationships. Treatment focus now shifts responsibility to the patient to contribute ongoing information that is related to the agreed-upon problem area. The patient must take a more active stance in bringing in the relevant information related to the identified problem area. In exploring these issues, the therapist has several tasks to accomplish:

1. Monitor depressive symptoms and consider adjunctive therapy such as medication if there is no improvement or a worsening.
2. Enable the patient to discuss topics relevant to the identified problem area.
3. Monitor feelings the patient associates with the events discussed and with the therapeutic relationship. Facilitate the patient's self-disclosure of his or her affective state.
4. Hold regular meetings with parents for counseling and education.
5. Maintain alliance with the parents so they will continue to support the treatment.

ROLE OF THE PATIENT

The role of the patient changes in the middle phase of treatment. It shifts from providing historical information to actively searching for solutions to the problem. By now, the patient should be feeling more comfortable with self-disclosure and be more at ease in discussing interpersonal relationships and feelings. The patient is encouraged to bring in feelings about events that occurred in between sessions so that the therapist and patient can relate these to the identified problem area. The therapist then assists the patient in clarification of the problem and discussion of ways to improve the situation, or the patient's approach to the situation. The patient is encouraged by continuous feedback from the therapist regarding progress in the use of the strategies or techniques and the reported decrease in depressive symptomatology. Changes in functioning are constantly being identified and reflected to the patient. The positive feedback bolsters self-esteem and a sense of competence in changing the social interactions and/or adapting to circumstances.

ROLE OF THE THERAPIST

The therapist's role in the treatment also changes in the shift from the initial to the middle phase. The therapist remains active in the session: patient and therapist, together, decide the focus of treatment, discuss the previous week's events or feelings, and clarify the conflicts and generate solutions. The therapist must continue to monitor the patient's self-disclosures to see if it is necessary to alter the focus of treatment. The therapist works collaboratively with the patient as a team facilitating the patient's engagement in problem formulation and clarification of feelings. As always, the therapist monitors improvement of depressive symptoms.

ADDRESSING THE PROBLEM AREAS

As stated previously, the patient is encouraged to select the topic of discussion as it relates to the problem area. The therapist begins the session by either waiting for the patient to initiate discussion or by asking a general question about what transpired since the previous session such as "What has happened in the past week since I saw you last?" or " What would you like to talk about today?" The patient's silence and/or difficulty starting a session is not interpreted except as it relates to the problem area.

For example, the therapist might say:

Last time we met we were talking about the fight you had with your mother over your boyfriend. She thinks you are "too young" to have a steady boyfriend and won't let you go out with him. We discussed ways for you to handle this kind of situation in the future. I am sure things have come up since I saw you last. Perhaps you can tell me about what has happened.

The therapist will usually conclude the session with a synopsis of themes brought out in the session and their relation to the identified problem area.

If peripheral material is introduced in the session or significant topics are being avoided, the therapist must decide if what is being discussed is somehow relevant to the problem and then bring the situation to the attention of the patient. The perceived tangentiality of the material should be discussed with the patient prior to shifting the focus to more pertinent information. It is important to allow time to explore for relevance because it does not necessarily emerge initially. If the patient actually presents information that does not appear related to the identified problem area, the therapist might say:

Today you are talking about [topic]. I'm not sure how this is related to the other issues we have been discussing in relation to your problem with [identified problem area]. How do you see the two topics as related? If they are not related, which issue do you feel is more related to your current depression? Let's focus on what appears most related to your current depression.

To clarify relevance, the therapist should refocus on what the patient is saying and explore its relationship to issues that previously have been the focus of treatment.

Case Example. Wendy was a 15-year-old girl with a major depression and an identified problem area of interpersonal role disputes, primarily with her mother. The initial treatment session focused on the difficulties in the relationship with her mother, her mother's dissatisfaction with Wendy's help around the house, and Wendy's anger over her mother's relationship with another adolescent girl in the neighborhood. During a session in the middle phase of treatment, Wendy initiated a discussion of her discomfort with males in their early 20s in reference to her discomfort with her young male science teacher and her poor grade in science. It wasn't readily apparent whether this was relevant to the conflict with her parents. After continuous questioning regarding the discomfort, Wendy revealed the memory of several episodes of attempted sexual molestation by a family friend and relative as a toddler. She reported that her parents' failure to believe her reports about the incidents had significantly contributed to her distrust of them and her reluctance to confide in them, especially her mother. She expressed much anger at her mother's failure to protect her from dangerous people when she was younger and asserted that the failure continued to the present. This anger appeared to underlie many of the disputes with her mother. [Note: As per New York State law, the therapist did not report this case to the children's protective service agency because the alleged abuse had occurred many years ago and was not currently occurring.]

It is not unusual for a patient initially to present minor issues and later in the treatment focus on more relevant issues. Conversely, it is not uncommon for a patient to withdraw from discussion and minimize a problem area that may be the one most related to his or her depression. Both reactions may stem from discomfort with intimate self-disclosure, lack of understanding about the problem, and/or distrust of the therapeutic relationship. In such instances, the treatment contract may need to be revised and renegotiated during the beginning of the middle phase of treatment. In general, though, the focus of the middle phase proceeds logically from the topics identified in the interpersonal inventory and in the delineated treatment contract. Discussion progresses from the general problems to the specific expectations and perceptions of the situation, to generation of alternative solutions, to the eventual efforts at changing behaviors and attempting new solutions.

During the middle phase of treatment, the therapist and patient continually assess the accuracy of the initial formulation of the problem in order to maximize the amount of change that can be accomplished in the treatment. The therapist must keep the patient's discussions relevant to the identified problem areas. If this is proving increasingly difficult, it may be necessary for the therapist to review with the patient the reasons for choosing the particular problem area and discuss the possibility of revising which problem area they will focus on.

Whereas the action takes place in the sessions, much of the focus of the middle sessions is on what occurs outside of the session. The patient is likely to begin to apply some of what is discussed to situations outside of the sessions. For example, after discussing negotiation strategies with the therapist, the patient may try the strategies out at home and then report the next week on their success or difficulty. The therapist should monitor the patients' outside functioning to obtain a better perspective on the problem and/or improvements. For adolescents, this may mean periodic school contacts with a guidance counselor to assess current school performance and family contacts to assess progress at home. The need for revision may occur as new information about the patient's interpersonal relationships becomes available.

CONDUCTING THE MIDDLE PHASE

Therapist–Patient Relationship

The middle phase also is a time in which the therapist should pay close attention to his or her own feelings toward the patient and to the progress of the treatment. This is especially true if the patient's identified problem area is interpersonal deficits. By monitoring one's own reactions to the patient, the therapist may be able to understand better the patient's interpersonal difficulties. It is the therapist's role to relate interpersonal strategies used in session to those that may be used in relationships outside of the session. The therapist fosters early discussion of interpersonal style seen within the therapist–patient relationship only if it pertains to an interpersonal style and problem that is occurring outside the session. Moreover, by working out the interpersonal problems in the relationship with the therapist, the patient is afforded a safe opportunity for role playing or communication clarification. These strategies resemble working with transference and countertransference issues. However, IPT differs from psychodynamic psychotherapy in its specific treatment of the therapist–patient relationship. Whereas psychodynamic psychotherapy would encourage the development of the transference, IPT brings these feelings quickly into the open to be discussed in relation to difficulties within the identified problem area. Therefore, the feelings are discussed earlier and more overtly and are directly related to current interpersonal functioning.

Involvement of Others in Sessions

Other family members or significant others may be asked to participate in one or two sessions during the middle phase of treatment. For example, in the case of a role dispute, the therapist may ask the patient and the other person in the dispute to attend a session together in order to assist in negotiation or to clarify the other person's expectations for the relationship. This is particularly helpful in cases where the patient is having trouble negotiating a relationship at home. Family members have been prepared for this possibility during the initial phase of treatment when they discussed the depression and the process of treatment with the therapist. The therapist must be vigilant in these sessions to ensure that all participants remain focused on the identified problem area and that the discussions are constructive rather than destructive.

Management of Crises

As a result of the uncovering and identification of many feelings associated with the significant relationship, crises sometimes arise. Feelings can become intensified as a result of increased communication between the patient and significant other. Concurrently, the patient's depression or anger may increase and result in acting-out behavior or suicidal ideation. It is important for the therapist to try and anticipate such a crisis by helping the patient to anticipate the consequences of the actions or discussion and the feelings that might be generated in the other person by the disclosures. The therapist should review with the patient possible reactions to the statements, how particular responses to the disclosures could be handled, and the feelings surrounding them. By preparing the patient for the possible outcomes, any expressions or behavior would be less shocking and disturbing and therefore less likely to precipitate a crisis situation. When this strategy fails and a crisis occurs, the crisis must take precedence and becomes the immediate focus of treatment. It is beneficial if the therapist can relate the crisis to the identified problem area, but this is not always immediately possible. In order to bring about a swift resolution of the crisis, sessions may be scheduled more frequently for a time. (Refer to section on crisis management in Chapter 16 for further explication.)

Use of the Brief Treatment Time Frame

One of the most important aspects of this phase of treatment is keeping the time frame of the brief treatment a salient aspect of the treatment. The therapist should place the treatment plan, strategies, and goals in a time frame and make the patient aware of how many more sessions are remaining. Researchers have written about changes in the rate of a patient's progress as the brief treatment continues. They have found that the most important activities of brief therapy that result in some degree of change occur during the first eight sessions of treatment (Garfield, 1986, 1989; Howard et al., 1986).

To assist the patient in completing treatment, the therapist should emphasize the patient's role in making changes in behavior and/or in understanding interpersonal relationships. The goal is to instill a sense of mastery and to maximize the patient's sense of competence to continue these improved interpersonal skills. Each of the phases of inter-personal psychotherapy builds on the previous phase, and the therapist must help the patient prepare for the next phase of treatment.

SUMMARY

In the middle phase, the therapist narrows the focus of therapy to a specific problem area, helps generate strategies, and suggests the applica-tion of techniques that will lead to clarification and resolution of the patient's problem. The therapist and patient play an active role together by collaborating on tasks that serve to provide support and direction for the adolescent. Formulated strategies may necessitate the involvement of significant others such as parents as they are brought to bear on situations both in and outside of the sessions. The expectation of a 12-week treatment duration must be emphasized as goals are targeted and interventions are implemented. It is also important to review con-tinuously the changes observed to increase the patient's feeling of com-petence. The patient's education continues throughout each phase of treatment illuminating the process of identifying problems, clarifying the issues, generating strategies, applying strategies for problem resolution, and acquiring skills that result in increased interpersonal self-confidence and improved functioning. By reviewing these steps with the patient at the end of the middle phase and at the beginning of the termination phase, the therapist assists in fostering the patient's independent use of interpersonal problem-solving techniques in future situations.

Chapters 8 through 13 focus on the five potential problem areas of IPT-A: grief, interpersonal role disputes, role transitions, interpersonal deficits, and single-parent families.

·8·

Grief

Grief is selected as the problem area of focus when patients describe the onset of depressive symptoms in association with the death of a significant person in their life. The death does not have to immediately precede the depression; the depression can be a delayed or distorted reaction to the loss. The significance of this relationship for the patient will have already been discussed in detail during the interpersonal inventory.

DEVELOPMENTAL ASPECTS OF GRIEF

Grief in Adults

Normal grief can resemble a depression in the nature of the symptoms experienced such as sad mood, increased tearfulness, disturbance in sleep and appetite, disturbances in daily functioning, and feelings of excessive guilt. In a normal grief reaction, these symptoms generally resolve without treatment in 6 months. If not, bereavement can lead to mood disorders such as depression.

Uncomplicated grief minimally disrupts normal functioning, whereas unresolved or pathologic grief is characterized by (1) inhibition, suppression, or absence of the grief process; (2) exaggeration or distortion of certain symptoms or behaviors that normally occur with grief; and/or (3) the prolongation of normal grieving (Raphael, 1983). IPT-A treats the depression associated with abnormal grief reactions and can also be used to negotiate a successful grief process.

Grief in Adolescents

In assessing the impact of the death of a loved one in adolescence, one must consider (1) the adolescent's role in the family system or peer group before and after the death; (2) the nature of the relationship lost; (3) the remaining social and familial support network; (4) the adolescent's psychological maturity and coping skills at the time of the death. Gray (1987) conducted a study of adolescent response to the death of a parent. He found higher levels of depression in those adolescents who experienced poor social support following the loss and in those who reported poor prior relationships with the surviving parents.

The few studies of bereavement in adolescents (Osterweis et al., 1984) highlight the many similarities in the mourning experiences of adults and adolescents. Horowitz (1976) identified themes in his research with grieving adults that are reported in clinical work with grieving adolescents (McGoldrick & Walsh, 1991). The most common feelings discussed by grieving adolescents include (1) sadness about having to cope with the actual loss of the relationship; (2) feelings of excessive guilt regarding activities or deeds they wish they had or had not done with the deceased; (3) anger at being left without the deceased; (4) not having had a chance to say good-bye; (5) feeling of responsibility, that maybe if they had done something different the person would still be with them; (6) concern that the same thing may happen to them; (7) overidentification with the deceased in order to maintain continuity of presence (Raphael, 1983).

The most intense grief response in early adolescence appears to be associated with the death of a parent. Common reactions include withdrawal, depressed feelings, denial, pseudomaturity, identification with the deceased, and care-eliciting behaviors (Raphael, 1983). Boys and girls appear to respond differently: boys may turn to stealing, drugs, or social withdrawal, whereas girls may more frequently increase their closeness with their sisters or sexualize their peer relationships as a means of finding the comfort and attachment they have lost (Osterweis et al., 1984). The adolescent may experience feelings of yearning for the parent, the intensity of which is determined by the former nature of their relationship and the degree of separation that had been achieved.

The impact of the death of others on the adolescent such as a close friend, grandparent, or teacher, similarly will be determined by the intensity of the relationship and the adolescent's preparedness for the death (Raphael, 1983). Sklar and Hartley (1990) found that difficulties triggered by the death of a close friend may be as severe as and in some cases more severe than those found in the loss of a family member. This results from the adolescent being in a developmental stage where friends rather than family have become the focal point. In addition, the deaths of young people are more likely to be sudden than from natural causes. Anxieties about the future play a prominent role in the adolescents' thinking, and death, separation, and loss only confirm their worst fears about what the future may hold (Rutter, 1979). Repression of the longing for the deceased may result in the adolescent's vulnerability to pathological mourning.

ABNORMAL GRIEF

Incomplete grieving can result in depression and/or dysfunction in daily living. The therapist's task in addressing abnormal grief is to help the adolescent acknowledge and express the feelings surrounding the death. Symptoms indicative of abnormal grief can appear during the normal grief period or they may surface at a future date, perhaps triggered by the anniversary of the death or an encounter with a belonging of the deceased. Pathological mourning of three general kinds is commonly noted in depressed adolescents: distorted grief, delayed grief, or chronic grief reaction (Raphael, 1983). The types of mourning are the same as in adults; however, the manifestations are informed by development. For example, grief in adolescents may lead to truancy rather than job problems. Adolescents may feel responsible for the death rather than be able to accept that it was out of their control.

TYPES OF ABNORMAL GRIEF

A *distorted grief reaction* can take many different forms. It may be characterized by behavioral problems rather than sad mood (Raphael, 1983). It can occur immediately following the death or at some distant time in the future. Distorted grief can come from unresolved feelings of desertion and guilt that can result in angry aggression or in self-punishing behavior. It may consist of guilty ruminations, anger, or fantasies about the deceased. Drug or alcohol abuse, sexual promiscuity, truancy, and other maladaptive behavior changes may occur. If the symptoms are physical, it is necessary to rule out a physiological basis (such as thyroid problem) to the complaints before proceeding to assess the psychological nature of the symptoms.

As implied in its name, a *delayed grief reaction* occurs at a time subsequent to the death and normal grieving period. The adolescent may have been unable to mourn adequately because the loss was too overwhelming or the associated feelings too frightening. Mourning also may be delayed until the adolescent is surrounded by secure relationships and feels supported (Raphael, 1983). When the feelings of sadness occur at a later date, the adolescent is often unable to make the connection between the presenting depressive symptoms and the past loss.

The delayed reaction can be triggered by many different types of experiences such as a second loss. In order to determine the presence of a delayed grief reaction, the therapist must obtain a complete history regarding the circumstance of the relationship with the deceased and the events surrounding the actual death. Often when adolescents are excluded from the events of the death, such as the funeral, their mourning can become delayed.

A *chronic grief reaction* is a protracted, often recurrent, triggered emotion, such as sadness, that was previously experienced upon the death of the loved one. It is often the result of the patient's difficulty in expressing grief and its associated emotions or of unresolved feelings about the deceased. One type of chronic grief reaction is an anniversary reaction in which the adolescent experiences significant sadness repeatedly at the same time of year as the original loss. The adolescent may experience chronic malaise, withdrawal, somatic symptoms, or frank depression without consciously connecting these symptoms to the previous loss.

ASSESSMENT OF ABNORMAL GRIEF REACTIONS

The assessment of whether an adolescent is experiencing an abnormal grief reaction should begin with a detailed review of the adolescent's significant relationships. This review should include current relationships, as well as past relationships with people who may now be deceased or who are no longer active participants in the adolescent's daily life. When asking questions about a relationship with someone deceased, it is important to obtain information on the adolescent's emotions surrounding the event, the actual event itself, and the impact of the event on the adolescent's life. Some questions that might be asked in the process of the assessment are:

> *Has anyone important to you died? Can you tell me about the death? When? Where? What circumstances? How did you hear about the death? What was your response when you were told? Did you cry? Did you miss any school? How much?. When did you start to feel better? How did others in the family deal with it?*

It is often necessary for the therapist to articulate some of the feelings before the adolescent is able to talk about them. The therapist might say:

> *It is normal to feel tremendous sadness when someone you are close to has died. That feeling can last for months, sometimes longer. Expressing*

and talking about those feelings is an important part of the process of mourning for [name of person] and of coming to terms with living your life without [name of person] being part of your life. When you don't mourn for the person you have lost, many problems can happen such as depression, anxiety, problems in your present relationships, and fears about getting close to people. By talking about your feelings, even though it may be difficult at first, you will be able to feel better again.

GOALS FOR TREATING ABNORMAL GRIEF

The main goal in the treatment for a depression resulting from abnormal grief is to facilitate the delayed normal mourning process. The therapist does this by helping the adolescent to (1) cope with the real loss (e.g., of a parent whose role was to provide nurturance and stability through the developmental process of adolescent separation and individuation); (2) resolve the positive and negative aspects of the specific relationship with the deceased; (3) find other relationships that can provide the support, nurturance, companionship, or guidance that has been lost.

STRATEGIES FOR TREATING ABNORMAL GRIEF

The main strategy employed by the therapist is to review in detail the adolescent's relationship with the deceased in order to free the adolescent from the disabling attachment to the deceased. In doing so, the therapist must review with the adolescent both the positive and negative aspects of the relationship, conflicts in the relationships, and special qualities of the relationship. The adolescent may be reluctant to discuss or acknowledge angry or hostile feelings toward the deceased or may feel somehow responsible for the death, a reaction that connotes guilt and self-blame.

The adolescent will need to be encouraged in a nonconfrontational manner to explore and express these feelings. The therapist should help guide the adolescent in a gradual expression and discussion of these negative feelings so as not to heighten the adolescent's guilt and/or anxiety. It is important for the therapist to educate the adolescent that this disclosure will be followed by more positive feelings and an understanding of the deceased that will enable him or her to further examine the relationship and its impact on his or her life. The disclosure is accomplished by eliciting feelings about the deceased and exploring the interactions between the deceased and the adolescent. The therapist might ask:

Tell me about your relationship with _____. *What kinds of things would you do together? Can you describe what you liked about [the person]? Most people have good and bad times in their relationship. Tell me about them. Were there times when the two of you had difficulty getting along? What would happen? How would you feel? Can you tell me about the time when you found out about the illness or death? What was it like for you? How did you feel?*

The therapist asks the adolescent to think about the loss, to discuss in detail the events surrounding the death and the emotional impact of the events on him or her.

The abnormal grief reaction may be a result of the loss of the adolescent's main support. It may be a realistic assessment of the loss of someone to care for the adolescent. In addition, the adolescent may experience a sense of isolation and the feeling that there is no one else to guide him or her through the normal process of mourning. Adolescents often feel unable to discuss the loss with peers because they feel peers may not understand their sense of loss and fear being looked upon as different. The grief reaction may also be a result of a secondary loss of the other parent through the surviving parent's own depression, remarriage, or dysfunction. Osterweis et al. (1984) found that one significant risk factor for psychological morbidity following the death of a parent is the psychological vulnerability of the surviving parent, which may result in the surviving parent's excessive dependence on the adolescent. A conflictual relationship with the deceased or an ambivalent reaction to the loss of a primary caretaker can further complicate the picture.

Treatment is basically the same for all types of grief reactions, that is, facilitating the mourning process. In treating distorted grief reactions, the therapist also helps the adolescent connect the acting-out behavior with the feelings surrounding the death. Treating adolescents with chronic grief reactions will often include more emphasis on increasing communication skills and applying those skills to the significant relationships that have been impaired as a result of the chronic grief. The therapist should monitor whether the adolescent with chronic grief has developed maladaptive patterns of relating and whether or not these patterns of relating have improved with treatment. If not, additional treatment may be recommended.

The purpose of having the adolescent review in detail the relationship with the deceased is to foster a better understanding of the complexity of their relationship in light of the difficult feelings experienced at the time of the person's death. It is an opportunity to clarify the relationship so that the adolescent can return to the normal mourning process. The adolescent can be helped to feel comfortable to express these feelings. The therapist might say:

> It's normal to have both positive and negative feelings toward a person. Your feelings can vary with situations and different periods in your life. It is important to be able to recognize the different feelings you may experience toward _____.

Reassurance

In exploring both the positive and negative aspects of the relationship, adolescents are often reluctant to mention events that have not been discussed in the family for a long time or of which they were at one time advised not to speak. They may fear punishment from another person for discussing them, hurting the other survivors' feelings, or losing control of their emotions in talking about the event. It is important for the therapist to reassure the adolescent that these fears are common and that it is rare for a person to lose control in psychotherapy by disclosing such feelings. The therapist should, however, also acknowledge how the adolescent's disclosure might be difficult. The therapist should monitor the patient's affect in the discussion and guide the speed or depth of disclosure accordingly.

Reintegration into Social Milieu

As adolescents begin to engage in the normal mourning process, frequently they feel as though they would like to resume more social interactions. They also may be vulnerable at this time to attaching to the first person who comes along to fill the empty space left by the deceased. The therapist can assist the adolescent in considering various ways to meet new people and in evaluating new social contacts for their potential to become significant participants in his or her life. The therapist can help the adolescent assess surroundings for new social opportunities such as after school activities, church, or youth groups by asking:

> What kinds of activities did you enjoy before the death of _____? How has your involvement changed? How would you like to get back involved with people? What kinds of activities could you participate in? Where do you feel you would be most comfortable? What would be your concerns, if any?

TREATING NORMAL GRIEF REACTIONS

In treating normal grief reactions, the therapist facilitates the adolescent's movement through the grief process by providing support and guidance on how to address the accompanying and often intense emotions. Education about normal bereavement patterns can be very beneficial for the adolescent. In addition, the therapist addresses the conflicts that may arise between the bereaved and other relationships as a result of the grief.

The strategies employed are similar to those for treating abnormal grief. The therapist assists the adolescent in discussing the relationship with the deceased, feelings surrounding the death, and the impact of the loss on his or her life. The therapist also may discuss the adolescent's transition back into the social milieu and participation in normal activities after a period of withdrawal. Together, they can address concerns about how to share the experience with others, for example, what to tell friends about a prolonged absence from school due to the death. Overall, the main focus is on the adolescent's feelings about the relationship with the deceased and the death and how current functioning is being affected.

SUMMARY

IPT-A can be used to help adolescents who are coping either with a normal or an abnormal grief reaction. The main tasks for the therapist are to assist the adolescent in a review of the relationship lost, the associated feelings, and the impact of the loss on current functioning. Following a resolution of feelings about the loss, attention can turn to establishing new interpersonal relationships and/or reestablishing relationships that had been interrupted by the reaction to the loss.

The following case example illustrates the use of IPT-A for the treatment of a chronic grief reaction complicated by significant family disruption.

CASE VIGNETTE: HELEN

Helen, a 17-year-old girl, was living with a friend of her mother, her third home since her mother's death 2 years before. Helen's parents had never been married, and she has had no contact with her father since she was an infant. Immediately following her mother's death from cancer, Helen lived with her 24-year-old half-sister who threw her out after approximately 9 months. She went to live with one of her mother's friends for several months. She was currently living with a second friend of her mother and was attending Catholic school, where she was closely cared for by one of the nuns.

Helen presented to the clinic with a major depression. She said she had been feeling depressed since her mother had died 2 years ago. She felt abandoned by her mother and half-siblings and angry at her forced independence. She reported sad mood, irritability, increased fatigue, concentration problems, decrease in grades, feelings of hopelessness and helplessness, and derealization. She felt no one loved her as her mother had. She denied any sleep or appetite disturbance but reported that she felt too lazy to prepare any food so she had been eating less. A child psychiatrist had recommended treatment with Prozac but Helen had refused to take the medication on a regular basis. Her symptoms resulted in increased sensitivity to criticism, mistrust, and rejection in her relationships, but the significant adults in her life continued to provide support for her.

Initial Phase (Sessions 1–4). During the initial sessions, discussion focused on the circumstances of the patient's mother's death and the unstable home life that her death had precipitated. She spoke with disbelief about her mother's death and her sister's lack of concern. She cried as she told the therapist that she thought of her mother's death throughout the day every day, since staying in the living room of a family friend. She did not feel able to confide her feelings to the family friend. She felt like a "boarder," alone in the world, rather than a part of the family with whom she was living. During this time, her half-brother who lived in Texas, invited her to come live with him. As much as she longed to be part of a family, leaving high school in her senior year to live with a brother who had always been described as "irresponsible" presented her with a significant conflict. The need to make this decision increased her anger at her mother for dying and leaving her with this difficult decision. The therapist speculated that a substantial part of Helen's difficulty coping with her present situation was the result of her failure to grieve her mother's death appropriately and to address the myriad of feelings toward her mother and the rest of her family. Helen and the therapist agreed by the end of the initial phase that the focus of the treatment should be on the relationship between the death of her mother and her current depression. Her relationship with the family friend was emotionally cold and distant. The therapist suggested that if she were to confide in the friend about her feelings, she would gain a sense of "belonging" and might begin to feel more a part of their lives.

Middle Phase (Sessions 5–8). A pressing decision for Helen at this time was whether or not to move to Texas to live with her half-brother or to stay at her school with the nuns and live with the family friend. By focusing on her feelings of abandonment and anger, Helen was better able to sort out her feelings and thoughts about this issue. Therefore, Helen and the therapist spent their time discussing Helen's feelings toward her mother, both positive and negative, in addition to the feelings about her relationship and interactions with her half-brother and half-sister. She expressed much anger at them for not supporting her more in dealing with her mother's illness, particularly against her half-brother who had disappeared for a time because the situation had been too much for him to bear. She spoke to her half-brother about her anger at him and was able to express her worries that he would not be able to care for her in the way she needed. Helen described her mother as being physically repulsive to her at the time of her death, as her abdomen was severely bloated from the cancer, and she had a sickly pallor, with numerous tubes going in and out of her body. She talked about the guilt she felt about her own difficulties looking at her mother when she was near death, her inability to stay in the hospital with her mother at the very end, and her absence from her mother's room when her mother finally died. She felt that she had not been loving enough in her mother's time of need and, as a result, had lowered her self-esteem accordingly. She was angry that her mother had not made better plans for her care after her death, which resulted in her sister feeling overwhelmed by the responsibility and rejecting her altogether. By sorting out her feelings in the sessions, Helen was better able to express her feelings about her mother's death to her half-brother. Through her self-disclosure with him, she gained a sense of closeness and "family" that she had been searching for in her relationships since her mother's death.

Psychoeducation regarding normal reactions to death and illness helped relieve Helen of some of the guilt. In addition, the therapist helped her to focus on the strengths she had demonstrated in coping with such a difficult situation. Helen worried that her mother's death and conflict with her sister were going to mar her future relationships. Treatment focused on how her fears of being abandoned and losing significant relationships could make her hesitant to enter new relationships or to be less open in her relationships, so that if she lost them the pain would not be as great. They were able to examine this in the context of her relationship with the family with whom she was living and in her initiation of a new relationship with a male friend. By the end of the middle phase of treatment, Helen was able to talk about her mother more easily, with less visible distress and was reporting a decrease in irritability, anger, and feelings of guilt. Her relationships with her half-brother and family friend were vastly improved as she was able to tell them about her fears and needs.

Termination Phase (Sessions 9–12). At the beginning of the termination phase, Helen reported that she had made the decision not to move to Texas to live with her half-brother. She stated that over the past few weeks he had shown through various unfulfilled promises that he still was irresponsible. She had been able to discuss her feelings about this with him. She reported that at the same time she had tried to talk more to the family with whom she was living and was feeling more comfortable there. She loved her school and the nuns who cared so much for her. She was feeling much happier, concentrating better in school, reporting improved eating and sleeping habits, less tearfulness, and fewer feelings of guilt and self-blame. She still thought a lot about her mother but without the anger she previously felt. She also felt proud about the way she was handling her life, making decisions, and taking care of herself in the absence of her mother. She was much more comfortable in talking about her feelings in relationships with her half-brother, her adopted family, and the nuns. She discovered that people responded positively toward her when she shared her feelings, which made her feel more cared for and supported. At the time of termination, Helen had completed the 11th grade and was eagerly awaiting her senior year, preparing to apply for college, and feeling confident that she was going to be able to develop good relationships in the future and to achieve her academic goals.

·9·

Interpersonal Role Disputes

EVALUATING INTERPERSONAL DISPUTES AS A PROBLEM AREA

An interpersonal role dispute is a situation in which the patient and at least one significant other person have "nonreciprocal expectations about their relationship" (Klerman et al., 1984, p. 104). Nonreciprocal expectations refer to disagreements about the terms and/or guidelines for behavior within the relationship. It is chosen as the identified problem area when adolescents describe their depression in relation to conflict within a significant relationship. This chapter focuses on how depression can distort expectations within a relationship and how IPT-A addresses the resulting problems.

The significant relationships in an adolescent's life usually include relationships with family members, teachers, best friends, and romantic attachment figures. The quality of these relationships can be significantly affected by the depression as well as be a precipitant of the depression. For example, depressed children frequently have persistent interpersonal problems with parents, siblings, and friends even after the depressed mood has been successfully treated (Puig-Antich et al., 1985b). Disputes with families and friends also can contribute to the development of a depressive episode. An example of a dispute occurring with a friend is the teenage girl who expects a best friend to be supportive of the time commitment inherent in her new-found love relationship; however, the best friend expects the friendship to take priority over romance. Role disputes in families can occur when parents expect their adolescent to confide in them fully about intimate feelings and details of life, whereas the adolescent feels the need to separate more from the parents and uses friends more than family as confidantes. One particularly common interpersonal dispute that occurs between adolescents and parents is the conflict between a conservative parent and the adolescent who is trying to behave consistently with his or her generation of peers. Often these conflicting values lead to different expectations for the adolescent's behavior.

Interpersonal role disputes become the identified problem area if the adolescent's depressive episode coincides with such a conflict. The type of dispute that is most likely to precede a depressive episode is one in which the adolescent feels helpless to resolve the conflict, and the dispute keeps being repeated in the relationship, generating feelings of increasing helplessness. Because the adolescent feels misunderstood, with no hope of mutual communication, self-esteem decreases, which results in further social withdrawal and lack of communication. An example is the adolescent who is having a dispute with a parent over permission to go out at night with friends. The parent, worried about safety, doesn't want to let the teen out of the house after dark. The teenager wants to be able to socialize with his or her peer group. They are unable to agree on what is a reasonable activity and/or curfew. The discussions escalate into yelling matches and end with each participant withdrawing, leaving the problem to reoccur at the next invitation. The adolescent expresses the feeling that the parent is never going to change and is never going to let him or her out of the house. As a result, the adolescent begins to withdraw from the peer group so that the inability to join his or her friends will not be noticed, and invitations will not need to be rejected.

Nonreciprocal expectation and disputes seem particularly acute in children of immigrant parents who are unfamiliar with the ways of their new country and even more acute for female children. For example, with female hispanic adolescents, the culture shock after immigration frequently results in increased parent–adolescent tensions about the appropriate female roles and behaviors (Hardy et al., 1982). In traditional hispanic families, the male and female roles are strictly defined; however, in the United States, the roles are not so clearly demarcated or similarly conceptualized. As a result of fear of the unknown, parents often become very rigid and overprotective of their children and the children attempt to rebel against this rigidity, viewing their parents' way of life as inferior to the American way (Ghali, 1977). Although specific disputes occur in immigrant families, similar ones can also be seen in the traditional adolescent rebellion against parental authority when the adolescent attempts to separate.

The perceived or real threat of loss of the relationship adds to the isolation and loneliness the depressed teen feels. Problems in resolving the disputes can be the result of an inability to see the other person's point of view, significant differences in expectations for the relationship, inability to communicate about feelings and expectations, or the feeling of pervasive helplessness that results in withdrawal from attempts at resolution.

In order to determine whether the issue of role disputes is the problem area, the therapist conducts a thorough history of the adolescent's significant relationships. Information to look for in diagnosing disputes includes conflicts with significant others that may elicit emotions such as anger, sadness, and/or frustration. Often the most salient feeling is the adolescent's sense that the situation will never change and that he or she will be forever misunderstood. Sometimes, however, the conflict may not be as overt. In such cases, the therapist needs to observe for nonverbal signs of repressed or denied emotions and to be alert if relationships with significant others are briefly mentioned, but the adolescent is reluctant to discuss them. If the adolescent shies away from discussion or appears to portray an ideal relationship, these may be clues that the adolescent is experiencing negative feelings that are uncomfortable to express. It is often helpful at this time for the therapist to educate the adolescent about the acceptability of having ambivalent and even negative feelings in relationships and how difficult relationships, can often make a person feel sad and precipitate a depression.

> *Case Example.* Liz presented with a major depression but was unable to identify what was making her so upset. In conducting the interpersonal inventory, the therapist asked her about her relationship with her mother. She reported that her relationship was great and that they got along very well. The therapist responded to this enthusiasm about their relationship by stating that most teenagers have some conflicts with their parents and she wondered if the patient did, too. This led to complaints by the patient about her mother's restrictiveness. Her mother wouldn't let her go out with friends after school or on weekends, and her phone calls were restricted and monitored by her mother. She felt unable to talk with her mother about her desire for more freedom. The therapist then reflected to Liz that it sounded as though she was feeling much anger toward her mother that might be contributing to her depression. This inventory and exploration of the initially idealistic relationship led to a more accurate accounting of the role dispute between mother and daughter.

There are three possible stages the dispute may be in when presented to the therapist (Klerman et al., 1984). These are:

1. *Renegotiation:* In this stage, the adolescent and significant other are still communicating with each other in attempts to resolve the conflict and are being open about the presence of a dis-

agreement. It is likely that they are being unsuccessful in their negotiations if coming to treatment.

2. *Impasse:* In this stage the adolescent and the significant other typically are no longer attempting to discuss the conflict. Communication has often ceased, and frequently social distancing between the two, known as "the silent treatment," exists.

3. *Dissolution:* In this stage, the adolescent and significant other have already decided that the dispute cannot be resolved and have chosen to terminate the relationship.

GOALS OF TREATMENT

The general goal for treatment of interpersonal role disputes is to help the adolescent define and resolve the dispute by identifying the significant people involved and the issue in conflict. At times, the goal may be complete resolution of the conflict, and at other times the goal may have to be more limited to understanding the nature of the dispute and/or revising expectations for the relationship. If the relationship has ended, mourning the loss of the relationship becomes one of the goals.

STRATEGIES FOR THE TREATMENT OF DISPUTES

Regardless of the stage of the dispute, there are several common strategies to the treatment. The therapist must facilitate discussion of the dispute focusing on the adolescent's expectations for the relationship. Whether or not the expectations are realistic, how do they differ from the expectations of others in the dispute, and how has the adolescent tried to resolve the dispute? The adolescent should learn that disputes often arise because the people in the relationship have nonreciprocal role expectations and that exploration of these expectations may reveal some areas of agreement that can be starting points for resolution or negotiation. In exploring role disputes the therapist may ask:

> *What do you and [name] fight about? How do your fights end? How would you like [name] to respond to you when you have these fights? How do you think [name] would like you to respond? What are your expectations for this relationship? In what ways have you been disappointed? Do you think you have disappointed [name]? How do you think your relationship with [name] can be helped or improved? If [name] can't change, how can you handle it? What other options or resources are available to you?*

The therapist and adolescent also explore communication patterns that may be complicating the resolution of the dispute. The disputes are difficult to resolve because the participants are reluctant to approach each other about the conflict, they do not know how to express their negative feelings in a nondestructive manner, they are stuck in their repetition of complaints, and/or they are unable to move into the reconstructive stage from fear of having to confront their individual roles in the dispute. An adolescent often acts out with disruptive, antisocial, or self-punishing behavior, rather than expressing his or her feelings directly. The aim here is to help patients recognize their complex, mixed feelings of anger, fear, and sadness and to devise strategies for managing these emotions, such as avoiding situations that will lead to disputes and anger, expressing feelings more directly, and reducing impulsive behavior that results from failure to verify one's understanding of the behavior of others. These strategies will enable the adolescent to make choices about modifying communication techniques and negotiating the actual details of the dispute. The therapist might say to the patient:

When you and [name] fight, it's clear that besides becoming angry you also feel very sad and disappointed. These feelings have been hard for you to acknowledge to yourself let alone talk about. Instead, you become angry and refuse to spend any time with your family. You go to your room and play your radio so loudly your mother comes in to yell at you. Have you ever tried to tell [name] what you are feeling and thinking? What do you think would happen if you told [name] how you really felt? How do you think [name] would respond? Would you be willing to try to tell [name] how you feel?

After achieving an understanding of the expectations or issues underlying the dispute, the therapist and adolescent move to the second stage of the treatment where decisions are made regarding specific solutions to dispute. At this stage the therapist might say:

Now that we understand the connection between your depression and your relationship with [name] and how the feelings you have lead to behaviors and actions that are ultimately self-defeating, let's see what things you can do to change this hurtful pattern in your life. What other options do you see for yourself? What do you think would happen if you handled the situation in these different ways?

The earlier sessions in the treatment of disputes at the renegotiation or impasse stage generally focus on communication patterns and exploration of the actual dispute, whereas the latter sessions focus on the specific negotiations and concomitant decisions about the issue in question. The length of time needed for the various steps may vary with the nature and complexity of the dispute. Strategies for treating disputes at the dissolution stage differ slightly in that the goals are to help the adolescent gain perspective on what occurred in the relationship and how it has ended and to help the adolescent feel competent and ready to establish new relationships that will be more successful. The therapist does attempt to preserve workable family relationships for the adolescent patient. If this is not possible, the therapist needs to provide alternative care, such as arranging for the adolescent to live with a relative.

If the therapist and patient determine that the role dispute is in the state of renegotiation, it might be handled as follows:

> You and [name] are fighting frequently. It seems to me that the underlying reason for your fights is that you expect something from [name] that [name] isn't giving to you and vice versa. No matter how hard the two of you try, you get stuck in the same battle, and neither one of you can find a solution. You both care about each other and want to find a solution. Let me try to help you by talking to you about finding new ways of communicating with [name] and maybe asking [name] to come in.

In the case of an impasse, the therapist might say:

> You and [name] are at odds with each other. Neither of you understands the other, and you each feel there is no solution to the problem. Now you don't even talk to each other. Maybe you're right that there is no solution, but I'd like to try to get the two of you to talk to each other again to see whether you can work out your problems. Maybe talking to someone outside the immediate situation will help you feel differently and help you find a better solution to your problems with [name] than not speaking. At first you and [name] may be fighting again, and it will feel like before. Once you understand your own feelings better and have tried everything you can to resolve the problem between you and [name], you will feel better and can then make a clear decision about whether this relationship can be helped or not.

If the therapist agrees with the patient that the relationship is irretrievably disrupted, the therapist's task is to help the patient successfully mourn the loss of the relationship and move on to other relationships. At this point the strategies employed by the therapist resemble those discussed in the chapter on grief. The therapist helps the patient to review the entirety of the relationship, to explore the impact of the loss of the relationship, and to explore ways to move on to new relationships from this experience.

It is important that the therapist not direct the adolescent to one or another of the solutions. The outcome of the therapy discussions may include changes in the adolescent's view of the dispute. These changes can take the form of revised expectations for the relationship, improvements in the parties' ability to communicate with each other, identification of other resources to fulfill certain needs that may take the pressure off this relationship, or, if necessary, an informed decision to end the relationship.

The therapist needs to consider whether direct intervention with family members will help alleviate the problems and whether outside social service resources are required. Ways in which social service resources may be helpful include sending a home health-care worker to relieve an overwhelmed mother, a visiting nurse to provide services for an ill family member, or public assistance to provide necessary material goods or housing.

Since many of the disputes of adolescents occur between the adolescent and the parents, there are sometimes less than optimal goals that have to be accepted if the parent is resistant to change. For example, the adolescent may need to understand the difficulties parents may be having that prevent them from fulfilling some of the expectations the adolescent has for them. In such a case, the adolescent's expectations may be reasonable, and those of the family may not be. Consequently, the goal of IPT-A is to help the adolescent clarify his expectations for the relationship, evaluate which expectations are realistic, and find strategies for coping with both the unreasonable and immutable expectations of the parent and the consequent feelings of anger and sadness engendered. It is very helpful for the adolescent to have another person verify his perceptions of the dispute in addition to finding ways to cope with the situation. It must be stressed that this is a less than optimal goal, but one that must sometimes be adopted when dealing with a resistant parent or any second party.

Case Example. John presented with a major depression precipitated by conflicts with his father who was described both by John and his mother as very rigid and short-tempered. John's depression revolved around his father's severe restrictions of his activities so that he was unable to participate in extracurricular activities and had very limited opportunities to make or spend time with friends. John's mother felt there was little she could do to influence the father, and the father refused to come for treatment with his son. Since the therapist was unable to assist in negotiations with the father, the goal of treatment was to identify methods of coping with the situation, realistic expectations for the father to eliminate repeated disappointments, activities that gave John pleasure that he could engage in with minimal contact from his father, and finally to identify an alternate family member to provide him with the nurturance, support, and interest in his activities that his father was unable to provide for him. This proved to be very beneficial for John. His depressive symptoms dissipated, and his self-esteem and school performance improved.

The therapist also needs to look for similar patterns of nonreciprocal expectations or communication problems in previous or other relationships to better understand the nature of the adolescent's difficulties. Such parallels include repeated conflicts with friends and earlier conflicts with parents that were difficult to resolve. Sometimes the similarities to other experiences may be more covert, such as the adolescent who describes many people having similar negative reactions to him. To better assess the scope of the particular dispute the therapist might ask:

> Have you ever had similar conflicts with other people? Have other people ever reacted to you in a similar manner? Would you say you get into disputes with people frequently? What happens?

When the dispute is discovered to be part of a larger pattern, it is important to explore what is happening to the adolescent as a result of these disputes. Is there any positive outcome for the adolescent? Is there a common misconception about relationships underlying the disputes? What keeps leading the adolescent to similar disputes?

ROLE OF THE PARENT IN THE TREATMENT OF ROLE DISPUTES

The therapist needs to explain to the adolescent and, at times the parents, how interpersonal role disputes contribute to depressive symptoms and how resolution of these disputes can alleviate the symptoms. For example, the therapist might say to the adolescent:

> The fights you are getting into with your father make you angry at first but then leave you with a feeling of hopelessness and helplessness. You feel powerless to change his attitudes and see no way out for yourself. As we talk about your relationship with your father, we will try to find other ways for you to relate to him. You may find that your father will change

toward you, but if he doesn't, then you may come to accept him as he is and find other ways of getting what you want.

The therapist might say to the parent:

The fights you and your child are getting into make him feel worse about himself, and I am sure they are upsetting to you as well. Your relationship with [name of child] at this point seems more than either of you can handle on your own, and perhaps I can be more useful to you and your child to help you communicate better so that you both feel understood. As this happens, your child will feel less depressed, which will be a relief to you, your child, and the rest of the family.

SUMMARY

Successful resolution of a role dispute occurs when the adolescent is able to communicate more openly, to engage the other person in direct nonconflictual discussion of the dispute, and to consider the other person's perspective in the renegotiations. In less optimal circumstances, successful resolution of the dispute may consist of developing more realistic expectations for the relationship that effectively remove the adolescent from the conflict. Either strategy should contribute to a decrease in depressive feelings.

The following two cases illustrate the course of treatment addressing the identified problem of a role dispute. The first case found the adolescent in the impasse stage of the dispute, and the second case found the adolescent in the negotiation phase of the dispute.

CASE VIGNETTE: ALICE—IMPASSE

Alice was a 15-year-old girl who was living with both her parents when she began treatment. She was attending a Catholic girls' high school. Her chief complaints were a lack of interest in her friends and school activities, and increasing moodiness. Her symptoms included sad mood, anorexia, insomnia, and difficulty sustaining attention in school. Her relationship with her parents had deteriorated over the previous year. She found her parents to be intrusive and restrictive. They were vigilant about her schoolwork and were restricting her activities to ensure academic improvement. There was a great deal of tension and fighting between her and her parents, and she began to withdraw more and more into her room. She vacillated between directing anger at herself for being angry at her parents and directing anger at her parents for their lack of understanding and their restrictiveness. She related her depression to her relationship with her parents but had little hope that they would change.

She dated the onset of her difficulties to the middle of her new year at Catholic school and the increasing tension and pressures she felt from her parents. She felt as though they did not trust her, had little consideration for her feelings, and little understanding of a 15-year-old's world.

Exploration of her interpersonal relationships revealed a paucity of social supports and close friendships. This was associated with her inability to express her needs and get them met in her relationships. She was an only child, had been born in South America, and had lived there with her mother and her mother's parents and 11 siblings until joining her father in the United States at the age of 6 years. At initiation of treatment her mother was pregnant with her second child after having been told previously that she couldn't have any more children. Alice felt close to her mother but very estranged from her father. The tension of her relationship with her father had adversely affected her relationship with her mother, as had her mother's pregnancy.

After gathering information about the current depression, the events surrounding the onset, and her perception of the difficulties in her relationship with her parents, the therapist tried to explore what Alice's goals were for therapy and how she thought therapy might be helpful to her. She reported that she wanted (1) to better understand her mood changes and how they were affected by her conflicts with her parents, and (2) to learn how to express her needs better so that she could negotiate better with her parents.

Although the interpersonal history made it clear that the patient had some role transition difficulties, the most pressing problem appeared to be an interpersonal role dispute with her parents to get them to treat her more like an adult and less like a child.

Initial Phase (Sessions 1–4). In the early sessions, Alice focused on her ambivalence regarding her parents' treatment of her as a young child. A part of her enjoyed times when she would look upset and she would be hovered over as if a young child. Another part of her was craving for some privacy. She expressed having the most conflicts with her father. She described a history of resentment for his strictness and an increasing sense of being hurt by his expectations and rigidness. She felt unable to please him. She felt her only options were withdrawal, secret disregard of his rules, or denial of her own interests and desires. An interpersonal inventory of her relationship with her parents revealed a pattern of withdrawal, denial, and/or indirect communication of her wishes. She felt they should be able to understand her merely from looking at her, to know instinctively how she felt, and then to react accordingly.

The focus of these sessions was to elucidate her expectations in her relationship with her parents and how she thought things would have to change for the situation to improve. Since she needed to live with her parents and finish school, her goal needed to be to find a way to improve communication with her parents, particularly her father.

Alice's pattern of communication was discussed first. She described a conflict they had recently about whether she could participate in an after-school activity. She acknowledged that her withdrawal made it more difficult for her parents to understand what it is that she wanted and why. Her anger toward her parents frightened her and she feared expressing it, so instead she would withdraw. She began to be able to discuss a bit more her dissatisfactions in her relationship with her parents and her unhappiness over their lack of trust in her. She said she would try to express her feelings more when in discussions with her parents, but she still believed that "it wouldn't change anything."

Middle Phase (Sessions 5–8). Alice began with a dispute she was having with her parents over their suspicion that she was smoking in her bedroom. She discussed how she told them it wasn't true. Despite their scanty evidence they were still convinced that it was true and lectured her extensively about her behavior. She did not respond to their lectures, although she was quite angry because she felt that they wouldn't change their minds no matter what she said. She felt one of the fundamental problems was their lack of trust in anything she said. The therapist decided it might be helpful to have her parents join them for a session, and both Alice and her parents agreed to do so.

When Alice's parents came for the family session, their communication difficulties were readily apparent. Alice's mother was very quiet throughout the session, leaving the discipline and discussion to her husband. Alice's father was very dogmatic in his discussion of Alice's behavior in terms of what he felt was appropriate or not, and he appeared to mistrust her ability to be more independent. Alice, in response to her father's punitiveness, refused to respond to his accusations and appeared resigned to her position in the family. The therapist attempted to encourage Alice to respond to her father and tried to help her father allow her a chance to express her feelings without belittling them.

In the following session, Alice began to discuss things she felt she would like to say to her parents, and she and the therapist rehearsed them in session. She reported that she was feeling more motivated in her schoolwork and having less trouble concentrating in class. She still expressed some fear about what her father's reaction might be to her new assertiveness. However, she had begun talking more with her mother, who was also encouraging her to express her attitudes and feelings more to her father, so she was feeling some added support. Much time was devoted to increasing her communication skills and assertiveness in a manner that could be received positively by her parents.

Termination Phase (Sessions 9–12). In the final sessions, Alice began to explore her communication patterns in settings other than her home, such as school, and to question herself about what might constitute more effective means of communicating both at home and at school. Alice was still having conflicts with her parents about the time spent in her bedroom, but she was feeling better able to respond to them and assert her position. She still wished that she didn't have to put any effort into her relationship with her parents, that they could just intuit what she was feeling and thinking.

During one of the sessions she returned to the reticent and withdrawing manner that she had evidenced in the initial sessions. We discussed the impact this behavior had on the therapist and how it might affect people similarly outside of the session. She was shown how her behavior affected the responses she received from people and how she could help change these responses through her own facial expression and tone of voice.

Alice was becoming more involved in the therapeutic process and would have benefited from follow-up treatment; however, her family called and said they wanted to try to work things out on their own. They were encouraged to return for treatment if there were any more difficulties.

CASE VIGNETTE: BECKY—NEGOTIATION

Becky was an 18-year-old girl who initially presented with chest pain and was referred for psychiatric treatment. Her chief complaints were dysphoric mood, increased emotional lability (i.e., crying), frequent headaches, lack of appetite, lack of energy, and suicidal ideation. She was having trouble making herself attend school because she couldn't get up in the morning. As a result she had flunked all her courses for the last semester and was not going to be able to graduate the following June.

Initial Phase (Sessions 1–4). Becky was the second-to-youngest child out of five in a large family. Her mother was the primary caretaker, as her father had not lived at home since she was 4 years old. He was a chronic alcoholic and had sporadic contact with the family. Becky reported that she had never been very close to her mother and that they had always had conflicts because she was a stubborn, often misbehaving, child.

Becky's depression had worsened the summer prior to treatment, when her mother had gone to Mexico for the summer and had left Becky home with her older sister. She reported that she had missed her mother a lot and had wanted to tell her about her new sexual experiences and development. When her mother returned, she did not show much interest in hearing about Becky's summer activities or feelings, and Becky felt she had no one to talk to. She felt that her mother only spoke to her when she was angry at her or checking up on her but that she wasn't really a mother to her. Becky decided that she would function independently in the household, rarely being at home or talking to her mother as a way of avoiding conflict with her. Becky's mother grew increasingly angry at Becky's withdrawal from the relationship and perceived her as becoming increasingly oppositional in their infrequent interactions. Becky initially did not want to discuss her relationship with her mother in therapy. Instead, in the initial sessions she focused on strategies for returning to school and graduating on time, and on her relationships with men.

Middle Phase (Sessions 5–8). After Becky felt she had readjusted to being in school and was working hard to graduate, she began to bring up conflicts with her mother in the sessions. She reported that she and her mother were increasingly getting into arguments and that she had heard her mother say to her relatives that she was impossible to handle. She was quite upset by this and started again to have trouble concentrating in school. The first step in the treatment was to try and identify what the conflict was between her and her mother. One factor appeared to be a conflict between her mother's desire for her to help with chores around the house versus her own feeling of being overwhelmed by all her school demands and unable to do chores as much as the mother expected.

The level of upset reported about the mother did not seem consistent with the unmet expectation identified by Becky. Becky was very angry about what she regarded as her mother's earlier abandonment of her motherly duties toward her, as Becky had been working and supporting herself since she was 14 years old. She appeared to be at an impasse with her mother, where her anger at her mother prevented her from communicating with her at all. The therapist discussed with Becky the possibility that her mother's expectations for her and their relationship were still unknown and that it would be difficult to master the situation until these were further delineated. The sessions focused on exploring her mother's possible expectations and wishes for the relationship and identifying her own expectations and wishes. Becky was encouraged to reinstate communication with her mother and to try and find out her mother's expectations and reasons for her attitude toward her. With knowledge of these issues, it would then be possible to explore whether there was some ground where the two of their expectations could meet.

The therapist tried to motivate Becky to communicate by stressing that the situation was not hopeless but rather was a failure of matching expectations and a lack of communication that exacerbated the situation. Similarly, it was important to legitimize her feelings in the situation so she would feel secure enough to explore her mother's position. Becky responded by engaging the mother in an in-depth conversation regarding the mother's expectations for her and discovered that her mother was upset at her since she had learned that Becky had lost her virginity. During this conversation they were both able to discuss what they wished for Becky's social activities and were able to make an agreement for Becky to ask permission before going out and to spend some more time at home with her mother. They had now moved into the negotiation phase of the dispute resolution as they were renegotiating the terms of their relationship. The therapist had facilitated the negotiations and was prepared to invite the mother in for a session to mediate any further negotiations that needed to take place.

Termination Phase (Sessions 9–12). Becky reported that her relationship with her mother was much better and that they had spent a pleasant Mother's Day together. She reported feeling less angry about helping out in the house and reported taking care of her mother when she was ill. During the final sessions, her focus returned to her concerns about graduating, her plans for the summer following graduation and attending college. She reported that she no longer felt that she needed to leave the city for college and that she was thinking of attending college in New York City, which might be less of a financial burden. She reported no sadness, decreased irritability, decreased fatigue, and no eating problems. She was attending school regularly and passing all her courses. She felt that she no longer needed treatment. She was eager to spend her time on her school work to ensure passing grades in all her courses and was looking forward to the summer. She had already arranged a summer job for herself in a department store and was planning on working until she could attend college in February. She reported enjoyment from her relationship with her mother and decreased conflict with her siblings as well. Becky and the therapist reviewed the strategies that had been used to address the conflicts and reviewed areas that she felt had improved emphasizing the utility of these strategies for other interpersonal conflicts that could arise in the future.

·10·

Interpersonal Role Transitions

A problem in role transition is defined as difficulty adjusting to a life change that requires a new or different role (Klerman et al., 1984). Role transitions mark the points between the major stages of life: from childhood to puberty, high school to college, single to married, student to worker, couple to parenthood, and married to widowed. Some transitions are biologically determined, whereas others are influenced by society and culture. Such changes are normative when they occur in a generally expected pattern that one can anticipate and prepare for psychologically and physically.

Time and circumstances can place people in different social roles. Events such as a sudden death or illness are unexpected, more difficult to prepare for, and may be more unsettling and difficult to accept. The impact of such events is strongly affected by the social context of the event and the other people involved in the person's social system.

Success in carrying out these roles affects a person's self-esteem and can affect personal, social, and professional relationships. Depression can impair a person's ability to successfully negotiate a role transition. Conversely, difficulties in making the transition from one role to another can result in depression. These problems may arise because (1) the role is thrust upon the person unexpectedly, (2) the role is an undesired one, (3) the person is not psychologically or emotionally prepared for the new role, and (4) the old role is missed. The social impairment and sense of loss can contribute to feelings of depression.

ADOLESCENT ROLE TRANSITIONS

Adolescents encounter role transitions as a normative part of their developmental process. Normal role transitions such as leaving school, planning work or career, or dating are expected and anticipated by adolescents and their family as rites of passage and are typically handled successfully. Problems arise when parents are unable to accept the concomitant changes to the transition (such as desire to spend more time with friends and less time with family) or when the adolescent is unable to cope with the changes. However, role transitions also can be thrust upon them as a result of unanticipated circumstances, for example, an illness in a parent. The ability of adolescents to cope with unforeseen circumstances rests on prior psychological development and current social supports.

Role transitions can occur from several pathways: (1) impairment in social functioning as a result of depression; (2) psychological and social immaturity; (3) adolescent–parent problems; and (4) changes caused by an unexpected event. Therefore, depression can contribute to role transition problems and vice versa.

Erikson (1968) delineates the changes and common significant tasks associated with the stages of adolescent and young-adult development. Normal role transitions for an adolescent include (1) passage into puberty, (2) the shift from group relationships to dyadic relationships, (3) initiation of sexual relationships or desires, (4) separation from parents and family to achieve increased independence, (5) having to find a first job to support self financially, and (6) taking responsibility for one's future by such things as work, career, or college planning. Problems that can occur during these transitions include loss of self-esteem, inability to meet expectations set by oneself or one's family, increasing pressures and responsibilities to achieve, peer pressure to fit in with the peer-group behavior, inability to let go of dependence on family because of lack of self-confidence, or family's reluctance to separate or inability to let go. Adolescents who become depressed in the latter years of high school are commonly troubled by the increasing pressure and responsibility to make decisions about their future; they may have been more comfortable in the earlier grades when they were still protected from making such decisions.

Depression may cause the adolescent to perceive even a normative role transition as a loss or failure. The adolescent may feel unable to perform successfully in the new role or may be dissatisfied with the limits or restrictions in the new role. Depression may exacerbate the problem and make the adolescent frequently feel hopeless, and unable to adapt to the new role and to find a way to modify the role to better suit his or her needs. The transition consequently contributes to a decrease in self-esteem, a confusion about identity, and a feeling of failure because of an inability to make this new role a success. These difficulties are often related to ideas about the new role that the patient is only partly aware of and that may be discovered through a systematic attempt in therapy to find out what the change means to the adolescent.

Unforeseen or imposed role transitions include (1) becoming a parent and (2) change in family role accompanied by increase or decrease in responsibility caused by parental divorce, remarriage, death of a parent, illness in the family, an impaired parent, or separation from parents. Problems that occur as a result of imposed transitions often are a result of the adolescent feeling overwhelmed by new responsibilities associated with the changed family structure and feeling unable to cope with the added pressures. Failure to cope with role transitions can result in feeling a loss of social support and difficulty dealing with concomitant feelings of sadness, anger, fear, and disappointment.

Alternatively, failure to grow into a new role because of parental disapproval or other externally imposed effects such as death or parenthood may result in depression. The adolescent's perception that he or she cannot successfully make the transition is, in large part, an accurate one. For example, despite their child's being in high school, an adolescent's parents may not want their child to go out after school or to go out with their friends on weekends. The adolescent, therefore, is not able to engage in the same activities as his or her peers and may consequently feel like a social failure resulting in depressive symptoms. IPT-A can help the adolescent to distinguish between real and misperceived abilities impairing successful role transition and to develop strategies to cope with each.

IDENTIFICATION OF ROLE-TRANSITION PROBLEMS

A therapist is likely to diagnose role transition as the identified problem area if the interpersonal history and review of life events suggests the onset of depression coincides with some type of social or role-change event. Often, the patient is able to identify such an event as being associated with decreased self-esteem that later impairs social functioning. In order to gain more information about the nature of the transition the therapist might ask:

> *What was it like for you to [leave school, have first romantic relationship, first job, etc.]? How did it affect how you felt about yourself? Did your life change in any way? How? Did the important people in your life change? In what way? How did you like being in this new role [as student, employee, boyfriend/girlfriend]? How did your mother react to this change in your life? Your father? Your brothers and sisters?*

Role transitions for adolescents affect and are affected by the family. It is important to question the parents as well as the child about the transition. At times, it is the family that is having trouble accepting the changes in the adolescent's role in the family, and family members' lack of acceptance can result in depression for the adolescent. At other times, the family may be pushing the adolescent to make a transition faster than is comfortable. Therefore, the therapist might ask the parent:

Could you tell me about the changes you see occurring with [name]? Are you comfortable with these changes? What do you like about the changes you see? What do you not like about the changes you see? Are there changes you would like to see in [name], new responsibilities you would like [name] to assume that you don't see happening? How do you feel about [name] [becoming more independent, or spending more time away from home, or having a boyfriend or girlfriend, or working at his or her first job]? What are your concerns? How have these changes affected your relationship with [name] or the rest of the family?

GOALS AND STRATEGIES FOR TREATMENT OF ROLE TRANSITIONS

Common strategies and goals for the treatment of major depression can be applied to many types of role transitions experienced by the adolescent. The main goal of the treatment is to help the adolescent relinquish the old role and accept the new one, or to find alternatives leading to a reduction of symptoms. In order to do so, the adolescent will need to review the feelings associated with the old role that were comforting and to express the feelings associated with the new role that make the transition problematic.

Case Example. Sally was a 13-year-old who presented with a major depression. Her depressive symptoms coincided with the remarriage of her father to her stepmother and the birth of her half-brother. Prior to the remarriage, Sally had lived alone with her father and enjoyed a close relationship with him. Following his marriage, she began to experience conflict with her stepmother. She did not like her stepmother telling her what chores to do around the house and telling her father how to discipline her. When she presented for treatment, she complained that she wished just she and her father were living together again. The therapist encouraged Sally to talk about her feelings regarding the remarriage and her new family, her fears of not being wanted by her stepmother, her fears that her stepmother would change the way her father felt about her, and the difficulty in losing some of her father's attention to the stepmother and new baby.

As seen in the above illustration, Sally needed to mourn the loss of her old role as her father's only responsibility and discuss what the problems were of her new role in her newly constituted family. Some of her difficulties stemmed from her reluctance to talk about her feelings with her stepmother as well as her father. The adolescent may need to develop new skills that would ease the transition and improve performance in the new social role. It is important while preparing for the transition to identify social supports for making and sustaining the transition.

Review of Social Role Expectations

The task of evaluating the old role resembles the task of reviewing the positive and negative aspects of relationships, a strategy that is used to treat grief reactions as well as interpersonal deficits. The therapist helps the patient examine the positive and negative aspects of the old role, what the adolescent is afraid will be lost by giving up that role, and the adolescent's perception of the new role. The review often provides the adolescent with an opportunity to develop a more realistic view of the old role, the positive as well as the negative aspects. The treatment is aimed at enabling the adolescent to relinquish the idealized version of the old role and mourn the loss of the real role. For example, one adolescent girl had a great deal of difficulty managing her separation from her parents and involvement in peer activities since she felt it was culturally expected of her never to challenge her parents' restraints on her activities. She felt that the normal role of being an active participant in peer activities after school was not acceptable to her parents whose native culture limited such a shift in focus. She suppressed the extent to which their restrictions made her unhappy, preventing her from pursuing activities, such as dance and theater, that she would have enjoyed at school. In this case, it was the parents' inability to accept a role transition that was normative in the adolescent's social environment that was contributing to the adolescent's inability to take on the new role that resulted in depression. The therapist thus needed to address the parents' concerns as well as those of the adolescent. This involved meeting with the parents to ascertain their fears as well as to provide psychoeducation about the adolescent's need for separation and individuation from the parent. Armed with knowledge of both parties' concerns, the therapist then set about to facilitate negotiation of a compromise. In this case, the family was able to agree to participation in certain activities with guidelines about curfews. Prior to such negotiations, the therapist needs to ask the adolescent:

> *How do your parents feel about your interests in these activities? How do you feel when your parents express concern about your participation? When you see the other students participating how do you feel? Even though we love our parents, sometimes they make decisions about us that make us unhappy. It is all right to love your parents and be angry at them too. Do you ever feel angry or hurt by their restrictions? Ideally, how would you like your parents to react to interests in these activities? Do you sometimes feel like doing them anyway? Do you feel guilty ever about having these desires to disobey your parents or about your anger?*

In reviewing the positive and negative aspects of the anticipated new role and parents' difficulty in accepting the transition, the therapist should try and elicit feelings associated with the change including fear of associated expectations or challenges, sadness about the loss of the old role, anger at the change if it is unexpected, and/or disappointment if the changes are more limited than desired. To get a better sense of what the transition means to the adolescent the therapist might ask:

> *Sometimes people feel a sense of loss when they give up old roles, even when they feel good about the changes. When this change occurred in your life how did you feel about it? What did you worry about? for yourself? for your parents? for your friends?*

Case Example. Kathy was having difficulty with her parents making the transition from being dependent on her family to being independent from family and spending more time with friends. While she felt her parents were not supportive of her transition, she herself experienced feelings of guilt when she thought about asserting herself to participate in more extracurricular activities in school. She felt guilty about challenging her parents' notion of what might be appropriate behavior at this age. In addition, she revealed concerns about her self-esteem and vulnerability if she tried out for the extracurricular activities and did not get accepted. Therefore, not only was she hindered by her parents' reluctance about the role transition, but she herself also had some anxiety about becoming more involved in peer activities and risking rejection. Prior to negotiating a compromise with her parents, the therapist needs first to address the patient's interpersonal anxieties and review the necessary social skills for entry into these peer activities.

Educating Parents about the Transition

In addition to educating the adolescent about role transitions, it is often important to educate the parents. It is not only the adolescent but other family members who can have a difficult time accepting the concomitant changes in their adolescent. The parents must be educated about normal developmental tasks for an adolescent, the feelings they may elicit in the parents, and ways to cope with these feelings. The therapist might say to the parents in a separate session:

> *Your child is growing up, having new experiences. Even though you realize the importance of these changes and are proud of your child, it can sometimes be hard for parents to see their child growing up and away from them. Is there anything that makes you uncomfortable about letting your daughter have these new experiences? What concerns you? You may feel a certain sadness and loss about these changes. Kathy needs to feel your support for these changes, and it's all right for Kathy to know that you feel sad as long as she knows you basically want these changes for her. Kathy needs to have your support and know that you are there for her. Without the feeling of support and permission to move on, she will feel conflict about making the transition, and this can lead to feelings of depression.*

Some parents have difficulty accepting these developmental changes. It is difficult for them to accept that their adolescent may want to spend more time with friends than with family or that the adolescent isn't sharing as much information about herself with the family.

The parents need to be educated as to what is appropriate behavior for an adolescent so they can recognize what behaviors to accept and what behaviors to be concerned about. The therapist needs to evaluate their concerns and fears, normalize them, and put them in the appropriate context. This can be done by asking the parents to recall their own experiences to help them empathize with their children. The therapist can tell the parents:

> *Your child is going through changes that you find hard to accept. This is part of growing up and is perfectly normal. These changes don't mean Kathy doesn't love you or care about the family any more. Sometimes children react with anger or pull away from the family because they love their families so much it is the only way they can become independent. Can you remember when you were Kathy's age and what you felt like and wanted for yourself? Well, Kathy is now feeling those same things and needs to feel your love and support through this change. You have*

given your child ideas about life and a sense of morals that are part of who she is, and you need to have faith in Kathy that she has learned well from you.

In circumstances where the adolescent is engaging in inappropriate behavior, the therapist needs to discuss these behaviors both with the adolescent and parent. Together they must negotiate guidelines for more socially acceptable behavior. Necessary groundwork for the negotiation will include clarifying the adolescent's expectations for his or her parents' behavior toward him or her, educating the adolescent about appropriate and/or safe behavior, correcting the adolescent's misperceptions about his or her behavior, and assisting the adolescent and the parents in finding activities that will be acceptable to each of them. This set of negotiations will involve sessions alone with the adolescent as well as joint sessions with the parents.

Social-Skills Assessment and Development

Frequently, the difficulty in making the role transition stems from a lack of self-confidence because of deficits in the skills necessary to make the transition. The adolescent either may not have the necessary skills or may have fears or unrealistic expectations about the role that prevents effective use of the skills. The therapist needs to explore the feelings surrounding the change and the status of their skills.

The therapist should also assist the adolescent in assessing which skills might be necessary to perform competently in the social role. Together they can review whether the assessment is realistic and compare the identified skills with those that the adolescent possesses and those he or she wishes to acquire. It is important for the therapist to clarify whether the adolescent is over- or underestimating his or her potential to perform the new role. Some of the skills may be on a very practical level such as how to apply to college or how to find a first job. Others may be more abstract such as the social self-confidence to ask another person to go out on a date. Often, the performance of the social role is adversely affected by anxiety about being successful or not. In order to relieve such anxiety, the therapist and adolescent can role play difficult situations associated with the anxiety and confront fears about the situation that can be discussed within the safety of the therapeutic relationship. The therapist might ask the patient:

Are there any social situations in which you feel more uncomfortable than most people? What are they? What is difficult about the situation? Is it hard for you to talk to people you don't know very well? If you need

help doing something, are you able to ask for help or do you struggle with
it alone? Is it hard to start a conversation with a person of the opposite
sex? What do you worry about? In this situation [on first date, first job]
what is the worst thing that could happen to you? How would you feel
if this happened? What could you do in such a situation? What are some
alternative ways to handle the situation?

Transitions also can be made difficult if the adolescent clings to
stereotyped assumptions about the new role. These assumptions may be
the result of peer discussion, and/or observation of and identification
with another individual in a similar role. The therapist's task is to
broaden the adolescent's expectations of the new role by identifying
other people who do not have the anticipated problems. For example,
Beth was a 15-year-old girl who presented with major depression that
was associated with the initiation of relationships with boys. She was
having considerable problems in her relationships with young men in her
class and was quite uncomfortable with them. In treatment she would
say "all boys were crazy, all were out to treat girls unfairly and take
advantage of them, and girls eventually just have to accept being treated
badly by boys or men." She described situations in which she felt she
could not assert herself with the boys and do what she felt was right. She
saw this as the state of women in general. The therapist tried to help her
recognize the possibility for relationships of a different nature by asking
her:

Whom do you know that is in a relationship with a boy? How do you see
their relationship? What do you see as the positive aspects of the relation-
ship? What do you see as the negative aspects of the relationship? What
do you think the women could do to improve their relationships with their
men? Can you think of anyone, even outside your community, who has
a different more positive type of relationship with a man? What makes
this relationship different? What would prevent you from having such a
positive relationship?

Social Support for Transition

Role transitions are often facilitated in adolescents if they can perceive
some system of social support or new friendship accompanying acceptance of the new role. Although the adolescent may have anxiety about
forming new attachments, the new role will appear more attractive if the
social rewards are desirable. In helping the adolescent to recognize the
potential for new relationships, the therapist will need to explore the
anxiety that often accompanies the prospect of new relationships and

new situations. This sort of change and anxiety may occur when a student enters the first year of high school. Although the student may have been successful in junior high school, the increase in the size of the school, the amount of work expected, and the change in fellow students and teachers may make the adolescent feel unprepared for the new environment. The adolescent will feel apprehensive about making new friends and becoming an active participant in school, although the adolescent is likely also to desire acceptance by a new social group.

In such a situation, the therapist will help the adolescent generate opportunities to get involved with students by joining an extracurricular activity of interest. This is an important task because, when depressed, people frequently lose interest in activities they ordinarily enjoy, and the negative outlook on life may result in missed opportunities. To help generate new opportunities the therapist might ask:

> Are there any activities going on in your school or community that you might enjoy? What kinds of things do you enjoy doing after school? Is there a club or class that you could join where you could do this with other people and meet people with similar interests? Have you ever done any volunteer work? Is that something you might enjoy? It is often enjoyable to meet people with similar interests as a start for forming friendships and having someone else to talk to about the ups and downs of daily life. Would you feel comfortable joining any of these activities? What are your concerns?

Together, these strategies help the adolescent feel more prepared to accept the new role by providing him or her with new skills, addressing anxieties about the transition, and correcting any unrealistic expectations about the social role that may make the transition undesirable or threatening.

SUMMARY

An impasse in a role transition can be successfully negotiated by defining the interpersonal relationships involved in the impasse and effecting changes in those relationships. Once the role transition is identified, the therapist helps the adolescent identify feelings and expectations of the new role. Communication with the significant people in the adolescent's life is supported and encouraged. The therapist helps the adolescent determine what is normal in a role transition and educates the parents about what can be expected from the adolescent as he or she relinquishes the old role and assumes the new role. Expectations of the parents and the adolescent about the new role are addressed. In this way, all parties can come to accept the adolescent's new role. Misconceptions about the anticipated role are corrected through education and observation of others in a similar role who have achieved the transition successfully. The therapist helps the adolescent attain the necessary social skills required for the new role. This can be accomplished through role playing or participation in new and varied social activities.

The following case vignette illustrates the work that must often be conducted with both the adolescent and the parents in order to improve the adolescent's adjustment to the role transition.

CASE VIGNETTE: PAM

Pam was a 13-year-old girl who presented to the clinic complaining of depressed mood, irritability, tearfulness, early and middle insomnia, increased fatigue, decrease in appetite, decrease in concentration, decline in grades, and frequent headaches. Pam was the only child of parents who had divorced when she was an infant. She had lived with her mother in the Dominican Republic until she was 8 years old, when she moved to the United States to live with her father. She still spent the summers with her mother. Her father had remarried a year ago, shortly before her half-brother was born. At the time of treatment, she was living with her stepmother, father, and half-brother. Pam's depression worsened as conflict between her and her stepmother and father increased about her role and responsibilities in the household. As a result of increasing arguments with her stepmother and father, she was spending the majority of her time alone in her room.

Initial Phase (Sessions 1–4). Pam did not like her stepmother. She did not like the way her stepmother spoke to her, and felt she was too critical of her. Her stepmother was never satisfied with her efforts to clean the house and would blame her for any mess that was made in the house. She wished her stepmother would just go away. She stated that her stepmother was crazy if she thought she could interfere in her relationship with her father. Her father acknowledged the stepmother's cruelty toward his daughter, but felt helpless to change the stepmother's attitude and was reluctant to leave the marriage because of the son they shared. Pam also did not like the way her stepmother and father related to each other, feeling that her stepmother was always yelling, putting him down, or bossing him around. It was apparent in the initial phase that Pam was having difficulty with the transition from being just her father's daughter to being a stepdaughter and acquiring a sibling. She agreed that this transition was difficult for her and was the cause of her unhappiness.

Middle Phase (Sessions 5–8). The focus of this phase of treatment was to examine the strategies Pam was using to better negotiate this transition. It became apparent that Pam did not communicate to anyone her feelings about what had happened and her concerns about her role in the family. Instead she would keep it all inside until she exploded in anger, which only exacerbated her problems with both her stepmother and father. To facilitate her comfort in expressing her feelings, she and the therapist first had to examine her expectations for her role in the family, whether or not they were realistic, and whether or not her fears were realistic. The therapist also met with Pam's father to discuss his perceptions of the problems that had occurred in the transition to this new family structure. It appeared that part of Pam's problem in making the transition was that her father had never worked out with his wife what roles they were to play in Pam's upbringing. Therefore, he was educated about his need to discuss with his wife what they felt were reasonable responsibilities for his daughter, what were acceptable punishments if she was remiss, who was to enforce the discipline, and generally how they wanted the household to function. Without this clarification of her family role, Pam was going to continue to have difficulty making the transition. While the father was working out these negotiations with his wife, the therapist was helping Pam learn to communicate her feelings to her parents so that they could better understand her needs.

Termination Phase (Sessions 8–12). Pam began to feel much better as she began to talk more with her father and see that he was sympathetic to her difficulties with her stepmother. Her parents' clarification of her role facilitated her ability to accept parts of the role and to negotiate with both of them the aspects of her role that she did not like. She learned to ask her stepmother for clarification of complaints voiced about her household chores. They negotiated a more reasonable set of responsibilities, and she and her father arranged to regularly spend some time alone together each week She reported feeling that she had a more secure place in the family and that she could still maintain a close relationship with her father, despite his remarriage. Her increasing communication skills resulted in a significant decrease in her irritability and angry outbursts, an increase in her ability to concentrate, and improvement in her grades, mood, sleep, and appetite. During termination, she and the therapist generated other problems that might arise with the transition, such as more focus on her brother and how she might handle the situation. She reported that she felt she had really learned the importance of talking about her feelings so that others could respond to her in a more desirable fashion and that this kind of communication should always be the first step in looking for a solution.

·11·

Interpersonal Deficits

Interpersonal deficits refer to a lack of social and communication skills that impairs the conduct of interpersonal relationships. Examples of interpersonal deficits include: inability to initiate relationships, inability to maintain relationships, inability to express one's feelings verbally, and/or difficulty eliciting information from others to establish communication. The arena of interpersonal deficits is selected as the problem area for IPT-A when the patient's interpersonal inventory reveals a history of social withdrawal with apparent difficulties in initiating and maintaining interpersonal relationships. These deficits may be apparent in some form prior to the depressive episode but are exacerbated by the depression and appear more severe at presentation for treatment.

Erikson (1968) identified the primary task of adolescence as that of establishing a unique identity or sense of self that requires one to interact with others to establish a set of personal values, attitudes, and goals. As a result of interpersonal deficits, the adolescent may be socially isolated from peer groups and relationships, a situation that can lead to feelings of depression and inadequacy. Interpersonal deficits may also be identified as a problem area when it appears that a depression has caused the adolescent to withdraw socially. The social withdrawal may result in a developmental lag in interpersonal skills that further perpetuates the depression by impairing social relationships. Puig-Antich et al. (1985b) found that although the symptoms of depression may be transient in children, the accompanying interpersonal impairments tend to persist even after the depression resolves. The persisting interpersonal deficits place the adolescent at risk for future episodes of depression.

Social isolation may be more problematic during adolescence than during other life stages because establishing social relationships is the focus of the developmental tasks of adolescence. Appropriate social behavior may become retarded or impaired by the isolation. Specific important developmental tasks of adolescence include making same-aged friends, participating in extracurricular activities, becoming part of a peer group, beginning to date, and learning to make choices regarding exclusive relationships, careers, and sexuality (Hersen & Van Hasselt, 1987). Withdrawal from social contacts may result in failure to learn and develop age-appropriate social skills. An adolescent with interpersonal deficits will find these tasks difficult to master. Interpersonal psychotherapy, because of its time-limited nature, is better suited to address those interpersonal deficits that are primarily a result of the current depressive episode than those that are of a more chronic nature.

DIAGNOSING INTERPERSONAL DEFICITS

An adolescent who was functioning well socially should have a network of close relationships with family members and friends, a satisfying number of acquaintances, and would feel comfortable socially in school. In contrast, the adolescent who was not functioning well usually would report a paucity of relationships or a history of disrupted relationships. The therapist must perform a thorough interpersonal inventory in order to diagnose the interpersonal deficit problem area. Later, during the middle phase of treatment, the therapist should investigate the adolescent's interpersonal problems, their chronicity, and their duration. The therapist might ask:

> *Who are your close friends? How long have you been friends? How did you meet? What makes [name] a good friend? How do you define a good friend? Have you had more difficulty being with friends since you have been feeling depressed? How did your friendship end? What is difficult about making friends for you? What is it like for you to begin conversations? Is it difficult to initiate friendships? Do you feel like you don't know what to do in a relationship once you have gotten past the initial meeting? What do you do to get to know someone better? What happens when you are with your friends? How do you feel? What was it like to be with your family and friends before you were depressed?*

In order to obtain a complete picture of the adolescent's social functioning, the therapist should conduct a thorough review of positive and negative aspects of past relationships.

The therapist should initially focus on the most current relationships and then progress to discussion of the past:

> *How do you find your friends and activities now? Have your relationships with them changed at all recently? How so? Are they less enjoyable?*

*more enjoyable? How do these present relationships differ from relation-
ships you had in the past?*

In reviewing the relationships, the therapist should be alert for evidence
of similar problems in multiple relationships, such as difficulties in deepening relationships or maintaining an ongoing relationship. Interpersonal deficits differs from other problem areas in that the interpersonal
problem is usually pervasive to the majority of the adolescent's relationships, whereas the dispute or role transition problem may be limited to
one.

GOALS AND STRATEGIES OF TREATMENT

Treatment of interpersonal deficits in adolescents must reduce the social
isolation and improve the relationships the patient has had and is
developing. To do this, the therapist must help to improve the patient's
self-esteem by directly addressing the deficits. Specific goals are (1) to
improve communication skills, (2) to increase the adolescent's social
self-confidence, (3) to improve quality of existing relationships, and (4)
to increase the number of satisfying relationships. If an adolescent presents with few current significant relationships, the therapist should
review past significant relationships looking for patterns of difficulties. If
a deficit such as maladaptive communication patterns is found in one
relationship, a subsequent session may explore the analogy to the patient's other relationships. Although the focus of treatment will be on
addressing the problems in one particular relationship, therapy will also
focus on how the use of these new interpersonal skills can generalize to
other relationships.

Given an extremely isolated patient, a therapist will have to use his
or her own relationship with the patient to explore the adolescent's
interpersonal deficits. The therapist should observe whether any interpersonal problems are evident in their relationship and be able to discuss
the positive aspects as well as the negative impact of any social-skills
deficits on the relationship. With specific patterns and deficits identified, the therapist can engage in education and role playing to expand
the adolescent's interpersonal repertoire. The therapist–patient relationship can act as a model for how to establish a more appropriate or
satisfying relationship in a given context (i.e., what are appropriate
expectations and conduct in particular types of relationships, and how
to communicate emotions more accurately).

Case Example. Dana was a 16-year-old girl who presented with a major
depression and identified problem area of interpersonal deficits. She

had a history of having friends in school and getting along with others until the previous year when she became depressed and more withdrawn. Her symptoms were depressed mood, suicidal ideation, increased fatigue, anhedonia, decreased appetite, low self-esteem, and feelings of helplessness and hopelessness. When questioned about her relationships with peers, Dana described her discomfort around males, stating that they were impossible to talk to and never treated women well. Dana's interpersonal inventory revealed that her depression had been precipitated by a problematic relationship with a boyfriend. Dana did not know how to initiate and deepen friendships gradually and/or how to remove herself from relationships (particularly with males) that were not satisfying for her. She did not know the appropriate boundaries in friendships and/or how to set limits for the relationship that were comfortable to her. For example, she would become sexually involved with boys even when she did not want to or feel comfortable doing so, because she did not know another way to communicate that she wanted to get to know them better. The focus of the treatment became the exploration of how to develop friendships, improvement of her self-image in relationships, appropriate self-assertion in relationships, education about intimacy, and the appropriate way to use her interpersonal skills. In session, Dana practiced expressing her feelings clearly by discussing the therapist's perceptions of her comments and discussing whether or not these were the messages Dana had meant to convey. This exercise helped Dana clarify her communications, thereby decreasing the misperceptions in her relationships and increasing the number of successful interactions outside the therapy.

In the session, the therapist is able to stop an interaction in progress and discuss what the adolescent was feeling at the time in relation to the behavior. In addition, the therapist is able to facilitate a discussion of the impact of the behavior on the other person in the relationship. In this manner, the therapist can identify unrealistic expectations for a relationship, help the adolescent understand the meaning of the words for another person, and correct any distortions in communication. It is also very important, where appropriate, for the therapist to relate the issues of their relationship to other relationships outside therapy in order to foster broader social confidence and social skills.

In conducting IPT-A, the negative feelings about the therapist are understood as transference phenomena but are not dealt with in a psychodynamic way. The therapist does not encourage the feelings in the patient or allow them to evolve fully. Instead, the therapist will intervene and test the patient's perceptions of reality. The therapist might say:

It seems as though you are feeling angry today? Are you feeling angry? With whom are you angry? Has something happened in the session that has upset you? If so, I think it is important to talk about it. By talking about it together we can see how it occurred, uncover any misunderstandings that may exist, and clarify our relationship so we can each have realistic expectations for each other. I wonder if this ever happens with other people?

The therapist needs to encourage the adolescent to examine the negative feelings for the therapist in a supportive atmosphere. Such direct exploration of the adolescent's feelings will prevent misunderstandings that could lead to premature termination. The experience also can provide a model, for the adolescent, of how to address negative feelings or problems in other significant relationships through similar types of open discussion.

It is very important to work with the adolescent on identifying repeated patterns of interpersonal difficulties so that the skills can be acquired or the difficulties resolved for future relationships. This information can only be obtained by comparing problematic relationships to successful relationships and analyzing verbal exchanges as they occur inside and outside the session. Adolescents may be reluctant to talk about relationships that have left them feeling badly, but they should be encouraged to do so to prevent future relationships from going awry.

Case Example. Working with Dana also revealed that she had a similar problem in initiating friendships with girls in school. For example, she would not talk to classmates unless they initiated the conversation. She felt she did not know what to say after "Hello, how are you?" This was discussed in the context of her entrance to a new school during treatment and anxiety over meeting new people. She frequently described how her difficulties in negotiating her relationships made her feel badly about herself and depressed. She felt helpless to make people understand what kind of person she was. A focus of discussion was the issue of self-disclosure, how much is appropriate and to whom. To assist in understanding methods of self-disclosure, patient and therapist role played various interpersonal exchanges. A repeated theme was how to establish boundaries in relationships and how these boundaries vary according to the type of relationship. Comparisons were made between relationships with family members, friends, teachers, acquaintances, and even her therapist.

Specifically, the techniques that are most helpful in educating the adolescent about interpersonal relationships are communication analysis and role playing. Through communication analysis, the therapist helps the adolescent understand the impact of his or her words on others, and the feelings conveyed by the words in comparison to the feelings that generated the verbal exchange. Role playing provides the adolescent with a safe way to practice the new communication skills and get feedback prior to applying what is learned to outside situations. In addition, successful role plays can increase the adolescent's social confidence. To initiate the role play the therapist may propose for example:

> *Let's pretend you are in school and you would like to join the group of kids sitting together in a group. What could you do to try and join these people? What could you say when you approach them?*

Or, in conducting communication analysis, the therapist might say:

> *How do you think the other girl felt when you said _____? How did you want her to feel? What had you wanted to say? How could you say it differently? How did you feel when she said _____ back to you? What do you think she meant?*

Because of the brief nature of the treatment, the therapist must be careful to focus on a circumscribed interpersonal deficit, such as how to initiate a social interaction, in order to make progress in the limited time of the treatment. The therapist must emphasize that the adolescent should begin to work on this problem and gain confidence during the treatment.

SUMMARY

The therapist's primary focus is on interpersonal deficits that have been exacerbated by the adolescent's depression and may additionally be playing a role in the perpetuation of the depression. Conducting a very throrough interpersonal inventory is crucial to the identification of this problem area. The goal of the treatment is to reduce the adolescent's social isolation and improve existing relationships. Strategies employed to achieve these goals include improving communication skills, increasing social confidence, and encouraging participation in more social activities. The therapist uses the therapist–patient relationship to illustrate difficulties in interpersonal functioning that may be apparent in the actual treatment sessions as well as in outside relationships. The specific techniques of communication analysis and role playing are employed to practice new social skills that will facilitate the development of new and or better relationships.

The following case example illustrates both how interpersonal deficits, such as difficulty communicating feelings, can result in depression and how interpersonal psychotherapy is used to treat the depression.

CASE VIGNETTE: CARMEN

Carmen was a 14-year-old girl who lived with her mother, father, and younger brother. Her mother was very worried about Carmen's withdrawal from family and friends and brought her for treatment. Carmen had been feeling depressed since her parents began to have marital problems resulting from her father's extramarital affairs approximately 2 years earlier. Three months prior to Carmen's evaluation, she began to feel worse after her parents began to fight more, and her father disappeared for 1 week. Around the same time, she broke up with her boyfriend, whom she had been seeing for several months. Carmen's parents did not know she had a boyfriend, so she was feeling both sad about the break-up and guilty about having the relationship without her parent's permission. Carmen presented with a major depression. Her symptoms included: depressed mood every day for most of the day, decreased appetite, early and middle insomnia, increased fatigue, suicidal ideation, headaches, tearfulness, feelings of guilt, and low self-esteem.

Initial Phase (Sessions 1–4). It was immediately apparent to the therapist in the initial sessions that Carmen had a very difficult time talking about her feelings. She confided in no one even though she reported having two close friends who were concerned and interested in her. Carmen's inability to talk about her feelings had begun when her father's affair disrupted the household. She had felt caught between her parents, angry at her father for the affairs, and angry at her mother for staying with her father. She stopped talking to her father altogether and stopped confiding in her mother. She decreased her communication to her mother because she did not want to add to her problems or worry. By not talking to her father, she was hoping he or the problem would just go away.

As a result of withdrawal from her family, Carmen had turned to a boyfriend to provide her with a feeling of importance and self-esteem. But given the secrecy of her father's affairs, Carmen began to feel increasingly guilty about her own secret relationship. She wanted to be able to tell her parents about the relationship, but her previous withdrawal from the family made her feel helpless to do so. The problem area was identified as that of interpersonal deficits, because it appeared that her inability to communicate her feelings to her parents was resulting in a feeling of isolation and guilt that was contributing to her depression.

Middle Phase (Sessions 5–8). The strategies used to ameliorate her interpersonal deficits included role playing, clarification of feelings, techniques of initiating and deepening relationships, and techniques of interpersonal problem solving within a conversation. The focus of the middle sessions was to help Carmen label her feelings and find the words to express those feelings. The therapist and Carmen explored what made it difficult for her to start conversations, what she was worried her mother or friends might think if she told them how she felt, and how she would feel if she expressed more of her feelings. Psychoeducation about relationships was provided regarding the types of negotiations that typically occur between two people in a relationship.

In the beginning, Carmen had much difficulty even relating to the therapist what had occurred since the previous session and how she had felt about the events. Using their own conversation in the sessions, the therapist demonstrated to Carmen how revealing information about herself could help others like the therapist and her family better respond to her needs and make her feel better about herself. In the sessions, Carmen role played with the therapist conversations she would like to have with her mother regarding her desire to date. She discussed how she would handle various reactions her mother might have. She also discussed her feelings about what had occurred in her parents' relationship and its effect on her ability to communicate with them. Carmen revealed she was afraid that if she wasn't the perfect daughter she would exacerbate her parents' marital stress. To try and maintain this image, she withdrew from talking about herself. By relating events to feelings, the therapist helped Carmen to see that the withdrawal was creating more problems in her relationships with her parents and making her feel worse about herself. Between sessions, Carmen experimented by talking more to her mother about her feelings. Her mother was able to successfully discuss the issue of boyfriends with her and negotiate a reasonable compromise that further encouraged Carmen to practice expressing her feelings to others. Her improvement was noticeable in her increased openness with the therapist as well.

Termination Phase (Sessions 9–12). As Carmen continued to practice her efforts at communication, she and the therapist discussed her increased sense of closeness and support within her relationships and the decrease in her depressed mood. She reported engaging in more social activities with friends and even found that her father was amenable to many of her requests to participate in particular social activities. Her parents, as a result of Carmen's treatment and the therapist's discussion with the mother about the contributing factors, made a commitment to work on their relationship. The mother reported that she and the father were trying to increase their communication with each other in the same way that Carmen was improving her communication with them. The therapist recommended that the parents seek marital counseling, but they refused. Carmen said that her parents appeared to be getting along better: There was a decrease in fighting and her father had not spent any nights out of the home.

During the final sessions, Carmen appeared less critical of herself and was finding people very accepting of her in social interactions. She was enjoying a new social self-confidence from the positive responses to her increased expressiveness. At termination, she reported no sad mood, no sleep difficulties or fatigue, no suicidal ideation, decreased guilt and self-blame, and increased self-esteem.

·12·

Single-Parent Families

Living in a single-parent family is the fifth problem area. It is added specifically for the adaptation of IPT for the depressed adolescent because of its high prevalence and the unique problems it creates in family functioning. The single-parent problem area is targeted when the adolescent's depression appears to be a result of family stress specifically caused by the single-parent structure of the family. Although the cause of the depression may appear to be conceptualized as role transitions or role disputes, the most salient factor is that it is precipitated by difficulties inherent in the family structure. We therefore feel it is necessary to recognize it as a separate problem area with its own strategies and goals. The identified dispute often is with the parent who is absent. The focus is on problems that develop when one parent who had been present is no longer present for any of a number of reasons. The inability to address the missing relationship puts significant stress on the remaining relationships in the family. We therefore feel it is important to establish this fifth problem area to emphasize the interpersonal difficulties unique to single-parent families and adolescents. In this chapter, we discuss the role of single-parent families in the development of depression and impaired interpersonal functioning. Causes of single-parent families will be reviewed with particular emphasis on the effects of divorce. Grief reactions to the loss of a parent are covered in a separate chapter.

ASPECTS OF SINGLE-PARENT FAMILIES

Causes of Single-Parent Families

In recent years, single-parent families have grown in incidence not only because of divorce and death but other interparental conflict. Some reasons include a parent being removed from the family following abuse allegations, more women having babies before marriage, drug abuse, or incarceration of one parent (Norton & Glick, 1986). In addition, there are situations where the parent just disappears, leaving the adolescent without knowledge of his or her whereabouts or if and when he or she will return. The single-parent family structure is not confined to lower socioeconomic classes but occurs in the middle class as well (Norton & Glick, 1986). Different reasons for the absence of a parent from the family can lead to different problems for the adolescent.

Parental Divorce and Single Parents

Parental divorce results in a range of family relationships and arrangements. For the majority of children, the most acute responses to parental separation diminish substantially within the first 6 months to a year after separation (Wallerstein & Kelly, 1980). In families where the conflict between parents ceases following divorce, children are shown to have few complications after the initial year. Children in families where the conflict continues show serious effects of the conflict. Wallerstein (1983) found that being in the custody of a psychologically disturbed parent or a parent who was neglectful or minimally invested in parenting responsibility was significantly linked to serious deterioration in behavioral, social, and academic functioning in children evident 5 years after parental separation. According to Hetherington et al. (1985), in the first few years following divorce, children in divorced families, regardless of the level of concomitant conflict, manifested more antisocial, impulsive, and acting-out behavior, more aggression, noncompliance, dependency, anxiety, depression, difficulties in social relationships, and had more problems in school.

Specific consequences of divorce such as the new interpersonal relationship between the parents or the absent father can result in depression, anxiety, physical complaints, and/or behavior problems in the children and adolescents. Forehand et al. (1989) have found an association between interparental conflict and the internalizing of problems in adolescents. Mechanic and Hansell (1989) report that higher levels of family conflict were associated with longitudinal increases in depressed mood, anxiety, and physical symptoms.

Parental conflict surrounding divorce can effect the child custody agreement, which in turn can have deleterious effects on the children. Parents, out of a sense of frustration at the limitations imposed on their time with their child, may resort to extreme acts such as kidnapping to satisfy their desire to see their child and to punish their spouse for limiting their involvement. When this happens, the child becomes a pawn between the parents and may experience conflicting loyalties and a desire to please both parents. The stress of this type of incident usually manifests itself in either internalizing or externalizing symptoms on the child's return to the custodial parent. It also is likely to have deleterious effects on communication with each parent and damage the child's sense of support and stability.

Often when the child's parents divorce, the child has to adjust to a very different type of relationship with the parents, especially the noncustodial parent. Frequently, intermittent parents feel they have legitimate authority over the activities of their children and can make rules for them to follow even when they are not around. Children, however, feel that if the parent is absent, he or she should have no say in their activities. The anger generated by such situations may also fuel an adolescent's depression and sense of helplessness to negotiate a better relationship with his or her parents.

Quality of Family Relationships

Children of single-parent families can function without significant difficulties, or they can experience a host of problems, one of which is frequently depression. The quality of the relationship between the parents, and of the child's relationship with each parent, affects the child's ability to cope with the divorce or physical separation from a parent. It is a better predictor of childhood adjustment than the structure of a single-parent home (Brody & Forehand, 1990). Specific factors that affect these relationships are the frequency, duration, and quality of time spent together.

Researchers have demonstrated that fathers, more frequently than mothers, fail to establish or maintain a continuous and stable visiting or parenting plan that would allow for a continuous relationship with their children (Kelly, 1981, 1988; Wallerstein & Kelly, 1980). Brody and Forehand (1990) found that close relationships with the noncustodial father are associated with the display of fewer internalizing problems, even in the presence of relatively high levels of interparental conflict. Coping methods are affected by the cause of the disruption and the mental health of both parents.

For adolescents whose parent has simply disappeared, the typical effects of separation can be exacerbated because the adolescents are often plagued with uncertainty as to the missing parent's future role in the family. The adolescent will ask questions such as: "Will Dad return?" "Is Mom alive?" There may be a persistent sense that the loss lacks finality and can be undone at any time. The adolescent therefore faces the loss of a relationship with the parent who remains, as well as with the parent who has left. The uncertainty of not knowing whether to accept the absence as temporary or final makes it difficult for the adolescent to cope with the loss and to try to make the remaining relationships work.

Effect of Single Parenthood on the Adolescent

Smollar and Youniss (1985), in a study of parent–adolescent relations in maternal-headed, single-parent homes, found that adolescents from such homes perceived themselves as more cautious in communicating with their parent and would hide feelings from their parent, particularly doubts and fears. Jacobson and Jacobson (1987) reported that the greater the length of separation from the parent with no contact, regardless of cause, the poorer the child's adjustment. Even when the child eventually did see the parent who had been in jail or who had abandoned him or her temporarily, the relationship was rarely the same. Expectations that each could pick up the relationship where they had left off often led to significant disappointment and anger. The intensity of the reaction on reunion or subsequent separation has been shown to be affected by the degree of separation, its abruptness, and whether it has happened before (Jacobson & Jacobson, 1987).

Schwartzberg (1981) found that loss of one parent often results in a blurring of the generational boundaries in which the adolescent prematurely takes on an adult role in the family. In such situations, the child usually feels the need to assume the missing parent's role in some manner, particularly if it is the same-sex parent who is absent. The parental separation or divorce can be associated with increased adolescent enmeshment with the remaining parent, an inability to separate appropriately from that parent, and an assumption of parental burdens such as financial concerns and social isolation (Glenwick & Mowrey, 1986). In addition, the child has to cope with two losses—the physical loss of the absent parent and the loss of the parental role of the present parent who is no longer functioning as such (Glenwick & Mowrey, 1986).

Problems that arise over the adolescent's conflicts with the parents can sometimes result in self-destructive behavior. For example, in response to loss of the father and decline in parental supervision, a teen may increase sexual activity to the point of promiscuity. As a possible reaction to feelings of abandonment or rejection, adolescent girls in particular seem to increase love-seeking behavior, seeking from other males affection that they are missing from their fathers. When a father is completely absent from the family structure, the adolescent's relationship with the mother has been found to be negative (Smollar & Youniss,

1985). Increasing school absences and a concomitant decline in grades are other problems that may be precipitated by parental separation (Blum et al., 1988).

GOALS OF TREATMENT

There are several tasks the adolescent must accomplish in IPT-A. They include: acknowledging that the parent's departure was indeed a significant disruption; addressing feelings of rejection and mourning the loss of family life; alleviating guilt about the ruptured relationship; accepting the permanence of the situation; and resolving issues in the relationship with the remaining custodial parent.

STRATEGIES FOR TREATMENT

The first step in achieving these goals, is to help the adolescent relate the depression to the single-parent circumstances by connecting the onset of the symptoms with a change in the family structure and/or relationships. The second step is to clarify the adolescent's expectation for the relationship with the custodial and noncustodial parent and the adolescent's perceptions of each parent's expectations for the new family structure. The third step is to address the feelings toward each of the relationships and the potential for negotiation. The fourth step is to define the adolescent's role in the new family structure, and the fifth step is to engage in negotiation or strategies that may lead to resolution of the problem.

In the second step of clarifying expectations, the therapist and adolescent need to be clear as to what the custodial as well as noncustodial parent would like out of the relationship with the adolescent. If the noncustodial parent maintains an intermittent relationship with the adolescent, it would be ideal to have the parent come for a session with the child so that they can negotiate their expectations for their relationship. The therapist can either assist them in making the transition to a new type of relationship or can assist the adolescent in mourning the lost relationship. The therapist would ask the adolescent:

> *How do you feel about not seeing your father or mother very frequently? What is it like when the visits don't occur regularly? How has it changed your relationship? The way you talk to him or her? What do you miss about the relationship? What do you still enjoy about the relationship? What type of relationship would you like to have with your father or*

mother if he or she were available to you? Did you ever wonder if the leaving of your father or mother was related to anything you did, or have you ever felt that you could have prevented it?

It is important to have the adolescent explore, in session, fantasies about his or her relationship with the absent parent. The therapist would assist the adolescent in putting his or her sense of abandonment in a context or perspective from which he or she can move on to other interpersonal relationships with some degree of trust.

If the parent is not available for such a discussion with the adolescent, then the patient might try to engage the custodial parent in speculating about the absent spouse's expectations in order to put the adolescent's expectations in a more realistic context. The therapist might ask the custodial parent:

What type of relationship do you think your spouse would like to have with your son or daughter? How possible is it for your spouse to have such a relationship with your son or daughter? What are some of the difficulties you could envision? What are the positive aspects of the arrangement that you could foresee?

It is important for the therapist to understand the custodial parent's ideas about what type of relationship the child could or should have with the noncustodial parent. It is necessary to see whether the adolescent's relationship with the noncustodial parent may be contaminated by the parent's feelings of anger and abandonment at the spouse.

It also is necessary to examine the adolescent's relationship with the custodial parent and the perceived role in the separation. The therapist could ask:

What type of relationship do you have with your father or mother who you live with now? Would you like things to be any different? How would you like them different? Do you ever blame your father or mother for your father's or mother's leaving your home? If so, how do you think he or she was involved in your being separated from your father or mother? Do you think anyone else had a part in causing this separation? How so?

It is important to try and uncover any misconceptions and/or incorrect assignment of blame for what has occurred in the family. There are some instances, particularly in circumstances of drug abuse allegations or incarceration, where the adolescent does not know the reasons for the parent's absence from home. In this instance, the therapist must work with the parent to find a way to properly inform the adolescent of the reasons for the absence in order to end the adolescent's incorrect self-blame or inappropriate anger at the remaining parent. Parents need to be reassured that it is better to help the adolescent address feelings about the truth than to worry about the adolescent hearing the truth inadvertently from someone else or having mistaken notions of responsibility. Particularly for an adolescent with parental absence resulting from incarceration or drug behavior, it is essential that the therapist and parent address the adolescent's feelings of demoralization and stigma that are associated with these behaviors (Lowenstein, 1986). This therapeutic work will enable the adolescent to continue functioning and to work through feelings about the absent parent in preparation for the parent's eventual return.

Once the expectations are clarified for the relationships, the adolescent may move into the negotiation phase. With the help of the therapist, the patient may generate various compromises or solutions to the identified problems in the relationship. The therapist might say to the adolescent:

> *Since you know you can only see your father or mother on weekends, what type of arrangements would you like to make for activities during these visits with him or her? How do you think this would work for your father or mother? What might be some of the difficulties? What are the things you like about this plan? How do you think this arrangement would be for [custodial parent]? What may be some other possibilities to consider?*

The therapist tries to help the adolescent examine the proposed solution from the perspective of everyone involved before presenting it to the other parties. The proposal can be presented in a session with the parents or the adolescent can try it at home on his own. Adolescents are encouraged to try out some of their ideas in between sessions and then may discuss, in session, why these failed or succeeded. As the patient moves into the negotiation phase, symptoms should decrease, and the adolescent should experience relief. If parents are unable to negotiate a custody agreement, the child or adolescent becomes caught in the middle. In such a situation, we recommend outside intervention for parents or assistance from the adolescent's therapist as is necessary to facilitate negotiation.

Often in cases of divorce, the adolescent gets entangled in issues of parental compliance with the custody agreement. It is important to explore any instances where the adolescent feels responsible for enforcing issues such as payment of child support. The adolescent may feel a need to stand up for the custodial parent who is perceived as helpless, but at the same time, the adolescent will find this a very stressful and unpleasant role to play.

Case Example. Janet, a 16-year-old girl, was an only child who lived with her mother. Her parents had been divorced since she was 2 years old. She presented with a major depression. She reported feeling depressed every day, crying frequently, suicidal ideation, difficulty falling asleep, waking frequently during the night, feeling tired, and difficulty concentrating in class since her parents began to have problems with the alimony agreement and visitation. The identified problem area was single-parent families.

Janet reported that she was having difficulty with her father's visits and his compliance with the custody agreement. She reported that when he visited he would expect her to drop all of her activities and plans and spend time with him, even when he did not give her advance notice. When she would express reluctance to do so, he would say, "You don't love me as much as you love your mother" or "You love your friends more than you love me." In addition, when they spent time together, he would behave inappropriately with her, wanting to wrestle and tease her as he would when she was a little girl. Exacerbating these conflicts was the fact that she and her mother were under financial stress, and her father was not contributing the appropriate alimony and child support payments. Janet observed that these stresses were making her mother depressed. She wanted to help her mother, and so she began to try to convince her father to make the appropriate payments. However, she became depressed and angry about their relationship. She was angry that he tried to make her choose between loving her mother or him, that he could not see she had grown up and should be treated differently, and that he would not give money to help support her and her mother.

The therapist began by helping Janet to express her feelings about the living arrangements she had, about the visitation arrangements, about feeling caught between her two relationships, and about her need to make her father meet the terms of the custody agreement. Because the father refused to participate in treatment, the next step was to see what type of relationship she would like to negotiate outside the sessions. Simultaneously, through a joint session with the mother, the therapist helped the mother communicate to Janet that she appreciated her efforts on their behalf, but it was no longer her job to pursue compliance with the custody agreement. In addition, the mother was able to discuss her feelings about the daughter's relationship with the father freeing Janet from maternal pressure to choose a certain type of relationship. With this freedom, Janet chose to renegotiate her visits with her father, explaining to him the importance of her friends. She discussed with him his need to make dates with her in advance so she could give him the appropriate attention without feeling he was interfering in her other social activities.

In such instances, it is important for the therapist to help the adolescent renegotiate this role, removing him- or herself from enforcement of the custody agreement. The therapist must support the parent in assuming more of the responsibility to reduce the pseudoparentification of the child.

The adolescent also must learn to negotiate with the custodial parent over issues of discipline, independence versus dependence, and responsibilities. Negotiations will be more successful if they first define their expectations for their relationship and for how the house will be run, now that there is only one parent. The therapist should encourage the adolescent to talk about his or her feelings upon seeing the custodial parent in a different role.

Prior to negotiation, the therapist must clarify whether the parental absence is permanent or temporary. If the noncustodial parent is not available for even intermittent contact and the absence is believed to be permanent, the main task is to achieve a realistic appraisal of the relationship, that is, to get the adolescent to accept that the parent may no longer play an active role in the family, and to mourn the loss of the desired relationship. If the absence might not be permanent, it is necessary to discuss reactions that might arise if or when the parent reappears. The adolescent should feel prepared to handle a variety of encounters with the parent. The therapist might ask:

> How do you think you would feel if your father or mother returned home in a few months or a year and wanted to be involved in your life? What do you think you might want to tell him or her? What do you think you would be worried about? What would you like to do when you saw him or her?

Discussions also might focus on how to reconcile the desire to have the parent return with the fear that the loss would be repeated.

SUMMARY

Several issues that must be addressed in the treatment are (1) the adolescent's feelings toward both the custodial and noncustodial parent, (2) identification of ways in which the adolescent's life has changed since the absence of a parent, (3) the adolescent's attitude and concerns about the single-parent structure of the family, and (4) redefinition of the adolescent's role in the new family structure. Therapy, hopefully, will increase expression of feelings and foster clearer communication. Both should help the adolescent and parent to resolve current family conflicts and provide some resolution for the adolescent's feelings of hurt and anger.

CASE VIGNETTE: SUSAN

Susan was a 16-year-old girl who was referred for treatment by her divorced mother. Her younger brother, 11 years old, had a different father, also divorced from Susan's mother. Susan and her brother lived with her mother. Her mother and father divorced when she was 3. When referred for treatment, Susan was feeling sad, lonely, and tired. She described having less of an appetite, decreased interest in school, decreased enjoyment from her normal activities, poor concentration, decreased memory capabilities, increased irritability in her relationships, and increased social withdrawal. Susan denied suicidal ideation, plan, or intent, and reported few social relationships. The onset of the symptoms was reported to be approximately 1½ years prior to initiation of treatment.

Following the parents' divorce, her mother was given custody and her father visitation rights. On a weekend visit when she was 4 years old, her father kidnapped her for approximately 6 months, taking her to live with his new wife. Susan reported that he could no longer take care of her when his second wife became pregnant, and so he returned her to her mother. Upon Susan's return, her mother fled with her from New York to Grenada to keep her away from her father. They returned to New York the following year, and her father resumed his weekly visitation. Susan reported that often he would fail to show up as he had arranged, and he rarely paid his child support. When she was 13 years old, her mother returned to Grenada to remarry, and they lived there for 2 years. Susan did not like her stepfather's restrictions on their activities and reported that she had convinced her mother to separate from him and return to New York when she was 15. Susan's mother confirmed that the stepfather had been unnecessarily strict with the children as well as with her. She confirmed that his strictness contributed to her decision to separate from him.

Susan reported that she had been looking forward to returning to New York, where her father was living with his second wife, her half-sister, and half-brother. Within 6 months after returning to New York,

Susan had a falling-out with her father. He expressed anger and disgust toward her for working at a drugstore after school. She would come home late at night sometimes and was trying to pursue a modeling career, both of which aggravated her father even more. Shortly after their argument, he moved his second family to Florida unexpectedly. Susan only found out he was gone when she went to look for him at his place of work. Her depression began shortly thereafter. At the time she entered therapy, Susan had had no contact with her father for a year. She also reported increased conflict with her mother, starting when Susan became involved in modeling and school activities and was spending less time at home.

Initial Phase (Sessions 1–4). After initiation of treatment, Susan reported in a session that her father had phoned her out of the blue to say he was in New York, and he wanted to see her. She went to meet him one afternoon. Since her visit with him, Susan reported feeling bored and "empty" a great deal of the time. The therapist helped Susan relate her recurrence of symptoms to the phone call, thereby demystifying the origin of the symptoms for her. They discussed the nature of the visit with her father, what issues had been discussed, and her feelings about the type of relationship she has had with her father to date. The therapist discussed with Susan what expectations she had for her relationship with her father and her perceptions of her father's desires for the relationship. Susan was able to discuss much of the hurt feelings stemming from her father and his past treatment of her. She spoke of disappointment when he did not show up for visits and when he would try and buy her presents without taking any time to get to know her. She also spoke of her resentment at him for trying to run her life on the occasions when he appeared after long absences. The therapist defined the problem area as single-parent family because it appeared that Susan's depression was a result of conflict with her father, the noncustodial parent, over his role in her life. The focus of the treatment was on resolving her conflictual feelings about her relationship with her father, her feelings about how her mother and father each had handled the kidnapping situation, and how her father could presently fit into her life. Susan and the therapist discussed whether there was a possibility of compromise for the terms of the relationship, and if not, how she would like to conduct their relationship.

Middle Phase (Sessions 5–8). Susan continued to be preoccupied with her father, all the more so because she had not heard a word from him since their previous visit, weeks earlier. The only knowledge she had of his activities was from her half-sister, who continued to telephone her.

The therapist questioned Susan as to what she perceived his rights to be in their relationship and whether she preferred to be completely independent of him altogether. Susan had decided that there was no way she could compromise with her father and that she would rather accept no relationship than a relationship on his terms. She felt as though she had not had a relationship with him in a long time, and she wanted to be able to accept the limitations of the relationship. Susan reported that she would rather not have him help her monetarily, because then she would feel she owed him, either in money or in having to engage in activities only with his consent.

The strategies the therapist chose to use sought to clarify Susan's feelings about her father and her expectations for the relationship, improve her communication skills for use during their encounters, and find strategies to cope with any undesirable responses. The therapist encouraged Susan to talk about the pain of having to accept this type of relationship with her father. Susan was able to discuss strategies she would use to handle future disappointments with her father, because it was likely that there would be other times when he would come and go in her life. She worked on revising her expectations for the relationship and on being able to communicate her feelings to him, even if he cannot respond to her as desired. In the process of adapting to the absence of the relationship, she discussed what she ideally would have wanted for their relationship, what she felt she missed, and what she received from her relationships with her mother and her modeling coach, who was like another parent to her.

At the same time, Susan worked on clarifying the terms of her relationship with her mother, which also needed renegotiating since their move back to New York. Because of the restrictions previously imposed on Susan by the stepfather, Susan had spent more time at home. Currently, she was very involved in school activities, an after school job, and modeling. Her mother felt left out of Susan's life and worried about her activities when Susan was not at home. Using the same strategies employed for working on her relationship with her father, Susan was able to clarify her mother's expectations for her, agree on some rules about when to be home and how many modeling assignments to accept during the school year, and to increase her understanding of her mother's new position as a single parent.

Termination Phase (Sessions 9–12). Susan reported much less irritability in her relationship with her mother than when she had begun treatment. She was able to negotiate with her mother in ways she could not with her father. She used these sessions to explore the feasibility of maintaining the adjustments she had made in her relationship with her mother. She felt that she was able to maintain a relationship with her half-sister for whom she cared deeply, independent of her relationship with her father. Susan was able to accept more easily her relationship with her father despite the disappointments and pain his behavior caused her. The acceptance was facilitated by her increased ability to discuss her feelings about her father and the revisions of her expectations for his behavior in the future. She had grown accustomed to supporting herself while attending school, so she did not have to readjust to financial independence from her father. Since she was worrying less about what he would do next and felt better prepared to handle his actions, she was able to redirect her attention toward her schoolwork and modeling career. Susan reported looking forward to the summer when she would relax a bit more, read nonschool books, and have time for other pleasurable activities. She reported no longer feeling sad, reduced conflict with her mother, decreased irritability, and feeling motivated to do well in school and eventually attend college. Although she had been unable to change her father through her own treatment, Susan felt ready to terminate because she felt armed with new strategies for handling her difficulties with both her father and her mother.

·13·

Termination Phase

A termination date is set with the patient at the beginning of treatment. The length of IPT-A has been designated as 12 weeks, and adolescent and family should be made aware of this from the beginning. The treatment length of 12 weeks was set for the clinical trial assessing the efficacy of IPT-A, but the actual number of weeks is not the most significant issue. The important issue is simply that the treatment is time-limited. Time-limited treatment is the goal because we feel the sick role of being in therapy is not typical for adolescents. So whether it is 12 or 16 weeks, the adolescent should be reminded about the termination date at least 2–4 weeks prior to its occurrence so that feelings surrounding the end of treatment can be addressed.

TERMINATION WITH THE ADOLESCENT

Although the therapist begins to focus on the issues of termination at week 9, this does not preclude continued discussion of the identified problem area. However, no new problem areas should be introduced after this point. The remaining time should focus on conclusion of problems and a review of the course of treatment—the strategies learned, the changes that have occurred, and future applications of the patient's newly learned skills.

During the sessions of weeks 9 and 10, the therapist should remind the adolescent that their work together will be coming to a close. The adolescent's feelings about this should be elicited. The therapist should discuss the end of treatment as a time of potential grieving or the possibility of a recurrence of feelings of depression. Throughout the termination phase, the therapist should help the patient recognize his or her competence by discussing accomplishments in the treatment. Adolescents may be hesitant to admit attachment to the therapist or the value of the therapy, particularly if they had been against the treatment initially. It is sometimes difficult for them to admit that they had really needed the help, that they may have grown to depend on the sessions, and that they have enjoyed the weekly meetings. It is often helpful if the therapist mentions some of the possible feelings the patient may be experiencing and allows the adolescents to acknowledge which ones "ring true." Adolescents may feel sadness at the end of therapy, which they may interpret as a return of their depression. They may either be upset by the return of the sadness and/or hope that it will allow them to continue their relationship with the therapist a little longer. The therapist needs to educate the adolescent about the difference between depression and sadness about ending the relationship. The therapist might say to the adolescent:

> *Feeling sad, worried, or even angry that we're stopping our work together are common feelings at this time. It's normal to feel these things. We've gotten to know each other, and you've told me very personal and important things about yourself. These feelings are not the same feelings you had when we started working together, and they do not mean you're becoming depressed again. I'll miss working with you, but I know it's important for you to be on your own and use what you've learned here in your other relationships.*

The therapist should make every reasonable attempt to link feelings about termination with the specified problem area. For example, feelings of termination may resemble feelings the adolescent experienced before the role transition or may be related to feelings experienced during a grief reaction.

The work of session 11 is to conclude the work on the specified problem area and to review the list of symptoms and interpersonal conflicts obtained during the initial clinical interview. These will include all positive responses given on the diagnostic interview affective disorders section as well as areas of interpersonal conflict obtained during clinical interview, interpersonal inventory, and treatment. The therapist might say to the adolescent:

> *Do you remember how you felt when you first began treatment? How did you know you were depressed? What was making it difficult for you to function? Describe the problems you were having in school? with your family? with your friends? Are you still having any symptoms of depres-*

sion like those described when you began treatment? How are these symptoms continuing to affect you?

The therapist and patient will put these symptoms and conflicts into one of four categories: symptoms specific to the depressive episode, symptoms secondary to the depressive episode, areas of conflict that are more enduring and representative of personality style, and areas of conflict between parent and adolescent that are part of a normal developmental process. Each category should be reviewed with respect to progress made during the course of treatment. Because IPT-A does not attempt to treat personality style disturbances, symptoms of this type should be explained to the adolescents as part of "who they are," as aspects of themselves that they can learn to cope with or that they may want to address in a future therapy.

The final session (12) should focus on the goals of treatment initially laid down, the progress made, and the strategies learned with a view toward independent application by the adolescent in the future. The therapist should ask the adolescent:

What is the identified problem that we have been focusing on? What changes have been made in this area during treatment? What were our goals? What strategies did we discuss and use to achieve these goals? Are there any goals that we did not meet? What are they? How might you continue to work on them after therapy is completed?

These goals are very specific to each patient and will have been achieved to varying degrees during the course of the therapy. Each problem area will be discussed in the context of the initial goals and final achievement of goals. Even more important, the therapist should review with the adolescent warning signs for a recurrence of depression and when it would be beneficial to seek additional treatment.

Typically, a major goal of therapy has been to improve the adolescent's self-esteem and feeling of confidence to negotiate interpersonal relationships. It is important in reviewing the accomplishments of the treatment, to help the adolescent see that the improvements were not solely the work of the therapist but, rather, were the result of hard work and changes by the adolescent. The therapist might say:

How do you think you are going to feel when you and I stop meeting? What might be difficult for you when you stop treatment? What will you miss? What will you worry about? Who else might provide you with support and guidance? Many times when patients leave therapy, they feel that the new ways of coping they've learned are dependent on keeping up the relationship with the therapist. That's not true. The changes you've made and things you've learned are part of you now, and when you leave therapy, you'll take them with you. When you've left and are on your own, you'll see that this is true, and you'll gradually feel more and more confident in yourself.

The therapist's role is to stress that the adolescent has acquired a mastery and/or competence in interpersonal skills that will be maintained beyond the end of treatment.

Throughout the treatment and termination, the therapist must continue to emphasize that the therapeutic work has been to foster more successful relationships for the adolescent outside of treatment. This will be easier to accomplish at termination if the therapist has employed certain strategies throughout the course of therapy. The therapist should always be identifying the changes observed in the adolescent, the efforts made to improve communication and see another person's point of view, the attempts made to negotiate a dispute, and improved insight into his or her own feelings about a relationship.

> *Case Example.* Sally presented with a major depression that appeared to be associated with role dispute with her stepmother and father. Sally was caught between her parent's disagreements about how to raise children as well as being caught in conflict with her stepmother over Sally's role in the newly constituted family. During the interpersonal inventory, it became clear that Sally never talked about her feelings until she had to explode. Over the course of therapy, one of the major changes Sally made was in her willingness and ability to talk about her feelings before they became uncontrollable. Therefore, during termination, the therapist reviewed with Sally (1) the new communication skills that she was using in her relationships; (2) her improved ability to assess the other person's perspective in the argument, now that the discussions took place before she was too angry to listen; and (3) her successful negotiations with her father and stepmother about her chores and responsibilities in the home.

Specific strategies employed by the adolescent should be identified so that they may be applied to other similar situations. It is important in the final session to review the patient's resources for support outside of therapy. In addition, it is helpful for the therapist and patient together to specify future situations that may be problematic for the adolescent and specifically review the application of the new skills to these other situations. The therapist may ask:

What situations are coming up that you anticipate might by difficult for you to negotiate or that may be stressful? What strategies have you learned in treatment that might be helpful in this situation? What are some of the steps you might take to handle this situation?

This type of review can help increase the adolescent's self-esteem, to enable him or her to feel equipped to handle future interpersonal situations. Situations that may be stressful, coping methods, and ways to remove stress should also be identified. It helps to identify people in the adolescent's environment who may be able to help with a future stressor or help the adolescent get further treatment if needed.

One of the most difficult issues facing the patient is the loss of the relationship with the therapist. Particularly with adolescents, the therapist often has become a role model of interpersonal functioning, in addition to becoming a source of guidance and support that previously may have been missing from the adolescent's life. The therapist must address an adolescent's concern about how he or she will do without this support; otherwise, the likelihood of a recurrence of the depressive symptoms will increase.

Case Example. Allison was a 14-year-old who presented with a major depression that appeared to be precipitated by conflict with her mother. Her identified problem area was a role dispute with her mother. Treatment focused on increasing her communication skills, thereby enabling her to better negotiate her relationship with her mother. Although showing improvement, Allison had become very attached to the therapist and was always eager to check the appropriateness of her behavior during the past week with the therapist. The therapist's goal during termination was to emphasize to Allison that she had been successfully negotiating her relationship with her mother on her own with less and less need for guidance from the therapist. The therapist emphasized Allison's skills and emphasized that she would be taking these skills with her when she left treatment. In addition, Allison and the therapist discussed other people she might turn to for guidance after treatment had ended. They were able to identify her sister and her current boyfriend as sources of support. Most important of all, though, was the therapist's review of Allison's recently demonstrated ability to generate solutions to her problems on her own, thereby increasing her sense of competence.

By emphasizing the adolescent's competence, the therapist will facilitate the adolescent's independence following termination.

TERMINATION WITH THE FAMILY

Terminating treatment with an adolescent also means terminating work with the family. Typically the therapist will conduct a final termination session with the adolescent alone and then have another joint termination session for the adolescent and family. The goals of the final session for the family are similar to those for the adolescent. They include a review of the patient's presenting symptoms, goals for the therapy, achievement of the goals, and discussion of the changes in the family interactions and functioning as a result of the therapy. It is important to discuss with the family the possible recurrence of some symptoms shortly after termination. Management of further treatment if that is indicated and management of future recurrent episodes of depression also are discussed.

Many of the interpersonal conflicts that the adolescent presented with will have involved the family and their relationships. The therapist might ask the family members:

> *How do you feel the family may have changed as a result of [name]'s treatment? What things are you doing differently? How do you feel differently about each other? What has improved? What do you feel helped bring out these changes?*

Hopefully, the therapy will have made significant changes in the adolescent's way of relating to the family and will have affected the family's way of relating to the adolescent. Also, as the depressive symptoms improved during the course of treatment, some interpersonal problems of the family may have been alleviated. These positive changes in the family interactions will be reviewed and supported by the therapist.

Family members need to be alerted to the possibility of a regression at termination of treatment. The distinction between a regression that will resolve in a few weeks and a recurrence of symptoms should be made. The former should be tolerated by the family who should provide support to the adolescent during this transition from dependence on the therapist to independence. The parent(s) should be informed that depressive episodes can recur at some point in the future, particularly during times of stress or change for the adolescent. Early warning signs and symptoms (general for depression and specific to the adolescent) are reviewed, and appropriate management including referral for treatment is outlined. If the adolescent's symptoms do not resolve in several weeks, the therapist should be contacted to determine if further treatment is necessary. Otherwise, if it is clear at termination that the adolescent needs further treatment, this is the time to arrange for appropriate referral. If a referral is needed, it should include a psychiatric evaluation to determine the need for medication and/or another course of interpersonal psychotherapy or another type of psychotherapy.

PROBLEMS ASSOCIATED WITH TERMINATION

Many patients have difficulty with termination. Therefore, the decision to recommend further treatment should not be based on the recent emerging discomfort but on a broader view of the patient's clinical history and course of his or her treatment. In cases where indications for further treatment are not clear, it is advisable to suggest to the adolescents that they wait several weeks and see how they are feeling. If they still are feeling a significant amount of discomfort, referral for additional treatment can be made. For adolescents who appear to be experiencing mild discomfort that is a result of concerns about termination, the therapist might tell them:

> It is very common for patients to feel apprehensive about ending treatment, particularly if they feel it has been helpful to them. It is our experience that this discomfort usually goes away several weeks after termination as you begin to recognize your ability to function successfully in the absence of treatment. That is why we usually suggest a 4-week waiting period before making a referral for additional treatment. How do you feel about trying the waiting period? What are your concerns? If possible, let's try the waiting period and see how you feel in a few weeks. If during that time you feel you need help, you can always call me, and treatment will be arranged.

If, after this waiting period, symptoms persist, further treatment recommendations might include individual psychotherapy or adolescent group therapy.

This waiting period is feasible for people who are experiencing mild discomfort, but it is not recommended for adolescents who continue to present with significant symptomatology and/or impaired functioning. In such cases, the adolescent should forego the waiting period and be referred immediately for additional treatment such as medication, a different type of psychotherapy, and/or a different therapist. Another possibility is to renegotiate for another time-limited course of IPT-A focusing on another identified problem area.

THE NEED FOR LONG-TERM TREATMENT

Even though a patient's major depressive symptoms may have resolved during the course of treatment, additional problems may require that they seek longer term treatment. IPT-A can help stabilize a patient and provide enough self-confidence to allow more intensive exploration of psychiatric issues that impair the adolescent. Other patients will need continued supportive psychotherapy. Additional psychotherapy is typically recommended for those adolescents who are experiencing other difficulties such as a mild eating disorder, adjustment to learning disabilities, problems coping with past history of sexual or physical abuse, coping with a chaotic family, or impaired personality traits that are not addressed in IPT-A. The frequency of recurrent depression in adolescents is still not clear. Many adolescents experience numerous transient episodes of depressive symptomatology and impaired functioning. For those adolescents who present with numerous such episodes, long-term treatment might prove useful in stabilizing their functioning. In addition, long-term treatment always is recommended for those patients who have not responded to the brief treatment.

In some cases, the adolescent may feel the need to take a break from therapy and choose to address these other problems at a later date.

> *Case Example.* Karen presented with a major depression that appeared to be precipitated by conflict with her parents, particularly her mother. Her identified problem area was role disputes. Through the course of treatment, the majority of her depressive symptoms remitted. She gained a better perspective and more realistic expectations for her relationship with her mother. However, she still had concerns about her relationship with her boyfriend and unresolved feelings about her sister's death 5 years before. At termination of IPT-A, Karen was referred for further treatment. She was unable to get herself to the appointments with the new therapist, and she decided that she did not want further treatment at this time. However, 5 months later, she recontacted the therapist to state that she was ready to reenter treatment. She did not present with a major depression but reported that she was worried about her relationship with her boyfriend and felt ready to talk about the death of her sister and its impact on her life.

In this case example, the adolescent did not return to treatment because of a relapse but, rather, because she felt ready to discuss these other issues. Perhaps, she felt ready as a result of resolving the other difficulties that had led to her depression. In this instance, the therapy was able to alleviate her depressive symptoms and to help her prepare to deal with other issues in future treatment.

In general, the initial treatment contract should be maintained unless the adolescent falls into one of the categories outlined above requiring long-term treatment. Options for long-term treatment include referral to another clinic, another therapist, a different therapeutic orientation, or a new and different contract with the same therapist focusing on different issues. This decision should be made jointly with the therapist, adolescent, and responsible parent.

Although we have been discussing IPT-A as a 12-week treatment, IPT-A may be used in several other ways. The 12-week time frame is our operating principle because it was chosen for our clinical trial assessing the efficacy of IPT-A. It was felt to be an optimal duration for adolescents who are reluctant to stay in treatment for any significant length of time. Twelve weeks gives a patient time to make some changes, but it also provides the patient with a finite time within which to try to achieve them. In general clinical practice, however, there may be adolescents who might feel the same way with 16 or 20 weeks of IPT-A. The important issue in modifying the length of treatment is to retain its time-limited nature by setting the initial treatment contract for whatever number of weeks seems most appropriate for that adolescent, and working within this time framework, maintaining the time allotments for the different phases of the treatment. Another possibility is using IPT-A as a once-a-month maintenance treatment following completion of the initial weekly treatment as has been done with adults (Frank et al., 1991). Although this has not yet been tried with adolescents, it may serve a similar purpose as it did with adults and provide enough support and continuity to decrease the rate of recurrent episodes. Whatever changes in duration of frequency of visits that are made following the initial treatment contract, it is important that therapist and patient always renegotiate a new treatment contract and that the treatment is never open-ended.

·III·

Special Issues in Treating Adolescents

·14·

Special Clinical Situations

Special clinical situations not specifically discussed in the previous chapter but that may occur are described here. They include: non-nuclear families, the suicidal teenager, the assaultive teenager, school refusal, substance abuse, notification of Special Services for Children in cases of physical and sexual abuse, learning disabilities, sexually active adolescents, and homosexual adolescents. These are issues that apply to some but not all adolescents and can cross all problem areas. Indications for medication will be discussed in a separate chapter. The other issues will be discussed in the following sections.

NON-NUCLEAR FAMILIES

With increasing frequency, adolescents may live in non-nuclear families, which include: homes of other relatives, foster homes or group homes, and single-parent families, which are discussed in Chapter 9. Reasons for these alternative arrangements include death, abandonment, intervention by protective services for children, irreconcilable differences among family members, and illness. Living with other relatives, such as grandparents or aunts and uncles, is a common alternative. Living with a known relative has the advantage of providing a familiar home for the adolescent. Still, the adolescent has become a new member of an existing family structure and needs to make a place for him- or herself. Foster care forces the adolescent to move into a preexisting family unit composed of many unfamiliar nonbiologically related members. Temporary placement causes stress for the adolescent who does not know how long the living arrangement will last and, consequently, how attached to become to the family, and whether to make an effort to find a role in the family. In a group home, the adolescent no longer has a primary caretaker, but is one of a group. The adolescent must learn to be part of a group and learn the rules of the community without the benefit of a parent. For the therapist, the task with these adolescents is to engage the relative, foster family, or leader from the group-home as the parents would be engaged. It is especially important in the group home situation to identify one responsible person who will act as a liaison between therapy and the home and also act as the adolescent's advocate/supporter in the group environment. As with the parents, these people are important in the adolescent's daily life and must be educated about the nature of depression, ways to support the adolescent's recovery, and if necessary, participate in the treatment to facilitate changes in the home environment that will play a role in the adolescent's recovery. If the therapist determines that the current home is not viable for the adolescent's recovery, alternative arrangements need to be found. The therapist can handle this directly or work with another mental health worker who can facilitate a move.

SUICIDAL ADOLESCENT

Although completed suicide in adolescence is an infrequent event, there has been a threefold increase in the rate of completed suicides among white males between the ages of 15 and 24 years. Overall, the incidence of suicide increases in each of the teenage years, peaking at age 23 years. Over the past decade, there has been a decrease in suicide rate for the middle-aged and elderly, whereas suicide has become more common in the young. In addition, suicide attempts and suicidal ideation are highly prevalent in adolescents (Shaffer, 1988). Evaluation for suicidality is a critical part of the initial evaluation, and suicidality should be monitored throughout the treatment. The adolescents should be asked about thoughts of death, wanting to die, and suicidal plans. Specific questions the therapist might ask include:

> Do you ever feel so bad that life isn't worth continuing? Do you think about death a lot? Do you think about your own death? Does death sometimes seem like a welcome relief from life? Do you think of killing yourself?

If the adolescent answers positively to these questions, the therapist should ask if the adolescent has ever made a suicide attempt, and if a current plan is being considered. The therapist should be very specific in questioning the adolescent to obtain specific answers about ideas, plans, and attempts. The therapist wants to assess the intention and lethality of past suicide attempts and future plans, for example:

Have you ever tried to kill or hurt yourself? When? What did you do? What happened? Did you receive medical treatment? Did you tell anybody? What did you think would happen?

Questions pertaining to future attempts would include:

What are you thinking of doing to hurt yourself now? How close have you come to doing it? What has stopped you? Would you be able to tell anyone before you hurt yourself?

Based upon the therapist's assessment of past suicide attempts, current suicidal ideation or plans, and the stability of the home and family, the therapist must determine whether the adolescent is an acute suicide risk. If the therapist is uncertain, a second opinion should be sought. Any adolescent who is an acute suicide risk is not a candidate for IPT-A and will in fact require psychiatric hospitalization. An adolescent with suicidal ideation may or may not be a candidate for IPT-A depending on the adolescent's capacity to establish and maintain a therapeutic alliance with the therapist. The cornerstone of this alliance is that the adolescent assures the therapist that no suicide plan will be attempted, but that if the suicidal urge becomes so compelling, the therapist will be notified immediately and, if the therapist is not available, the adolescent will go to an emergency room immediately. The task of the therapist is not only to monitor the adolescent's suicidality but also to address the inappropriate use of suicide as a coping mechanism. The therapist might connect the patient's suicidal feelings with feelings of anger, despair, frustration, and hopelessness. The therapist might say to the adolescent:

It sounds as though you think about hurting yourself when you feel hopeless to change your situation. It also sounds as though you feel very angry about the way you are treated. In your anger and hopelessness, you are unable to see alternatives to resolve the situation other than by killing yourself. I believe that there are other ways to handle these feelings and that there are better solutions to your problems. Let's try and work on some other solutions together.

ASSAULTIVE ADOLESCENT

There are occasions when adolescents are so upset that they know no other way of venting their frustration than through aggressive and violent behavior. Assessment for thoughts of hurting other people should be done in conjunction with the assessment of suicidal behavior. The therapist might ask:

> *Have you ever had thoughts of hurting another person? If so, whom? Have you ever lost control and hit someone? Do you ever feel life could get so bad that you would consider doing so? Do you have a plan for how you would do it? What is your plan?*

As in the assessment of suicide, it is very important for the therapist to ask highly specific questions about the intent and the feasibility of carrying through with the action. Based upon the assessment, the therapist must determine whether the adolescent is at risk of harming another person. If this is deemed so, the therapist, according to the law, must hospitalize the patient and has a duty to warn the intended victim of the patient's wishes (*Tarasoff* decision—Southard & Gross, 1982). An adolescent who is at serious risk for homicidal behavior is not a candidate for IPT-A. An adolescent who expresses anger and hostility in vague threats to others may be a candidate for IPT-A if a therapeutic alliance with the therapist can be established, if the adolescent has the capacity to control assaultive behavior, and if the adolescent is capable of making an agreement with the therapist that violence will not be enacted while treatment is on-going. The therapist also should educate the adolescent to more appropriate methods of problem solving and ways to diffuse anger. The therapist might say:

> *When you make those threats to [e.g., to hurt your father] it sounds as though you are very angry and would like to get him to change his behavior with you. However, violence is not an acceptable solution to most conflicts and is not an appropriate expression for feelings of rage and anger. What other ways do you think you could address your anger with [name]? What conflict precipitated the anger? What other ways could you solve the conflict? What could you do when you get angry to help yourself calm down so you could discuss your feelings more rationally [e.g., listen to music, go for a walk, call a friend]?*

SCHOOL REFUSAL

As a result of their feelings of fatigue, poor concentration, and anhedonia, some adolescents who are depressed find themselves unable to get themselves to school each day. Moreover, when they find that they have been out of school for a week or two, they then conclude that they are too behind to catch up, are embarrassed to go back to school after their absence, and consequently remain home from school for an extended period of time. It is important that the therapist question the adolescent and parent about school attendance during the initial evaluation. The therapist should ask:

> *Are you attending school? Do you go every day? How many days have you missed this month? Are you regularly late to school? What are your grades? Are they the same or better than those you received before you became depressed?*

It also is important for the therapist to make contact with the school to confirm the adolescent's report. The therapist's role should be to stress the importance of returning to school and enlisting the assistance of the parents or school in ensuring the adolescent's return. The therapist should explain to the adolescent that although reluctance to return to school and embarrassment are common, the embarrassment will dissipate after the first day, and being productive in school will improve the adolescent's mood. In addition, the adolescent should be told that as the depression resolves, concentration will improve. Throughout the treatment, the therapist should continue to check on the adolescent's school attendance and performance and be in contact with the school as necessary.

SUBSTANCE-ABUSING ADOLESCENT

Part of a screening and history should include a complete history of drug and alcohol use and abuse. Other family members should be interviewed about drug use as well, even though family members may be ignorant of such abuse. For example, the therapist might ask:

> *Have you ever used or experimented with any drugs or alcohol? Have you ever tried marijuana? Not even once? What about cocaine or crack? Hallucinogens? When did you first try marijuana? How often did you use it? Does it interfere with your school or family life? Have you ever tried to stop using marijuana? What happened? Has using marijuana ever caused you to do things you might not ordinarily do? Give me an example. Have you ever sought treatment because of your marijuana problem? What happened? Do any of your friends use marijuana? What about your family, does anyone use any drugs or alcohol?*

If necessary, the adolescent should be referred for drug treatment before IPT-A is started. In order to participate in IPT-A, the adolescent must not be abusing or using any substances and must make a commitment to maintaining a drug-free life. The therapist might say:

> For me to work with you and use IPT-A to treat your depression, it is very important that you not use drugs during the time you are in therapy. If you do, the therapy will not be effective. Can you stay drug-free during this time? If you do use drugs, it is important that you tell me so I can help you most effectively. IPT-A may not be the right therapy for you now. Will you be able to tell me if you use drugs?

With some adolescent patients, the therapist might suggest a weekly drug screen to monitor possible drug abuse. The therapist could suggest this as a way to alleviate any difficulty the patient might have in telling the therapist about drug use, difficulty that could engender guilt about not having revealed this information to the therapist. The therapist should present this therapeutic maneuver as nonpunitive. If the adolescent does use drugs during the time of IPT-A, that is a clear indication that the therapy is not providing the help the patient needs for this problem, and alternative treatments should be suggested. If the therapist feels that the drug abuse is a primary problem and the depression is secondary to the drug abuse, the adolescent should be referred to a drug treatment center.

Within the IPT-A framework, the therapist can help the adolescent to deal with peer pressure and family dynamics that lead to drug use and to engage a family member as another source of support for the adolescent's abstinence from drugs. The therapist might ask:

> What happens when you see other kids your age using drugs? How do you feel when you join them? How would you feel if you didn't join them? How does the [substance] make you feel different about yourself? Is it difficult to say no when someone offers it to you? What makes it difficult? What goes on at home when you get the feeling of needing to find some drugs? Does it make the problems go away? What is another way to deal with these problems? Is there anyone you feel close to who doesn't use drugs to whom you could talk when you feel an urge to get high or when you feel upset?

PROTECTIVE SERVICE AGENCIES

Protective service agencies have the purpose of protecting the welfare of children when their environment is harmful. Each state has its own agency for accepting and dealing with reports and its own laws governing when and how to report a case. A child may already be in the jurisdiction of a protective service agency when therapy begins, or it may be the duty of the therapist to report the child to a protective service agency if information about possible harm to the child is raised in the course of treatment. Contacting a protective service agency can disrupt the therapeutic alliance with the child or parent. The therapist must be alert to this possibility and work with the adolescent and parent to help them understand the reasoning behind the actions. Parent and adolescent should be told that the report is being made to alleviate a stressful situation for both of them and to provide help. The therapist should emphasize that the protective service agency is a means to provide them with increased social support so that the family can function better.

SEXUAL ABUSE

The therapist should carefully evaluate the adolescent for any past history of sexual abuse or current abuse. The therapist should ask:

> *Has anyone ever made you uncomfortable to be alone with him or her? How so? What happens when you are alone with him or her? Has [name] ever touched you in a way that made you uncomfortable? What did he or she do? When does or did it happen? How many times? Is it still going on now? When did it stop? Does anyone else know about it?*

Frequent symptoms that might indicate a past history of abuse include depression, suicide attempt, sexual promiscuity, and conduct problems. Evaluating for sexual abuse requires sensitivity and time. The adolescent may not reveal the abuse during the initial visit but instead may reveal it during the course of treatment, as the patient begins to trust the therapist. If the abuse is currently ongoing, the therapist is required by law to contact the protective service agency for children to intervene with the family, and to provide the appropriate social services to the family and the adolescent. If the abuse is current, the adolescent may not be appropriate for treatment with IPT-A because IPT-A is not designed to deal with the acute or long-term consequences of sexual abuse. If the abuse has been in the past, the therapist still needs a detailed history of the interpersonal context in which the abuse occurred so that an accurate picture of the familial relationships can be created.

LEARNING DISABILITIES

Depression is commonly associated with cognitive impairments that appear most pronounced during the acute stages of depression. A psychosocial history will help the therapist distinguish between long-standing learning disabilities and impairments secondary to the depressive episode. The therapist should ask:

> When did you begin to have trouble in school? How were your grades when you were younger? When did you begin to have trouble concentrating in class and/or doing your homework? Does it seem like it has gotten worse since you have been feeling sad or that it is about the same? What is difficult about doing your schoolwork, concentrating or not understanding the material? Can you give me an example?

The task of differentiating between learning disability and depression is made more difficult when the patient has long-standing depressive symptoms or a personality style that presents what appear to be cognitive limitations. Psychological or educational testing can be useful in identifying learning disabilities. When learning disabilities are diagnosed, special educational resources are necessary, and the therapist will need to arrange for this in conjunction with the school system. Cognitive impairments secondary to the depression will resolve when the depressive symptoms resolve. The child and parents should be told of the etiology of the child's impairments and revise their expectations accordingly.

SEXUALLY ACTIVE ADOLESCENT

Adolescence is a time in which there is an increase in sexual feelings and behavior and often a first intimate sexual encounter. The therapist should question as to whether the adolescent is sexually active and, if so, whether he or she is using birth control and practicing safe sex. The therapist should explore knowledge of sexual issues such as pregnancy and sexually transmitted diseases. For example, the therapist might ask:

> Are you currently in a relationship? Do you have a physical relationship with your partner? Do you practice birth control? What type? Are you aware of how sexual diseases are transmitted? Do you take precautions to prevent this from happening to you? If so, what kind of precautions? If not, what prevents you from practicing safe sex?

If the sexually active female adolescent appears to lack such knowledge and has not been using birth control, it is important to make the appropriate referral to a gynecologist or pediatrician. The therapist may also discuss the importance of birth control with the adolescent, both male and female. It is important for the therapist to explore the adolescent's feelings about sex, sexual fantasies, and fantasies about pregnancy. Although it is important for the therapist to impart factual information about sexual behavior, the therapist should also connect sexual feelings and/or behavior to the adolescent's feelings about his or her relationship with his or her parents, boy- or girlfriend, and to the adolescent's feelings of loneliness and self-worth. In this manner, the therapist may be able to assist in identifying interpersonal conflicts that may be contributing to inappropriate or risky sexual behavior.

HOMOSEXUAL ADOLESCENT

Adolescence is a time when individuals begin to form intimate relationships usually with partners of the opposite sex and, for some adolescents, with partners of the same sex. Exploration of sexual relationships with different partners is common. Those adolescents who find their sexual interest is exclusively with partners of the same sex can feel isolated and alone. It also is possible that the adolescent is comfortable with and has accepted his sexual orientation. In such a situation, the therapist must be supportive of the decision. Those adolescents who feel attracted to both same- and opposite-sex partners may feel confused about their sexual orientation. The role of the therapist is to help the adolescent explore his or her sexual feelings and concerns about orientation in a nonjudgmental context. In addition, it may be appropriate to identify the association between the adolescent's state of confusion and the depression.

·15·

Issues in the Therapist–Patient Relationship

The original manual for treating depressed adults with interpersonal psychotherapy has a Special Issues section (Klerman et al., 1984). The majority of those issues are applicable to the treatment of adolescents as well. Several issues, however, are handled differently with adolescents. These are discussed in the ensuing section.

THERAPIST AS SUBSTITUTE FOR FRIEND OR FAMILY

For many adolescents who feel alienated from family and friends and who are in need of support, the therapist can become a substitute for these missing relationships. Often the therapist does take on some roles with the adolescent that might have been performed by a family member in order to serve as a bridge while the adolescent tries to reestablish family connections or find outside support. For example, when an adolescent does not have a parent who is able to act as an advocate, the therapist often acts on behalf of the adolescent with the school, by providing the adolescent with alternative role models for adult behavior, and so forth. Sometimes it becomes necessary to clarify with the adolescent the limits of the therapeutic relationship and how it differs from a friendship. In addition, the therapist should encourage the adolescent to find appropriate sources of support and/or role models outside the therapeutic relationship.

PATIENT MISSES APPOINTMENTS OR IS LATE

When working with adolescents in IPT-A, the therapist takes a different stance on missed appointments or lateness than when working with adults. As stated previously in the manual, the therapist allows greater flexibility of scheduling sessions and does not interpret missed sessions as resistance. Nonetheless, it is important for the therapist to examine whether the adolescent is not attending the session because he or she feels worse or is unable to get out of the house, or whether the adolescent is feeling better and has returned to involvement in numerous activities with peers and/or family that hinder attendance. The therapist is similarly nonjudgmental about lateness. The therapist might say:

> *These past few weeks I've noticed you have been [missing sessions or late], and I was wondering how you are feeling about coming for therapy? Have you been feeling better? Worse? How so? What do you think keeps you from getting here [on time]?*

Again, the therapist explores the reasons for the lateness to ensure that it is not a sign of worsening of the depression. The therapist should review the patient's depressive symptoms specifically to see if there is a worsening or improvement. If not, the therapist stresses that the more time they have together, the more they can accomplish.

In treating the adolescent, the therapist often relies on the telephone as a means of staying in contact with the adolescent either between initial sessions or when sessions are missed. In the beginning, telephone contact is believed to enhance the development of the therapeutic alliance. If the adolescent has failed to attend a session, the therapist can hold a brief session over the telephone to maintain continuity until the adolescent comes in for a session. However, therapy should not regularly occur on the telephone. If such a pattern begins to develop, it is necessary to have the adolescent attend a session to discuss these therapeutic difficulties.

PATIENT IS EXCESSIVELY DEPENDENT

Depressed adolescents frequently experience such fatigue or malaise that they feel unable to act upon any initiative and feel unable to make any decisions on their own. They may ask for specific advice about how to resolve a problem or may try to have the therapist do some of the negotiating with their parents instead of doing it themselves. The therapist must be wary of intervening too directly because the therapist does not want to deprive the adolescent of developing his or her own coping/negotiation skills to use in the future. Still, adolescents often need the added support and authority of the therapist when trying to negotiate and/or communicate with their parents, and the therapist should assist them. If the adolescent's demands on the therapist are inappropriate, such as wanting to go places together outside of treatment, the therapist must explore the reasons for these needs and explain to the adolescent the appropriate boundaries for the relationship. The therapist might say:

> It is not unusual for patients to feel a closeness to their therapists, but it is important to remember that there is a difference between your friendships and your relationship with me. I am here to support you, to help you learn new ways of coping with conflicts and situations outside the therapy, but my goal is to enable you to find fulfilling relationships outside of therapy. Maybe we should talk about how you can establish friendships with other people who could engage in these activities with you.

PATIENT WISHES TO TERMINATE EARLY

Before reacting to an adolescent's desire to terminate early, the therapist must investigate the reasons the patient wants to do so. It is important to discern whether the adolescent is terminating because he or she feels better, whether it is because the treatment has not satisfactorily met his or her therapeutic needs, or whether it is because the parents want termination. Adolescents often have what appear to be transient episodes of depression that may remit quickly and/or spontaneously. In such a case, the therapist would be wrong to force the adolescent into continuing the treatment and perpetuating the sick role. The therapist should support the adolescent's feelings of well-being, review the changes that may have occurred in the time that the adolescent did receive treatment, and inform the adolescent that he or she may return for treatment at a later date if the feeling of well-being does not last and if the adolescent desires a return to treatment. If the adolescent wishes to terminate because of dissatisfaction with the treatment, the therapist must examine the therapeutic contract in light of the adolescent's expressed needs and either renegotiate the contract if possible, or refer the adolescent for treatment that may be more congruent with his or her needs.

If it is the parents who wish the adolescent to terminate the therapy, a meeting should be set up between parents and therapist. If the parents refuse to come in, the problem should be discussed over the telephone with the goal of arranging a face-to-face meeting. The reasons parents may wish to terminate their child's treatment may include: feeling threatened by the therapist and worrying that their role is being usurped; thinking that because their child is in therapy they are bad parents; worrying that a "family secret" such as incest or alcohol abuse may be revealed; and feeling threatened by the changes the adolescent is making in the treatment, even if these are beneficial changes. The therapist must try to determine which of these reasons are responsible for the parents' desire to have their child leave treatment. Depending upon the particular reason, the therapist will need to respond with reassurance, clarification, assurance that their involvement is welcomed, and perhaps a referral for family or individual treatment for other family members. If the parent persists in wanting the child to terminate, the therapist is obliged to do so unless there are clear indications that termination of therapy constitutes neglect. Such indications include severe depressive symptoms, suicidal ideation, or indications of sexual or physical abuse in the household. Referral to another therapist and/or notification to a protective service agency is mandatory in such cases.

CONFIDENTIALITY

Confidentiality is an important issue when working with adolescents. Adolescents under the age of 18 are still legally considered minors. However, when working with adolescents and their families, the therapist should emphasize to the family that the therapy will be more effective if the adolescent can feel that the conversations are confidential. Both the adolescent and family are instructed that the information from the sessions will be kept confidential unless the therapist feels that the adolescent is at risk or may harm someone else. If the therapist feels the need to share some information from the session with the parents, he or she should discuss this with the adolescent, allow the adolescent to express his or her concerns, explain the reasons for discussing it with the parents, and plan the best way to inform the parents. The parents should be informed that any information they wish to provide to the therapist is welcome and may be beneficial. However, all phone calls and information from the parents will be told to the adolescent. The therapist cannot maintain confidentiality with the parents because it would jeopardize the therapist's alliance with the adolescent. These strategies will help the adolescent feel that the therapy session is a safe and secure place to talk.

PATIENT WANTS TO SHARE THERAPIST

Sometimes an adolescent may bring along a family member or friend to therapy and would like the therapist to treat the other person. Reasons for this are complex and are often unconscious. It is not the role of the IPT-A therapist to explore this. The therapist should explain to the adolescent that he or she is that adolescent's therapist and is there to help the adolescent. Consequently, the therapist is interested in the other people in the adolescent's life, but the therapist must refer the other person for an evaluation for treatment by another therapist.

CHILD FINDS PARENTS ENGAGING IN INAPPROPRIATE BEHAVIOR

Often an adolescent may catch a parent engaging in behavior that is considered bad or dangerous to the parent, such as using drugs or stealing. This presents the adolescent with a conflict. The adolescent is often torn between wanting to confront the parent with the inappropriate behavior and wanting to forget he or she ever saw it. It is important for the therapist to explore the adolescent's feelings surrounding the incident, reason through the different options, and discuss the possible consequences of his or her actions so the adolescent can make an informed decision about what to do. The therapist should support whatever reasonable manner in which the adolescent decides to handle the situation. If the therapist determines that the parent's behavior is such that the welfare of the child is in danger, the protective service agency must be notified. Therapist and adolescent need to inform the parents that this will happen and explain the reasons for their decision to report the situation. Again, as discussed in Chapter 14, it should be emphasized that this action is being taken as a way to get the support and help that the adolescent and family need to address their problems.

·16·

Crisis Management

Crises are not infrequent during the treatment of a depressed adolescent. The crisis can be a direct result of the adolescent's family or a social problem, and it can pose a direct threat to the adolescent's treatment. Crises should be handled swiftly and decisively to protect the adolescent and the treatment. A crisis is a major change in the patient's living situation, interpersonal relationships, family relationships, or emotional well-being that jeopardizes the patient's psychological well-being and overwhelms the patient's capacity to cope with the situation. The IPT-A therapist's approach to and management of a crisis are presented here. Specific crisis situations are then discussed.

ASSESSMENT OF THE CRISIS

The first task facing the IPT-A therapist is to determine the nature and etiology of the crisis. This should be accomplished by speaking to the adolescent and other parties involved. The initial contact should be in person but can be over the telephone. Frequently, the first word of a crisis is communicated by telephone. The IPT-A therapist needs to elucidate the events surrounding the crisis and assess the adolescent's reaction and the family's response to the crisis. It must first be determined whether the crisis is a response to the therapist or to issues being addressed in the therapy. Did the therapist miss early warning signs that such a crisis was likely, or was the patient or family concealing information that would have allowed the therapist to anticipate and prevent the crisis? Alternately, the event may have been unpredictable and a response to events out of the control of therapist, patient, and family.

The next step for the therapist is to bring the patient in for an emergency session as soon as possible. In the case of suicidal or homicidal ideation, if an appointment cannot be set up soon enough, the patient should be sent to the nearest emergency room. When meeting in the emergency session, the therapist must determine the need for and level of family involvement. When dealing with an adolescent under 18 years of age, it is mandatory for the therapist to notify the parent if there is a significant risk to the patient and the crisis is verified. The level of involvement will vary with the different type of crises and the nature of the patient's relationship with the family members. The therapist must be careful to elicit the entire story from the adolescent regarding the precipitant and the accompanying emotions. After hearing the whole story, the therapist must again assess whether there is a need for hospitalization because of risk of the patient getting hurt or hurting others. In addition, the therapist must evaluate whether there is a need to involve other agencies or parties, such as medical or legal consultations or protective services for children, in evaluating or intervening in the situation.

If the patient is evaluated as being able to remain in outpatient treatment, the IPT-A treatment contract should be reexamined and revised as necessary. Such items in the contract that may change include the frequency of the sessions, involvement of the family, frequency of phone calls between therapist and patient, and the identified problem area that is the focus of the treatment. At times the crisis may suggest that a significant problem area was overlooked, or there may be an interaction between two problem areas, thus requiring a shift in the focus of the sessions. The therapist also may choose to meet more frequently in the weeks following the crisis until the patient's situation stabilizes.

Management of the individual crises varies by the situation. The most significant decision the therapist must make is whether to hospitalize the patient and/or whether IPT-A must be terminated and another form of treatment begun. If the decision has been made to involve the family, it is important to meet with the family separately as well as conjointly with the patient to see how the problem is understood and how it can best be resolved. The therapist might conduct several sessions with the family to assist in negotiating the resolution of the precipitating conflict and then resume individual treatment with the patient. If the protective service agency is notified, the therapist should work with the agency to rectify the patient's situation so that no further harm can come to the patient.

In this chapter, management of the following specific issues will be presented: runaways, pregnancy, illness in patient or family, involvement with the law, violence, and premature termination by the patient. The other issues that can require crisis management, such as suicidal behavior and homicidal behavior, are discussed in the chapter on special issues in working with adolescents.

TYPES OF CRISES

Running Away

It is not uncommon for adolescents who are experiencing a significant amount of conflict in the home to threaten to run away. In such a situation, the therapist must do a careful assessment as to the intent of the adolescent and the anticipated consequences. For example, the therapist might ask:

> *Are you thinking of running away? Where would you think of going? Have you ever run away before? If yes, where to and for how long? What was it like for you and for your family? Now, what are you trying to get away from? What do you think will happen back home if you run away? What do you think running away would be like for you? What do you hope would be different for you?*

The therapist needs to obtain a history of previous attempts to run away in order to better assess the likelihood of the patient actually running away. To assist in finding an alternative action, the therapist and patient together should generate a list of options. These options might include writing a list of people (friends or relatives) the patient could call when distressed, identifying a friend or relative's house the patient could go to for a "cooling off" time, visiting the emergency room to speak with a mental health profession, calling a hotline for runaways (assuming one is available), going for a walk, writing feelings down, or any one of a number of suggestions to help the adolescent either find alternative care or to vent feelings rather than act on them in a potentially destructive manner. In addition, the therapist should examine the likelihood of the event occurring in light of the therapeutic relationship. The therapist should ask the patient to tell the therapist if he or she is running away, where he or she is going, and to maintain contact if he or she does run away. If there is a good therapist–patient alliance, the therapist should try and get a commitment from the adolescent that he or she will sign a contract stating he will not run away in between sessions. With such a contract, the therapist can then begin to work on understanding the desire and/or need to run as a maladaptive communication style perhaps within the problem area of interpersonal role disputes. If possible, the therapist should try to help the patient to generate alternative solutions to the problem that would not entail running away. Treatment should assist the patient in acquiring more adaptive communication skills and problem-solving techniques.

Pregnancy

Adolescent pregnancy can be a desired event sought by the adolescent. It may also be one thrust upon her by the absence of adequate birth control measures or by a violent sexual act such as rape. The situation can be further complicated by the family's response to the pregnancy and by the quality of the relationship with the boy. Regardless of the type of situation it is, the first question to address is whether the patient is really pregnant. At the first suspicion of pregnancy, the patient should be referred for a gynecological exam and pregnancy test. Once the pregnancy has been confirmed, it is the therapist's role to help the patient evaluate her options: to have and keep the baby, to have the baby and give it up for adoption, to have an abortion, to make the decision on her own, or to involve the other biological parent. Given the patient's feelings, the therapist needs to discuss how the pregnancy or abortion would affect the adolescent's life and to explore the feelings associated with the various actions. The therapist must also discuss with the adolescent the realities of taking care of an infant. The therapist might say to the adolescent:

> What do you imagine it will be like to have a baby at your age? What would you like about it? What would you not like about it? How would you feel around your friends? How do you feel it will change your relationships with your friends? your family? How do you feel about the father of the baby? What do you expect from your relationship with him?

The therapist must also discuss whether or not the patient's parent(s) are aware of the pregnancy and if so, what their attitudes are toward the patient. It is often helpful if a parent is notified early on in the pregnancy, particularly if the patient chooses to carry to term and may be expecting support from the family. The therapist should help facilitate discussion between parent and patient regarding who will take care of the child, expression of each of their concerns about the situation, and alternative solutions. The patient must be educated as to the impact the infant will have on her life. Ultimately it is the patient's choice as to whether or not to keep the baby. The therapist's role is to make sure it is an educated decision.

Illness in Patient or Family

When the patient presents with a medical illness, it is important for the therapist to make sure the appropriate medical care is being received. The therapist needs to consult with the treating physician so treatments can be coordinated if necessary. A similar strategy should be undertaken when coping with an illness in a family member. The therapist should consult with the physician to ensure a complete understanding of the situation so he or she can better help the patient cope with the illness and its implications. The treatment will likely focus on coping with the illness and the feelings it elicits in the patient and any subsequent conflicts that may arise with family members.

Involvement with the Law

An antisocial act necessitating legal intervention committed by the adolescent in IPT-A could jeopardize the treatment. Incarceration obviously puts an immediate end to treatment. If the patient is not incarcerated, the therapist should contact the involved law enforcement agents, frequently a probation officer, in an effort to assess all the facts surrounding the incident. The severity and consequences of the act should be taken into consideration by the therapist, who will need to decide if IPT-A can continue or whether another type of treatment, including residential treatment or hospitalization, would better meet the patient's needs. If it is determined that IPT-A can continue, the therapist will need to address the antisocial act with the adolescent and help the patient understand that further antisocial acts may not only disrupt treatment but will have serious legal consequences as well. The therapist might ask the adolescent:

> *What were you feeling when this occurred? What led up to it happening? What did you feel when it was over? What were you hoping would result from this behavior? Do you feel it might happen again? What else could you do in such a situation if it happened again? How does this relate to the problems we have been talking about in therapy?*

The initially agreed-upon problem area should be reassessed at this time, and the new act included in the relevant problem area. Treatment will need to focus on acquiring other more adaptive problem-solving and communication skills, in addition to focusing on management of emotions.

Violence

Violent acts against persons or objects by the adolescent can occur without legal involvement. Here too, the IPT-A therapist must thoroughly assess the event by talking to the adolescent, the family, and any other involved parties (i.e., school, siblings). Can the patient continue living in the present household or is another act of violence likely to occur? The adolescent who has become out of control may need hospitalization or placement in a residential treatment facility. The therapist must assess the patient's intent to commit future violence and whether there is a specific target for the violence. If the patient reports specific intent and target, the therapist is obligated to hospitalize the adolescent. If the adolescent, the family, and the therapist feel the patient can control further violent impulses, IPT-A can continue, but there must be a renegotiation of the treatment contract. The violent act will need to be understood by the adolescent and the therapist in the context of one of the defined problem areas. Connections will need to be made between the patient's depressed and angry feelings and the violent behavior. Specifically, a clear plan of action regarding how to handle another violent incident must be elucidated and agreed on by patient, therapist, and family. The plan may include termination of IPT-A treatment, referral for residential treatment, or hospitalization following a second incident, depending on the severity of the behavior. A primary focus of treatment should be increased communication of feelings in a nonviolent manner and acquisition of better problem-solving skills.

Premature Termination by Parent

There are times when a patient's family will sabotage the treatment by withdrawing the patient from treatment abruptly and unexpectedly. In such cases, if possible, it is important for the therapist to meet with the patient's family to inquire about their treatment concerns and discuss whether termination is believed to be an appropriate disposition at this time. The therapist might say:

> It appears that you have some concerns about your son or daughter continuing in treatment. I felt it might be helpful for you and your son or daughter if we could talk about some of these concerns. What are you feeling that is causing you to withdraw your son or daughter from treatment? What aspects of the treatment are you unhappy with? What aspects of the treatment are you pleased with? What are your plans for your son or daughter following removal from treatment? How can we work together to best help [name]?

The discussion and/or meeting allows the therapist the opportunity to correct any misperceptions about the treatment that might be causing the termination. If the therapist is unable to alter the family's decision to terminate and believes that the patient is not a risk for harm to self or others and that it would not constitute medical neglect, the therapist is obligated to abide by the family's decision. If the therapist feels that termination is contraindicated and is a risk to the patient, the therapist must report the case to a protective service agency to try and ensure that the patient is provided with the appropriate treatment either with him- or herself or another mental health provider.

SUMMARY

Crises may arise with adolescents in brief treatment. The therapist's most important decision is whether or not the adolescent can remain in IPT-A or whether the adolescent must receive other types of services either at the same or another facility. Once the decision has been made for the adolescent to remain in IPT-A, the therapist's first step must be to renegotiate the therapeutic contract in order to better address the crisis-related interpersonal problem. With the new contract, the therapist can move forward to address the new information about the patient's interpersonal relationships and the context of the depression.

· 17 ·

Use of Antidepressant Medication in Conjunction with IPT-A

Antidepressant medication is not contraindicated during IPT-A and, in fact, may be a useful adjunct treatment for severely depressed adolescents whose symptoms do not remit during the initial phase of treatment. The practice of prescribing medication for adolescents is standard clinical procedure. This chapter reviews the guidelines used to decide if antidepressant medication is indicated. The types of antidepressant medications currently in use for depressed adolescents and their administration are also reviewed. A review of efficacy studies on pharmacological treatment of adolescent depression was presented in Chapter 3. This chapter is written for the adolescent clinician who may or may not be familiar with the clinical use of antidepressant medication.

THE DECISION TO TREAT WITH ANTIDEPRESSANT MEDICATION

Although the efficacy studies to date of tricyclic antidepressants do not support their use for treating adolescent depression, most clinicians will give some adolescents a trial of medication if, in their clinical judgment, the medication may provide relief to the adolescent. The definitive data on the efficacy of antidepressants for the treatment of adolescent depression are still being collected, and the decision to medicate, therefore, is based on the adolescent psychiatrist's clinical judgment, experience, and wisdom.

Any adolescent who has depressive symptoms meeting DSM-III-R or Research Diagnostic Criteria for major depression or dysthymic disorder should be considered for medication. Patients who are suicidal and/or severely impaired are frequently hospitalized. However, with the availability of newly developed serotonergic antidepressants (i.e., fluoxetine) that have a low lethality potential, suicidality is no longer a mandate for hospitalization. Our outpatient clinical experience has been that a substantial percentage of adolescents who initially present for treatment with signs and symptoms of major depression improve during the course of several weeks with nonspecific psychotherapeutic intervention alone. Therefore, most adolescents who can be treated on an outpatient basis are monitored closely for several weeks before being started on antidepressant medication.

Adolescents who are receiving IPT-A are monitored clinically by the treating therapist and through self-report scales (Beck Depression Inventory; BDI) and clinician-rated scales (Hamilton Rating Scale for Depression; HRSD) on a weekly basis. This information is systematically reviewed every 4 weeks and sooner if the treating clinician thinks it necessary to do so. If by week 4 of IPT treatment the adolescent remains significantly depressed, based on clinical impression and substantiated by BDI > 15 and/or HRSD > 20, antidepressant medication is recommended as an adjunctive treatment to IPT. If there has been little to no improvement in the adolescent's presenting signs and symptoms of depression, and if the adolescent remains significantly impaired in the areas of school and interpersonal relationships after 4 weeks, medication should be tried. In addition, a family history of affective disorders responsive to antidepressant medication argues in favor of such medication. The decision to medicate is a clinical decision made by the child psychiatrist. Rating scales are used to inform and guide this decision.

If the primary clinician is not a child psychiatrist, a referral should be made to a child psychiatrist. The clinician should discuss with the adolescent and the parents the reasons for a medication consultation. They should be told that the adolescent is still showing significant signs of depression and that in such instances medication can often be beneficial. A child psychiatrist is the professional who assesses the need for medication and prescribes the medicine.

PHARMACOTHERAPY

Pharmacological Agents

The major classes of medications used for the treatment of adolescent depression include tricyclic antidepressants (e.g., nortriptyline, imipramine, desipramine), serotonergic antidepressants (e.g., fluoxetine and sertraline), antianxiety agents (e.g., lorazepam, alprazolam, klonopin), and neuroleptics. Neuroleptics are used to treat psychotic symptoms such as delusions and hallucinations, but they will not be reviewed here because psychosis precludes treatment with IPT-A. Antianxiety agents may be used in conjunction with antidepressants in the early stages of pharmacological treatment. Indications include nervousness, agitation, anxiety, severe insomnia, and concurrent panic attacks.

Administration of Antidepressant Medications

The procedures for administering medication are basically the same whether the child psychiatrist is the primary clinician, or whether the treatment is split between the primary clinician who is doing IPT-A and the child psychiatrist who is prescribing medication. If the treatment is split, communication between the two clinicians is the cornerstone of successful management and treatment. This section will be presented as if the treatment were split.

The roles of therapist and psychiatrist need to be clearly delineated to the adolescent and the parents. The therapist will be conducting the therapy in which the adolescent discusses feelings, thoughts, and solutions to problems. The psychiatrist prescribes medication and monitors efficacy and side effects. All problems with the medication should be reported to the psychiatrist. The clinician should inform the psychiatrist of any medication problems that have come to his or her attention. Similarly, the psychiatrist should inform the therapist of any psychological or social issues the adolescent has revealed. The adolescent should be told that the therapist and psychiatrist will be communicating with each other regularly.

The adolescent is referred to a pediatrician for a medical exam if one has not been obtained within the past 3 months. The baseline laboratory tests can be ordered by the child psychiatrist for an adolescent with no medical problems and a recent physical exam. The tests include routine blood count, biochemical screen including evaluation of liver function, thyroid function studies, and an electrocardiogram. When the adolescent is medically cleared for a trial of antidepressant medication, there should be a meeting with the adolescent and parents to review the expected benefits, possible side effects, and the proposed course of treatment.

Prescriptions are given to the parents or another responsible adult who will be instructed on appropriate administration of the medication. The adolescent patient is not made responsible for his or her medication, but rather the filling of prescriptions and supervision of daily dosing is under the direction of the parent. Depression is associated with significant morbidity and mortality. Impulsiveness and availability of means constitute significant risk factors for suicide attempts and completion in adolescence. Therefore, all medications are to be kept in a locked cabinet out of reach of the depressed adolescent and other children in the household.

The recommended dose of tricyclic antidepressants for children is 5 mg/kg per day in divided doses (Ambrosini et al., 1984). We start our adolescents on 25 mg two times a day to a maximum of 200 mg per day. Doses are increased by 25 mg two times a day every 4 days. Each dose increase is preceded by an electrocardiogram. If the PR interval exceeds 2 msec, the dose is lowered. Blood pressure, pulse, side effects, and positive therapeutic response are monitored during weekly visits. Serum levels of medication are obtained biweekly to monitor compliance and aid in dose regulation. A positive response is usually seen in 2–4 weeks on a stable dose. Six months on a steady dose is the recommended course of treatment (Ambrosini et al., 1984).

Side Effects and Complications of Antidepressant Medication

Antidepressants are frequently accompanied by side effects. The side effects in adolescents are basically the same as those reported in adults. Unfortunately, the side effects precede the beneficial effects of the medication and are felt in the very early stages of treatment. The most commonly reported side effects of tricyclic antidepressants include dry mouth, sedation, dizziness, constipation, and appetite disturbance. Less frequent side effects include tremors, sweating, insomnia, nausea, flushed face, tiredness, and listlessness (Puig-Antich, 1987; Rapoport et al., 1974; Saraf et al., 1974). Blurry vision and urinary hesitancy have also been reported. These side effects will often resolve if the dose is lowered and will certainly resolve if the medication is discontinued. More serious, albeit rare, side effects include cardiotoxicity, reduced seizure threshold (Petti & Campbell, 1975), and the occurrence of seizures in previously unaffected children (Brown et al., 1973; Petti & Campbell, 1975). Side effects associated with fluoxetine include headaches, stomach upset, reduced appetite, and, less commonly, rash and agitation. These side effects subside or disappear with a lower dose or discontinuation of the drug.

A major concern in the administration of antidepressant medications is an overdose. There are no reports of lethal overdoses with fluoxetine, and this is a factor to consider when prescribing an antidepressant to a suicidal and impulsive patient. The possibility of an overdose occurring is minimized by careful and continuous assessment of the patient's suicidality, a strong therapeutic alliance in which the adolescent assures the therapist that no suicidal action will be performed without seeking help first, and by following the guidelines listed in the preceding section on storage and administration of medication.

Overdoses require immediate medical care because they can result in serious medical complications such as arrhythmias, seizures, coma, and death. Treatment is administered in an emergency room. The patient who has overdosed is treated with ipecac (which induces vomiting) or gastric lavage (which washes out the contents of the stomach) up to 18 hours after ingestion. The patient is encouraged to drink large amounts of fluids because the drug circulating in the bloodstream is in gastric fluids. Activated charcoal, which will absorb the drug, can be given in water as well. The child should be kept in the intensive care unit for 24 hours with a cardiac monitor, since the QRS complex is the best gauge of cardiac toxicity. Dialysis is not useful since the drug is protein-bound.

Antidepressant medication is not an addictive medication, and the patient does not build up a tolerance to the drug. However, there have been reports of withdrawal symptoms when tricyclic antidepressants are suddenly stopped. Symptoms reported include nausea and vomiting, abdominal cramps, drowsiness or fatigue, decreased appetite, tearfulness, apathy, headache, agitation. A syndrome resembling a gastrointestinal flu has also been reported. Withdrawal symptoms are best treated with a small dose of medication (25 mg imipramine) and may be repeated as necessary. To avoid the possibility of withdrawal symptoms, it is best to taper the medication over a 2-week period. This also allows for the psychiatrist and clinician to monitor carefully the resumption of depressive symptoms that would indicate that a longer course of treatment is necessary.

INTEGRATING PHARMACOLOGICAL TREATMENT WITH IPT-A

It is important for the pharmacological therapy and the IPT-A to be coordinated. If both treatments are being administered by a child psychiatrist, this obviously is an easier task. If, however, there are two treating therapists, a plan of communication throughout the course of dual treatment should be agreed upon. The adolescent and parent both should be informed what role each therapist plays in the treatment. The psychiatrist will be prescribing and monitoring medication, whereas the treating clinician will be conducting psychotherapy.

Appointments should be made so as to enhance the adolescent's participation in the treatment and maximize his or her return to a full and active life. Appointments should be coordinated by the therapists so that the adolescent is not faced with the same appointment time for each therapist. Appointments scheduled for the same day in succession may be best for this purpose, except in instances where a clinical decision is made to provide multiple visits in a given week. This is done when an adolescent is severely depressed and minimally functioning in school.

The child psychiatrist should inform the clinician about the medication before the clinician's next appointment with the adolescent. The treating clinician should know the dose the adolescent is on, any reported side effects, and the expected timetable for improvement. In turn, the treating clinician should inform the psychiatrist about any information relevant to the adolescent's mental status or to the adolescent's taking of medication. Such information should include changes in mood or suicidal ideation, side effects, missing doses or failure to take medication, and stressful life events. Weekly telephone contact between the psychiatrist and clinician is usually adequate for communication.

SUMMARY

The rationale for the clinical use of antidepressant medication for the treatment of depressed adolescents is presented, and the guidelines for the judicious administration of medications are reviewed. IPT-A is not a contradiction to prescribing antidepressants, and some psychotherapeutic intervention is a recommended adjunct for any depressed adolescent receiving psychotropic medications. To be most effective, treatment with IPT-A and medication must be carefully coordinated.

·18·

The Future Direction of IPT-A

The purpose of this book is twofold: (1) to educate the reader about the epidemiology, nature, and current treatment practices of adolescent depression; and (2) to introduce the experienced adolescent therapist to the theoretical formulation and practical application of IPT-A to the treatment of depressed adolescents. Specifically, we also present the manual for IPT-A in an effort to standardize treatment for adolescents in the manner in which it has been done for adults. We caution that results on the efficacy of IPT-A as demonstrated in a controlled clinical trial are not yet available. One clinical trial is currently under way, and more clinical trials are needed. Presently, there are no formal training programs independent of the research setting. Still, we believe highly experienced clinicians with extensive experience in the treatment of adolescents will be able to adopt elements of the IPT-A approach by reviewing the manual presented here. Thus, it is our hope that not only will this book form the basis for training therapists to participate in other clinical trials assessing the efficacy of IPT-A, but that experienced clinicians will find the approach useful in their own clinical practice.

Our experience in training therapists in IPT-A has been for the purpose of testing the efficacy of the treatment in clinical trials. Whereas there are certain procedures that are required by research, the general training strategies have application to the training of clinicians in general and are described.

SPECIFICATION OF TREATMENT BY MANUAL

Psychotherapy manuals are now required for clinical trials of psychotherapy and are necessary components of therapist training for research.

The manuals enhance the consistency and reliability of psychotherapy procedures among psychotherapists and facilitate clinical training of psychotherapists as well. They specify the aims, tasks, and sequence of procedures. Scripts and case examples provided in the manuals may be supplemented by video tapes of actual sessions. The first manuals were designed for behavior therapy (Lewinsohn et al., 1982). It was the ability of the behaviorists to specify with precision interventions such as desensitization that gave impetus to the development of other manuals for specific psychotherapeutic modalities. Beck developed the first comprehensive manual specifically for the cognitive therapy treatment of depression (Beck et al., 1979). Since then many manuals have been developed.

Treatment manuals, however, are not just applicable to psychotherapy. For example, Fawcett and Epstein (1987) have developed a manual for the administration of pharmacotherapy. In order to study the efficacy of a psychotherapy, it is necessary to specify the treatment and how it differs from other psychotherapies and procedures. Psychotherapies that have very different procedures may have a similar outcome; however, this does not negate the value of specifying the different procedures. Rounsaville et al. (1988) have shown that IPT therapists were able to adhere to the manual, without reverting to their usual treatment modality, over the course of the 16-week NIMH Collaborative Study on the Treatment of Depression (Rounsaville et al., 1988). DeRubeis et al. (1982) and Hollon et al. (1984) have shown that blind raters were able to differentiate between IPT and cognitive therapies and clinical management (see Rounsaville et al., 1988, for review). Future work is necessary to elucidate what makes certain treatments efficacious, what are the common denominators of different treatment strategies that are not preferentially effective, and which treatments are selectively efficacious in specific disorders. The most obvious common denominator for any psychotherapy is the therapist.

SELECTION OF PSYCHOTHERAPISTS

A critical question for psychotherapy researchers and clinical practice is what personal qualities or characteristics make a good therapist. Factors that have been examined include personal warmth, supportiveness, and empathy. Efforts to identify individual characteristics of the therapist that are most promising as predictors of patients' outcome in psychotherapy have not yet yielded consistent results. Another line of investigation has looked at the effect of therapist's level of experience on therapeutic outcome. The NIMH Collaborative Study on the Treatment of Depression and its therapist training program provided an opportunity to examine the relationship between therapist experience and quality of treatment.

In the NIMH Collaborative Study on the Treatment of Depression, the described psychotherapist applicants were prescreened to meet certain preliminary selection criteria. Each prospective therapist was interviewed as part of a prescreening procedure to assess his or her overall clinical experience, commitment to the approach and general suitability (Chevron et al., 1983). The initial requirements included being fully qualified as a psychiatrist or Ph.D. clinical psychologist, training in a psychodynamic framework, prior treatment of a minimum of 10 depressed patients in psychotherapy. All therapists were required to submit a videotape of their psychotherapy sessions with a depressed patient, using their customary treatment approach.

Blind to the therapists' credentials, three independent evaluators (psychiatrists and psychologists) viewed the videotapes from training cases to evaluate each therapist's potential. Agreement between independent evaluators was excellent. The one variable that differentiated between therapists was experience. Psychotherapists with over 10 years of experience, regardless of discipline, were consistently judged as more skilled. The results of this one study suggested that selection criteria should be specified and that attention should be paid to the therapist's level of experience.

TRAINING OF PSYCHOTHERAPISTS

Standardized training programs based on manual-specific procedures are also a requirement for efficacy studies of psychotherapies. The training programs that are developed for psychotherapy clinical trials are not designed to teach inexperienced persons how to become therapists or to teach fundamental skills such as empathy, handling of transference, or timing. They are designed to modify practices of fully trained, competent therapists to conduct the psychotherapy under study as specified in the manual. The goal is to develop a shared language and a specified procedure in an agreed-upon sequence among the therapists participating in the trial.

If there is a careful selection of the therapist, namely one experienced in psychotherapy and committed to the particular approach to be tested, then training can be brief. The sequence adopted in the NIMH Collaborative Study on the Treatment of Depression (Elkin et al., 1989), which has become a model for subsequent studies (Frank et al., 1990b), includes a brief didactic phase in which the manual is reviewed. This is followed by a longer supervised practicum component during which the therapist treats patients under supervision monitored by actual video tapes of the sessions (Weissman et al., 1982; Rounsaville et al., 1986, 1988). Rounsaville et al. (1986) subsequently demonstrated that therapists who performed well on their first supervised case did not require further intensive supervision.

EVALUATING THE QUALITY OF THE IPT PSYCHOTHERAPIST

Chevron and Rounsaville (1983) evaluated different methods for assessing psychotherapy skills during a clinical trial of IPT, including didactic examinations, global ratings by trainers, supervised ratings based on psychotherapists' retrospective process notes, therapists' self-rating, and independent evaluators' ratings of observation of actual psychotherapy sessions as recorded on video tape. The results showed poor agreement among the assessment of therapists' skills based on the different sources. More important, ratings based on the review of the videotape sessions were not correlated with those based on the process notes. Of the five types of ratings of psychotherapists' skill, only the supervisors' ratings of the actual video tape sessions were correlated with patient outcome. The authors concluded that therapists' self-ratings may serve an important function in encouraging therapists to think about their work in terms of prescribed techniques and strategies, but they may be biased. Supervisors' ratings that are based on the process notes seem to reflect patient improvement rather than therapists' expertise. Results of this study underscore the importance of incorporating video or audio tape review of actual therapy sessions into the clinical training. The results also raise questions about the customary reliance on process reporting as a sole basis on which to make judgments about the therapist's skills. Certification criteria for the therapist should be developed and applied following the training period.

In the NIMH Collaborative Study on the Treatment of Depression, certification was carried out by an independent evaluator, a highly experienced IPT therapist (minimum of 5 years experience) who viewed the video tapes of the training sessions to determine if the therapists had met competence. Independent monitoring of selected video tapes throughout the course of the clinical trial ensured that the quality and standards of the therapy were being maintained. If there was drift in adherence to technique, supervisory sessions were held. In all cases, the manual was the guide and was used as the standard to which the therapist adhered.

CURRENT WORK

While IPT for depressed adults has been formally tested in clinical trials, IPT-A is in an earlier phase of assessment. An open clinical trial of IPT-A was conducted with 14 adolescents who had a diagnosis of major depression or dysthymic disorder and who had sought treatment at an outpatient clinic of a metropolitan hospital. The adolescents were treated with a 12-week trial of IPT-A. Two of the 14 adolescents terminated treatment early: one no longer wanted treatment after week 3; and one no longer felt depressed and in need of treatment after week 7. In addition, one adolescent was dropped from the study at week 2 because of noncompliance. All of the adolescents completed a full assessment battery that included the K-SADS semistructured interview, the Beck Depression Inventory (BDI), the Hamilton Rating Scale for Depression (HRSD), and the Children's Global Assessment Scale (C-GAS). Of the 11 patients who received 12 weeks of IPT-A, nine reported a significant decrease in depressive symptoms on the BDI (scores less than 9). The remaining two patients showed a decrease, but they were not as significant. According to their scores on the HRSD at week 12, 10 patients no longer met criteria for major depression according to their scores on the HRSD (scores less than 6), and the remaining patient had a score of 8. In addition, all the adolescents were rated as significantly improved in their daily functioning on the C-GAS.

Although these results suggest a positive effect of IPT-A on the treatment of depressed adolescents, they must be viewed with caution for several reasons: (1) there was only one therapist conducting all of the treatment so that it is unknown as to whether the effects are due to IPT-A or to the specific therapist; and (2) the preliminary study did not account for the high percentage of adolescents who may have improved without any treatment.

These questions are being addressed currently in a second study that is a controlled clinical trial of IPT-A for adolescents meeting criteria for a major depression. In this study, adolescents will be randomly assigned to either IPT-A or a nonscheduled treatment group. The latter is a minimal treatment group. The study will be conducted with several IPT-A therapists who will be fully trained prior to participating in the research project. The training program is modeled after the NIMH training program, includes a 5-day didactic program, and requires supervised treatment of three adolescents prior to certification. A completed assessment of adolescent patients who will participate in the study includes evaluations of depressive symptoms, social functioning, medical history, and family history. These same factors will be assessed at specific points during the course of treatment, at the conclusion of the study, and at 6-month follow-up to determine what variables, if any, change with IPT-A. The results of this study will be forthcoming.

CONCLUSION

Our clinical work with depressed adolescents provided the impetus for this project and the writing of this book. We are acutely aware of the potentially crippling effects of depression on adolescents, and we have often been frustrated by the paucity of effective treatments. Many depressed adolescents will improve within the first few weeks of nonspecific psychotherapeutic interventions and will leave treatment despite concerted efforts on the therapist's part to maintain the therapy. Many of these adolescents will return with future depressive episodes, but many others will not return to receive necessary treatment. Instead, the latter group will suffer the impairing social and interpersonal consequences of their depressive episode until many years later when they may again seek treatment as adults. We hope that IPT-A, specifically tailored to the adolescent's developmental tasks, will address the need for effective treatments for adolescent depression.

References

Albert, N., & Beck, A. T. (1975). Incidence of depression in early adolescence: A preliminary study. *Journal of Youth and Adolescence, 4,* 301–307.

Alessi, N., & Robbins D. R. (1984). Symptoms and subtypes of depression among adolescents distinguished by the dexamethasone suppression test: A preliminary report. *Psychiatry Research, 11,* 177.

Alessi, N. E., Robbins, D. R., & Dilsaver, S. C. (1987). Panic and depressive disorders among psychiatrically hospitalized adolescents. *Psychiatry Research, 20,* 275–283.

Altman, E., & Gotlib, I. (1988). The social behavior of depressed children: An observational study. *Journal of Abnormal Child Psychology, 16*(1), 29–44.

Ambrosini, P. J., Rabinovich, H., & Puig-Antich, J. (1984). Biological factors and pharmacologic treatment in major depressive disorders in children and adolescents. In H. S. Sudak (Ed.), *Suicide in the Young* (pp. 81–96). Boston: John Wright PSG.

American Psychiatric Association. (1987). *Diagnostic and Statistical Manual of Mental Disorders* (3rd ed., rev.). Washington, DC: American Psychiatric Press.

Angold, A. (1988a). Childhood and adolescent depression I. Epidemiological and aetiological aspects. *British Journal of Psychiatry, 152,* 601–617.

Angold, A. (1988b). Childhood and adolescent depression II. Research in clinical populations. *British Journal of Psychiatry, 153,* 476–492.

Angold, A. *DSM-IV Review.* Unpublished manuscript, Duke University, Durham, NC.

Angold, A., Weissman, M. M., John, K., Merikangas, K. R., Prusoff, B. A., Wickramaratne, P., Gammon, G. D., & Warner, V. (1987). Parent and child reports of depressive symptoms in children at low and high risk of depression. *Journal of Child Psychology and Psychiatry, 28*(6), 901–915.

Angst, J., Merikangas, K., Scheidegger, P., & Wicki, W. (1990). Recurrent brief depression: A new subtype of affective disorder. *Journal of Affective Disorders, 19,* 87–98.

Barkley, R. (1988). Child behavior rating scales and checklists. In M. Rutter, A. H. Tuma, & I. S. Lann (Eds.), *Assessment and Diagnosis in Child Psychopathology* (pp. 113–155). New York: Guilford Press.

Barrera, M., Garrison, J., & Carolynne, V. (1988). Properties of the Beck Depression

Inventory as a screening instrument for adolescent depression. *Journal of Abnormal Child Psychology, 16*(3), 263–273.

Beardslee, W. R., Bemporad, J., Keller, M. B., Klerman, G. L., Dorer, D. J., & Samuelson, H. (1983). Children of parents with major affective disorder: A review. *American Journal of Psychiatry, 140*(7), 825–832.

Beardslee, W. R., Keller, M. B., Lavori, P. W., & Klerman, G. L. (1988). Psychiatric disorder in adolescent offspring of parents with affective disorder in a non-referred sample. *Journal of Affective Disorders, 15*, 313–322.

Beck, A. T. (1967). *Depression: Clinical, Experimental and Theoretical Aspects.* New York: Harper & Row.

Beck, A. T. (1976). *Cognitive Therapy and the Emotional Disorders.* New York: International Universities Press.

Beck, A. T., Rush, A. J., Shaw, B. F., & Emery, G. (1979). *Cognitive Therapy of Depression.* New York: Guilford Press.

Bemporad, J. (1988). Psychodynamic treatment of depressed adolescent. *Journal of Clinical Psychiatry, 49*(9) (Suppl.), 26–31.

Bemporad, J., & Lee, K. W. (1988). Affective disorders. In C. Kestenbaum & D. Williams (Eds.), *Handbook of Clinical Assessment of Children and Adolescents* (Vol. II, pp. 626–650). New York: New York University Press.

Bernstein, G. A., & Garfinkel, B. D. (1986). School phobia: The overlap of affective and anxiety disorders. *Journal of the American Academy of Child and Adolescent Psychiatry, 25*, 235–241.

Biederman, J., Munir, K., Knee, D., Armentano, M., Autor, S., Waternaux, C., & Tsuang, M. (1987). High rate of affective disorder in probands with attention deficit disorder and in their relatives: A controlled family study. *American Journal of Psychiatry, 144*, 330–333.

Blos, P. (1961). *On Adolescence.* New York: Free Press.

Blum, H. M., Boyle, M. H., & Offord, D. R. (1988). Single-parent families: Child psychiatric disorder and school performance. *Journal of the American Academy of Child and Adolescent Psychiatry, 27*(2), 214–219.

Boszormenyi-Nagy, I., & Kranser, B. R. (1986). *Between Give and Take: A Clinical Guide to Contextual Therapy.* New York: Brunner/Mazel.

Bowlby, J. (1969). Attachment. In *Attachment and Loss* (Vol. I, pp. 177–257). London: Hogarth Press.

Bowlby, J. (1980). Loss: Sadness and Depression. In *Attachment and Loss.* (Vol. III, pp. 265–433). London: Hogarth Press.

Brodaty, H., & Andrews, G. (1983). Brief psychotherapy in family practice: A controlled perspective intervention trial. *British Journal of Psychiatry, 143*, 11–19.

Brody, G., & Forehand, R. (1990). Interparental conflict, relationship with the noncustodial father and adolescent postdivorce adjustment. *Journal of Applied and Developmental Psychology, 11*, 139–147.

Brown, D., Winsberg, B. G., Bialer, I., & Press, M. (1973). Imipramine therapy and seizures: Three children treated for hyperactive behavior disorders. *American Journal of Psychiatry, 130*, 210.

Brown, G. W., & Harris, T. (1978). *The Social Origins of Depression: A Study of Psychiatric Disorder in Women.* New York: Free Press.

Brown, G. W., Harris, T. O., & Bifulco, A. (1986). Long-term effects of early loss of parent. In M. Rutter, C. E. Izard, & P. B. Read (Eds.), *Depression in Young People: Developmental and Clinical Perspectives* (pp. 251–297). New York: Guilford Press.

Cadoret, R. J. (1978). Psychopathology in adopted-away offspring of biological parents with antisocial behavior. *Archives of General Psychiatry, 35,* 176–184.

Campbell, M., & Spencer, E. K. (1988). Psychopharmacology in child and adolescent psychiatry: A review of the past five years. *Journal of the American Academy of Child and Adolescent Psychiatry, 27*(3), 269–279.

Carlson, G., & Cantwell, D. (1980). Unmasking masked depression in children and adolescents. *American Journal of Psychiatry, 137*(4), 445–449.

Carlson, G., & Strober, M. (1979). Affective disorders in adolescence. *Psychiatric Clinics of North America, 2,* 511–526.

Carroll, B. J. (1982). Use of dexamethasone suppression test in depression. *Journal of Clinical Psychiatry, 43,* 44–48.

Carroll, B. J., Curtus, G. C., & Mendels, J. (1976). Neuroendocrine regulation in depression II. Discrimination of depressed from nondepressed patients. *Archives of General Psychiatry, 33,* 1051–1058.

Carroll, K. M., Rounsaville, B. J., & Gawin, F. H. (1992). A comparative trial of psychotherapies for ambulatory cocaine abusers: Relapse prevention and interpersonal psychotherapy. *American Journal of Drug and Alcohol Abuse, 17*(3), 229–247.

Chambers, W., Puig-Antich, J., Hirsh, M., Paez, P., Ambrosini, P. J., Tabrizi, M. A., & Davies, M. (1985). The assessment of affective disorders in children and adolescents by semistructured interview: Test–retest reliability of K-SADS-P. *Archives of General Psychiatry, 42,* 696–702.

Chess, S., Thomas, A., & Hassibi, M. (1983). Depression in childhood and adolescence: A prospective study of six cases. *Journal of Nervous and Mental Disease, 171*(7), 411–420.

Chevron, E., & Rounsaville, B. J. (1983). Evaluating the clinical skills of psychotherapists: A comparison of techniques. *Archives of General Psychiatry, 40,* 1129–1132.

Chevron, E., Rounsaville, B., Rothblum, E. D., & Weissman, M. M. (1983). Selecting psychotherapists to participate in psychotherapy outcome studies: Relationship between psychotherapist characteristics and assessment of clinical skills. *Journal of Nervous and Mental Disease, 171,* 348–353.

Chien, C., & Chang, T. (1985). Depression in Taiwan: Epidemiological survey utilizing the CES-D. *Seishin Shinkoi Gaku Zasshi, 87,* 355–338.

Clarke, G., & Lewinsohn, P. M. (1989). The coping with depression course: A group psychoeducational intervention for unipolar depression. *Behavior Change, 6,* 554–569.

Coble, P., Kupfer, D. J., Spiker, D. G., Neil, J. F., & Shaw, D. H. (1980). EEG sleep and clinical characteristics in young primary depressives. *Sleep Research, 9,* 165–165.

Corey, G. (1981). *Theory and Practice of Group Counseling* (2nd ed.). Monterey, CA: Brooks/Cole.

Cytryn, L., & McKnew, D. H. (1985). Treatment issues in childhood depression. *Psychiatric Annals, 15*, 401–403.

Cytryn, L., McKnew, D. H., Zahn-Waxler, C., & Gershon, E. S. (1986). Developmental issues in risk research: The offspring of affectively ill parents. In M. Rutter, C. E. Izard, & P. B. Read (Eds.), *Depression in Young People: Developmental and Clinical Perspectives* (pp. 163–189). New York: Guilford Press.

DeRubeis, R. J., Hollon, S. D., Evans, M. D., & Bemis, K. M. (1982). Can psychotherapies for depression be discriminated? A systematic investigation of cognitive therapy and interpersonal therapy. *Journal of Consulting and Clinical Psychology, 50*, 744–756.

DiMascio, A., Weissman, M. M., Prusoff, B. A., New, C., Zwilling, M., & Klerman, G. L. (1979). Differential symptom reduction by drugs and psychotherapy in acute depression. *Archives of General Psychiatry, 36*, 1450–1456.

Downey, G., & Coyne, J. (1990). Children of depressed parents: An integrated interview. *Psychological Bulletin, 108*(1), 50–76.

Edelbrock, C., & Costello, A. J. (1988). Structured interviews for children. In M. Rutter, A. H. Tuma, & I. S. Lann (Eds.), *Assessment and Diagnosis in Child Psychopathology* (pp. 87–112). New York: Guilford Press.

Edelbrock, C., Costello, A. J., Dulcan, M. K., Conover, N. C., & Kalas, R. (1986). Parent–child agreement on child psychiatric symptoms assessed via structured interview. *Journal of Child Psychology, Psychiatry, and Allied Disciplines, 27*(2), 181–190.

Eissler, K. R. (1958). Notes on problems of technique in the psychoanalytic treatment of adolescents. *Psychoanalytic Study of the Child, 13*, 223–254.

Elkin, I., Shea, M. T., Watkins, J. T., Imber, S. D., Sotsky, S. M., Collins, J. F., Glass, D. R., Pilkonis, P. A., Leber, W. R., Docherty, J. P., Feister, S. F., & Parloff, M. B. (1989). National Institute of Mental Health treatment of depression collaborative research program: General effectiveness of treatment. *Archives of General Psychiatry, 46*, 971–983.

Emery, G., Bedrosian, R., & Garber, J. (1983). Cognitive therapy with depressed children and adolescents. In D. P. Cantwell & G. A. Carlson (Eds.), *Affective Disorders in Childhood and Adolescence—An Update* (pp. 445–471). New York: Spectrum Publications.

Erikson, E. (1968). *Identity, Youth and Crisis.* New York: W. W. Norton.

Fairburn, C. G. (1988). The current status of the psychological treatments for bulimia nervosa. *Journal of the Psychosomatic Research, 32*(6), 635–645.

Fairburn, C. G., Jones, R., Peveler, R. C., Carr, S. J., Solomon, R. A., O'Connor, M. E., Burton, J., & Hope, R. A. (1991). Three psychological treatments for bulimia nervosa: A comparative trial. *Archives of General Psychiatry, 48*, 463–469.

Fawcett, J., & Epstein, P. (1987). Clinical management of imipramine and placebo administration. *Psychopharmacology Bulletin, 23*(2), 309–324.

Fendrich, M., Warner, V., & Weissman, M. M. (1990). Family risk factors, parental depression and psychopathology in offspring. *Developmental Psychology, 26*(19), 40–50.

Fine, S., Forth, A., Gilbert, M., & Haley, G. (1991). Group therapy for adolescent depressive disorder: A comparison of social skills and therapeutic support.

Journal of the American Academy of Child and Adolescent Psychiatry, 30(1), 79–85.

Fine, S., Gilbert, M., Schmidt, L., Haley, G., Maxwell, A., & Forth, A. (1989). Short-term group therapy with depressed adolescent outpatients. *Canadian Journal of Psychiatry, 34,* 97–102.

Fisher, P., Wickes, J., Shaffer, D., Piacentini, J., & Lapkin, J. (1992). *National Institute of Mental Health Diagnostic Interview Schedule for Children (NIMH DISC, version 2.3): User's Manual.* New York: Division of Child and Adolescent Psychiatry, New York State Psychiatric Institute.

Fleming, J. E., & Offord, S. R. (1990). Epidemiology of childhood depressive disorders: A critical review. *Journal of the American Academy of Child and Adolescent Psychiatry, 29*(4), 571–580.

Fleming, J. E., Offord, D. R., & Boyle, M. H. (1989). Prevalence of childhood and adolescent depression in the community: Ontario Child Health Study. *British Journal of Psychiatry, 155,* 647–654.

Foley, S. H., Rounsaville, B. J.,Weissman, M. M., Sholomskas, D., & Chevron, E. (1990). Individual versus conjoint interpersonal psychotherapy for depressed patients with marital disputes. *International Journal of Family Psychiatry, 10,* 1–2.

Forehand, R., Wierson, M., McCombs, A., Brody, G., & Fauber, R. (1989). Interparental conflict and adolescent problem behavior: An examination of mechanisms. *Behaviour Research and Therapy, 27*(4), 365–371.

Frank, E., Frank, N., & Reynolds, C. F. (1988). *Manual for the Adaptation of Interpersonal Psychotherapy to Maintenance Treatment of Recurrent Depression in Late Life (IPT-LLM).* Pittsburgh: University of Pittsburgh School of Medicine.

Frank, E., Kupfer, D. J., Cornes, C., Carter, S., & Frankel, D. (1990a). *Manual for the Adaptation of Interpersonal Psychotherapy to the Treatment of Bipolar Disorder (IPT-BP).* Pittsburgh: University of Pittsburgh.

Frank, E., Kupfer, D. F., & Perel, J. M. (1989). Early recurrence in unipolar depression. *Archives of General Psychiatry, 46,* 397–400.

Frank, E., Kupfer, D. F., Perel, J. M., Cornes, C., & Jarrett, B. B. (1990b). Three-year outcomes for maintenance therapies in recurrent depression. *Archives of General Psychiatry, 47*(12), 1093–1099.

Frank, E., Kupfer, D. J., Wagner, E,F., McEachran, A. B., & Cornes, C. (1991). Efficacy of interpersonal psychotherapy as a maintenance treatment of recurrent depression: Contributing factors. *Archives of General Psychiatry, 48*(2), 1053–1059.

Freud, A. (1958). Adolescence. *Psychoanalytic Study of the Child, 16,* 225–278.

Friedman, R. C., Hurt, S. W., Clarkin, J. F., Corn, R., & Aronoff, M. S. (1983). Symptoms of depression among adolescents and young adults. *Journal of Affective Disorders, 5,* 37–43.

Garber, J., Kriss, M. R., Koch, M., & Lindholm, L. (1988). Recurrent depression in adolescents: A follow-up study. *Journal of the American Academy of Child and Adolescent Psychiatry, 27*(1), 49–54.

Garfield, S. L. (1986). Research on client variables in psychotherapy. In S. L. Garfield & A. E. Bergin (Eds.), *Handbook of Psychotherapy and Behavior Change* (3rd ed., pp. 113–156). New York: Wiley.

Garfield, S. L. (1989). *The Practice of Brief Psychotherapy*. New York: Pergamon Press.

Garfinkle, B. D. (1986). Major affective disorders in children and adolescents. In G. Winokur & P. Clayton (Eds.), *The Medical Basis of Psychiatry* (pp. 308–330). Philadelphia: W. B. Saunders.

Garrison, C. Z., Schucter, M. D., Schoenbach, V. J., & Kaplan, B. K. (1989). Epidemiology of depressive symptoms in young adolescents. *Journal of the American Academy of Child and Adolescent Psychiatry, 28*(3), 343–351.

Geller, B., Chestnut, E. C., Miller, M. D., Price, D. T., & Yates, E. (1985). Preliminary data on DSM-III associated features of major depressive disorder in children and adolescents. *American Journal of Psychiatry, 142*, 643–644.

Geller, B., Cooper, T. B., Graham, D. L., Marsteller, F. A., & Bryant, D. M. (1990). Double-blind placebo controlled study of nortriptyline in depressed adolescents using a "fixed plasma level" design. *Psychopharmacology Bulletin, 26*(1), 85–90.

Geller, B., Cooper, T. B., McCombs, H. G., Graham, D. L., & Wells, J. (1989). Double-blind placebo controlled study of nortriptyline in depressed adolescents using a "fixed plasma level" design. *Psychopharmacology Bulletin, 25*(1), 101–108.

Gershon, E. S., Hamovit, J., Guroff, J. J., Dibble, E., Leckman, J. F., Sceery, W., Targum, S. D., Nurnberger, J. I., Goldin, L. R., & Bunney, W. E. (1982). A family study of schizoaffective bipolar I, bipolar II, unipolar, and normal control probands. *Archives of General Psychiatry, 39*(10), 1157–1167.

Ghali, S. B. (1977). Culture sensitivity and the Puerto Rican client. *Social Casework, 58*(8), 459–468.

Gibbs, J. T. (1985). Psychological factors associated with depression in urban adolescent females: Implications for treatment. *Journal of Youth and Adolescence, 14*, 47–60.

Gillin, J. C., Duncan, W., Pettigrew, K. D., Frankel, B., & Snyder, F. (1979). Successful separation of depressed, normal, and insomniac subjects by EEG sleep data. *Archives of General Psychiatry, 36*, 85–90.

Glenwick, D. S., & Mowrey, J. D. (1986). When parent becomes peer: Loss of intergenerational boundaries in single-parent families. *Family Relations, 35*, 57–62.

Goldberg, D. P. (1972). *The Detection of Psychiatric Illness by Questionnaire* (Institute of Psychiatry Maudsley Monographs 21). Oxford: Oxford University Press.

Gray, R. E. (1987). Adolescent response to the death of a parent. *Journal of Youth and Adolescence, 16*(6), 511–525.

Gurman, A. S., & Kniskern, D. P. (1978). Research on marital and family therapy: Progress, perspective, and prospect. In S. L. Garfield & A. E. Bergin (Eds.), *Handbook of Psychotherapy and Behavior Change* (pp. 242–281). New York: Wiley.

Gutterman, E. M., O'Brien, J. D., & Young, J. G. (1987). Structured diagnostic interviews for children and adolescents: Current status and future directions. *Journal of the American Academy of Child and Adolescent Psychiatry, 26*(5), 621–630.

Haley, J. (1976). *Problem-Solving Therapy: New Strategies for Effective Family Therapy*. New York: Jossey-Bass.

Hall, G. S. (1904). *Adolescence: Its Psychology and Its Relations to Physiology, Anthropology, Sociology, Sex, Crime, Religion, and Education.* New York: D. Appleton.

Hammen, C., Burge, D., Burney, E., & Adrian, C. (1990). Longitudinal study of diagnoses in children of women with unipolar and bipolar affective disorder. *Archives of General Psychiatry, 47,* 1112–1117.

Hardy, J., Fanta, C., & Montana, P. (1982). The hispanic female adolescent: A group therapy model. *International Journal of Psychotherapy, 32*(3), 351–366.

Harrington, R. C. (1989). Child and adult depression: Concepts and continuities. *Israel Journal of Psychiatry and Related Sciences, 26*(1–2), 12–29.

Harrington, R. C., Fudge, H., Rutter, M., Pickles, A., & Hill, J. (1990). Adult outcomes of childhood and adolescent depression. *Archives of General Psychiatry, 47,* 465–473.

Henderson, S., Byrne, D. G., Duncan-Jones, P., Adcock, S., Scott, R., & Steele, G. P. (1978). Social bonds in the epidemiology of neurosis. *British Journal of Psychiatry, 132,* 463–466.

Herjanic, B., & Reich, W. (1982). Development of a structured psychiatric interview for children: Agreement between child and parent on individual symptoms. *Journal of Abnormal Child Psychology, 10,* 307–324.

Hersen, H., & Van Hasselt, V. B. (Ed.). (1987). *Behavior Therapy with Children and Adolescents: A Clinical Approach.* New York: Wiley.

Hetherington, E. M., Cox, M., & Cox, R. (1985). Long-term effects of divorce and remarriage on the adjustment of children. *Journal of the American Academy of Child and Adolescent Psychiatry, 24*(5), 518–530.

Hoeper, E. W., Nycz, G. R., Regier, D. A., Goldberg, I. D., Jacobson, A., & Hankin, J. (1980). Diagnosis of mental disorder in adults and increased use of health services in four outpatient settings. *American Journal of Psychiatry, 137,* 207–210.

Hollon, S. D., Evans, M. D., Elkin, I., & Lowery, M. A. (1984). *System Rating Therapies for Depression.* Paper presented at the annual meeting of the American Psychiatric Association, Los Angeles.

Horowitz, M. (1976). *Stress Response Syndromes.* New York: Jason Aronson.

Howard, J. I., Kopata, S. M., Krause, M. S., & Orlinsky, D. E. (1986). The dose effect relationship in psychotherapy. *American Psychologist, 41,* 159–164.

Hudgens, R. (1974). *Psychiatric Disorders in Adolescents* (pp. 38–89). Baltimore: Williams & Wilkins.

Inamdar, S. C., Siomopoulos, G., Osborn, M., & Bianchi, E. (1979). Phenomenology associated with depressed moods in adolescence. *American Journal of Psychiatry, 136*(2), 156–159.

Jacobson, G., & Jacobson, D. S. (1987). Impact of marital dissolution on adults and children: The significance of loss and continuity. In J. Bloom-Feshbach & S. Bloom-Feshbach (Eds.), *The Psychology of Separation and Loss* (pp. 316–327). San Francisco: Jossey-Bass.

Kandel, D. B., & Davies, M. (1982). Epidemiology of depressive mood in adolescents: An empirical study. *Archives of General Psychiatry, 39,* 1205–1212.

Kandel, D. B., & Davies, M. (1986). Adult sequelae of adolescent depressive symptoms. *Archives of General Psychiatry, 43,* 255–262.

Kaplan, S. L., Hong, G. K., & Weinhold, C. (1984). Epidemiology of depressive symptomatology. *Journal of the American Academy of Child and Adolescent Psychiatry, 23*(1), 91–98.

Kashani, J. H., Burbach, D. J., & Rosenberg, T. K. (1988). Perceptions of family conflict resolution and depressive symptomatology in adolescents. *Journal of the American Academy of Child and Adolescent Psychiatry, 27*(1), 42–48.

Kashani, J. H., Carlson, G. A., Beck, N. C., Hoeper, E. W., Corcoran, C. M., McAllister, J. A., Fallahi, C., Rosenberg, T. K., & Reid, J. C. (1987). Depression, depressive symptoms, and depressed mood among a community sample of adolescents. *American Journal of Psychiatry, 144*(7), 931–941.

Kashani, J. H., Hodges, K. K., & Shekim, W. O. (1980). Hypomanic reaction to amitriptyline in a depressed child. *Psychosomatics, 21*, 867–872.

Kashani, J. H., Orvaschel, H., Burke, J. P., & Reid, J. C. (1985). Informant variance: The issue of parent–child disagreement. *Journal of the American Academy of Child and Adolescent Psychiatry, 24*(4), 437–441.

Kashani, J. H., Rosenberg, T. K., & Reigh, N. C. (1989). Developmental perspectives in child and adolescent depressive symptoms in a community sample. *American Journal of Psychiatry, 146*, 871–875.

Kashani, J. H., & Sherman, D. D. (1988). Childhood depression: Epidemiology, etiological models and treatment implications. *Integrative Psychiatry, 6*, 1–21.

Kashani, J. H., Sherman, D. D., Parker, D. R., & Reid, J. C. (1990). Utility of the Beck Depression Inventory with clinic-referred adolescents. *Journal of the American Academy of Child and Adolescent Psychiatry, 2*, 278–282.

Kashani, J. H., Whekim, W. O., & Reid, J. C. (1984). Amitriptyline in children with major depressive disorder: A double-blind crossover pilot study. *Journal of the American Academy of Child and Adolescent Psychiatry, 23*(3), 348–351.

Kazdin, A. E., Esveldt-Dawson, K., Sherick, R. B., & Colbus, D. (1985). Assessment of overt behavior and childhood depression among psychiatrically disturbed children. *Journal of Consulting and Clinical Psychology, 53*, 201–210.

Kazdin, A. E., French, N. H., Unis, A. S., & Esveldt-Dawson, K. (1983). Assessment of childhood depression. *Journal of the American Academy of Child and Adolescent Psychiatry, 22*, 157–164.

Keller, M. B., Beardslee, W. R., Lavori, P. W., & Wunder, J. (1988). Course of major depression in nonreferred adolescents: A retrospective study. *Journal of Affective Disorders, 15*, 235–243.

Keller, M. B., Lavori, P. W., Beardslee, W. R., Wunder, J., & Ryan, N. (1991). Depression in children and adolescents: New data on "undertreatment" and a literature review on the efficacy of available treatments. *Journal of Affective Disorders, 21*, 163–171.

Kelly, J. B. (1981). Visiting fathers: Observations on adolescent relationships five years after divorce. *Adolescent Psychiatry, 9*, 133–141.

Kelly, J. B. (1988). Longer-term adjustment in children of divorce: Convergent findings and implications for practice. *Journal of Family Psychology, 2*(2), 119–140.

Kestenbaum, C. J., & Kron, L. (1987). Psychoanalytic intervention with children and adolescents with affective disorders: A combined treatment approach. *Journal of the American Academy of Psychoanalysis, 15*(2), 153–174.

Klerman, G. L. (1988). The current age of youthful melancholia. *British Journal of Psychiatry, 152,* 4–14.

Klerman, G. L., Budman, S., Berwick, D., Weissman, M. M., Damico-White, J., Demby, A., & Feldstein, M. (1987). Efficacy of a brief psychosocial intervention for symptoms of stress and distress among patients in primary care. *Medical Care, 25,* 1078–1088.

Klerman, G. L., DiMascio, A., Weissman, M. M., Prusoff, B., & Paykel, E. S. (1974). Treatment of depression by drugs and psychotherapy. *American Journal of Psychiatry, 131,* 186–194.

Klerman, G. L., Lavori, P. W., Rice, J., Reich, T., Endicott, J., Andreasen, N. C., Keller, M. B., & Hirschfeld, R. M. A. (1985). Birth-cohort trends in rates of major depressive disorder among relatives of patients with affective disorder. *Archives of General Psychiatry, 42,* 689–693.

Klerman, G. L., & Weissman, M. M. (1992). Interpersonal psychotherapy: Efficacy and adaptations. In E. S. Paykel (Ed.), *Handbook of Affective Disorders* (2nd ed., pp. 501–510). New York: Guilford Press.

Klerman, G. L., Weissman, M. M., Rounsaville, B. J., & Chevron, E. S. (1984). *Interpersonal Psychotherapy of Depression.* New York: Basic Books.

Kovacs, M. (1979). The efficacy of cognitive and behavioral therapies for depression. *American Journal of Psychiatry, 137,* 1495–1501.

Kovacs, M. (1982). *The Children's Depression Inventory.* Unpublished manuscript, University of Pittsburgh, Pittsburgh, PA.

Kovacs, M. (1985). The Children's Depression Inventory (CDI). *Psychopharmacology Bulletin, 21*(4), 995–998.

Kovacs, M., Feinberg, T. L., Crouse-Novak, M. A., Paulauskas, S. L., & Finkelstein, R. (1984). Depressive disorders in childhood I. A longitudinal prospective study of characteristics and recovery. *Archives of General Psychiatry, 41,* 229–237.

Kovacs, M., Gatsonis, C., Paulauskas, S. L., & Richards, C. (1989). Depressive disorders in childhood IV. A longitudinal study of comorbidity with and risk for anxiety disorders. *Archives of General Psychiatry, 46,* 776–782.

Kovacs, M., Paulauskas, S., Gatsonis, C., & Richards, C. (1988). Depressive disorders in childhood III. A longitudinal study of comorbidity with and risk for conduct disorders. *Journal of Affective Disorders, 15,* 205–217.

Kovacs, M., Rush, A. J., Beck, A. T., & Hollon, S. D. (1981). Depressed outpatients treated with cognitive therapy or pharmacotherapy: A one year follow-up. *Archives of General Psychiatry, 38,* 33–39.

Kramer, A. D., & Feiguine, R. J. (1981). Clinical effects of amitryptiline in adolescent depression: A pilot study. *Journal of the American Academy of Child and Adolescent Psychiatry, 20,* 636–644.

Kupfer, D. (1976). REM latency: A psychologic marker for primary depressive disease. *Biological Psychiatry, 11,* 159–174.

Kupfer, D., & Foster, F. G. (1979). EEG sleep and depression. In R. L. Williams & I. Karacan (Eds.), *Sleep Disorders: Diagnosis and Treatment* (pp. 163–204). New York: Wiley.

Kupfer, D. J., Frank, E., & Perel, J. M. (1989). The advantage of early treatment intervention in recurrent depression. *Archives of General Psychiatry, 46,* 771–775.

Leon, R. G., Kendall, P. C., Garber, J. (1980). Depression in children: Parent, teacher, and child perspective. *Journal of Abnormal Psychology, 8,* 221–235.

Levy, J., & Deykin, E. Y. (1989). Suicidality, depression and substance abuse in adolescence. *American Journal of Psychiatry, 146,* 1462–1467.

Lewinsohn, P. M., Clarke, G. N., Hops, H., & Andrews, J. (1990). Cognitive–behavioral treatment for depressed adolescents. *Behavior Therapy, 21,* 385–401.

Lewinsohn, P. M., Sullivan, J. M., Grosscup, S. J. (1982). Behavioral therapy: Clinical applications. In A. J. Rush (Ed.), *Short-Term Psychotherapies for Depression* (pp. 50–87). New York: Guilford Press.

Lewinsohn, P. M., Weinstein, M., & Shaw, D. (1969). Depression: A clinical-research approach. In R. Rubin & C. Frank (Eds.), *Advances in Behavior Therapy* (pp. 231–240). New York: Academic Press.

Liebowitz, J. H., & Kernberg, P. F. (1988). Psychodynamic psychotherapies. In C. J. Kestenbaum & D. T. Williams (Eds.), *Handbook of Clinical Assessment of Children and Adolescents* (Vol. II, pp. 1045–1065). New York: New York University Press.

Lobovitz, D. A., & Handal, P. J. (1985). Childhood depression. *Journal of Pediatric Psychology, 10,* 45–54.

Locke, H. J., & Wallace, K. M. (1976). Short-term marital adjustment and prediction tests: Their reliability and validity. *Marriage and Family Living, 38,* 15–25.

Loosen, P. T. (1985). The TRH-induced TSH response in psychiatric patients: A possible neuroendocrine marker. *Psychoneuroendocrinology, 10,* 237–260.

Lowenstein, A. (1986). Temporary single parenthood: The case of prisoners' families. *Family Relations, 35,* 79–85.

Markowitz, J. C., Klerman, G. L., & Perry, S. (1992). Interpersonal psychotherapy of depressed HIV seropositive patients. *Hospital and Community Psychiatry, 43,* 885–890.

Marriage, K., Fine, S., Moretti, M., & Haley, B. (1986). Relationship between depression and conduct disorder in children and adolescents. *Journal of the American Academy of Child and Adolescent Psychiatry, 25*(5), 687–691.

Mason, B. J., Markowitz, J. C., & Klerman, G. L. (1993). Interpersonal psychotherapy for dysthymic disorders. In G. L. Klerman & M. M. Weissman (Eds.), *New Applications of Interpersonal Psychotherapy* (pp. 242–281). Washington, DC: American Psychiatric Press.

Matson, J. L. (1989). *Treating Depression in Children and Adolescents.* New York: Pergamon Press.

McGoldrick, M., & Walsh, F. (1991). A time to mourn: Death and the family life cycle. In F. Walsh & M. McGoldrick (Eds.), *Living beyond Loss: Death in the Family* (pp. 30–50). New York: W. W. Norton.

Mechanic, D., & Hansell, S. (1989). Divorce, family conflict and adolescent well-being. *Journal of Health and Social Behavior, 30,* 105–116.

Meyer, A. (1957). *Psychobiology: A Science of Man.* Springfield, IL: Charles C. Thomas.

Minuchin, S. (1974). *Families and Family Therapy.* Cambridge: Harvard University Press.

Mitchell, J., McCauley, E., Burke, P. M., & Moss, S. J. (1988). Phenomenology of depression in children and adolescents. *Journal of the American Academy of Child and Adolescent Psychiatry, 27*(1), 12–20.

Moreau, D. L. (1990). Major depression in childhood and adolescence. *Psychiatric Clinics of North America, 13*(2), 355–368.

Moreau, D., Mufson, L., Weissman, M. M., & Klerman, G. L. (1991). Interpersonal psychotherapy for adolescent depression: Description of modification and preliminary application. *Journal of the American Academy of Child and Adolescent Psychiatry, 30,* 642–651.

Moretti, M., Fine, S., Haley, G., & Marriage K. (1985). Childhood and adolescent depression. *Journal of the American Academy of Child and Adolescent Psychiatry, 24,* 298–302.

Mueller, P. S., Heninger, G. R., & MacDonald, R. K. (1972). Studies on glucose utilization and insulin sensitivity in affective disorders. In T. A. Williams, M. M. Katz, & J. A. Shield (Eds.), *Recent Advances in Psychobiology of Depressive Illnesses* (pp. 235–245). Washington, DC: U.S. Department of Health, Education and Welfare.

Mufson, L., Moreau, D., Weissman, M. M., Klerman, G. L., & Martin, J. (1992). *An Open Clinical Trial of Interpersonal Psychotherapy for Depressed Adolescents.* Unpublished manuscript, New York State Psychiatric Institute.

Murphy, G. E., Simons, A. D., Wetzel, R. D., & Lustman, P. J. (1984). Cognitive therapy and pharmacotherapy singly and together in the treatment of depression. *Archives of General Psychiatry, 41,* 33–41.

Nichols, M. (1984). *Family Therapy: Concepts and Methods.* New York: Gardner Press.

Nissen, G. (1986). Treatment for depression in children and adolescents. *Psychopathology, 19*(Suppl. 2), 152–161.

Norton, A. J., & Glick, P. C. (1986). One parent families: A social and economic profile. *Family Relations, 35,* 9–17.

Offenkrantz, W., Altshul, S., Cooper, A., Frances, A., Michels, R., Rosenblatt, A., Schimel, J., Tobin, A., & Zaphiropoulos, M. (1982). Treatment planning and psychodynamic psychiatry. In J. M. Lewis & G. Usdin (Eds.), *Treatment Planning in Psychiatry* (pp. 3–41). Washington, DC: American Psychiatric Association.

Offer, D. (1969). Adolescent turmoil. In *The Psychological World of the Teenager: A Study of Normal Adolescent Boys* (pp. 174–193). New York: Basic Books.

Offer, D., Ostrov, E., & Howard, K. (1982). The mental health professional concept of the normal adolescent. In S. Chess & A. Thomas (Eds.), *Annual Progress in Child Psychiatry and Development* (pp. 593–601). New York: Brunner/Mazel.

Offord, D., Boyle, M. H., Szatmari, P., Rae-Grant, N., Links, P. S., Cadman, D. T., Byles, J. A., Crawford, J. W., Blum, H. M., Byrne, C., Thomas, H., & Woodward, C. A. (1987). Ontario Child Health Study: II. Six month prevalence of disorder and rates of service utilization. *Archives of General Psychiatry, 44,* 832–836.

Orvaschel, H. (1990). Early onset psychiatric disorder in high risk children and increased familial morbidity. *Journal of the American Academy of Child and Adolescent Psychiatry, 29*(2), 184–188.

Orvaschel, H., Weissman, M. M., Padian, N., & Lowe, T. L. (1981). Assessing psychopathology in children of psychiatrically disturbed parents: A pilot study.

Journal of the American Academy of Child and Adolescent Psychiatry, 20, 112–122.

Osterweis, M., Solomon, F., & Green, M. (Eds.). (1984). *Bereavement: Reactions, Consequences and Care* (pp. 99–145). Washington DC: National Academy Press.

Paykel, E. S., DiMascio, A., Klerman, G. L., Prusoff, B. A., & Weissman, M. M. (1976). Maintenance therapy of depression. *Pharmakopsychiatrie Neuropsychopharmakologie, 9*, 127–139.

Pearlin, L. I., & Lieberman, M. A. (1979). Social sources of emotional distress. In R. Simmons (Ed.), *Research in Community and Mental Health* (pp. 217–248). Greenwich, CT: JAI.

Petti, T. A. (1983). Behavioral approaches in the treatment of depressed children. In D. P. Cantwell & G. A. Carlson (Eds.), *Affective Disorders in Childhood and Adolescence. An Update* (pp. 417–444). New York: Spectrum Publications.

Petti, T. A., & Campbell, L. M. (1975). Imipramine and seizures. *American Journal of Psychiatry, 132*(5), 538–541.

Petti, T. A., & Unis, A. (1981). Imipramine treatment of borderline children: Case reports with a controlled study. *American Journal of Psychiatry, 138*(4), 515–518.

Poznanski, E. O., Kaahenbuhl, V., & Zrull, L. P. (1976). Childhood depression: A longitudinal perspective. *Journal of the American Academy of Child and Adolescent Psychiatry, 15*, 491–501.

Preskorn, S. H., Weller, E. B., Hughes, C. W., Weller, R. A., & Bolte, K. (1987). Depression in prepubertal children: Dexamethasone nonsuppression predicts differential response to imipramine versus placebo. *Psychopharmacology Bulletin, 23*(1), 128–133.

Puig-Antich, J. (1980). Affective disorders in childhood: A review and perspective. *Psychiatric Clinics in North America, 3*, 403–424.

Puig-Antich, J. (1982). Major depression and conduct disorder in prepuberty. *Journal of the American Academy of Child and Adolescent Psychiatry, 21*(2), 118–128.

Puig-Antich, J. (1987). Affective disorders in children and adolescents: Diagnostic validity and psychobiology. In H. Y. Meltzer (Ed.), *Psychopharmacology: The Third Generation of Progress* (pp. 843–860). New York: Raven Press.

Puig-Antich, J., Goetz, R., Hankon, C., Davies, M., Thompson, J., Chambers, W. J., Tabrizi, M. A., & Weitzman, E. D. (1982). Sleep architecture and REM sleep measures in prepubertal children with major depression. *Archives of General Psychiatry, 39*, 932–939.

Puig-Antich, J., Lukens, E., Davies, M., Goetz, D., Brennan-Quattrock, J., & Todak, G. (1985a). Psychosocial functioning in prepubertal depressive disorders I. Interpersonal relationships during the depressive episode. *Archives of General Psychiatry, 42*, 500–507.

Puig-Antich, J., Lukens, E., Davies, M., Goetz, D., Brennan-Quattrock, J., & Todak, G. (1985b). Psychosocial functioning in prepubertal depressive disorders II. Interpersonal relationships after sustained recovery from affective episode. *Archives of General Psychiatry, 42*, 511–517.

Puig-Antich, J., Orvaschel, H., Tabrizi, M. A., & Chambers, W. (1980). *The Schedule for Affective Disorders and Schizophrenia for School-Age Children—*

Epidemiologic Version. New York: New York State Psychiatric Institute and Yale University School of Medicine.

Puig-Antich, J., Perel, M. P., Lupatkin, W., Chambers, W. J., Tabrizi, M. A., King, J., Goez, R., Davies, M., & Stiller, R. L. (1987). Imipramine in prepubertal major depressive disorders *Archives of General Psychiatry, 44*, 81–89.

Puig-Antich, J., & Weston, B. (1983). The diagnosis and treatment of major depressive disorder in childhood. *Annual Review of Medicine, 34*, 231–245.

Raphael, B. (1983). *Anatomy of Bereavement* (pp. 139–177). New York: Basic Books.

Rapoport, J. L., Quinn, P. O., Bradbard, G., Riddle, D., & Brooks, E. (1974). Imipramine and methylphenidate treatment of hyperactive boys. *Archives of General Psychiatry, 30*, 789.

Reinherz, H. Z., Stewart-Berghauer, G., Pakiz, B., Frost, A. K., Moeykens, B. A., & Holmes, W. M. (1989). The relationship of early risk and current mediators to depressive symptomatology in adolescents. *Journal of the American Academy of Child and Adolescent Psychiatry, 28*(6), 942–947.

Reynolds, C., & Imber, S. (1988). *Maintenance Therapies in Late-Life Depression* (MH#43832). Washington DC: National Institute of Mental Health.

Reynolds, W. M., & Coats, K. I. (1986). A comparison of cognitive–behavioral therapy and relaxation training for the treatment of depression in adolescents. *Journal of Consulting and Clinical Psychology, 44*, 653–660.

Robbins, D. R., Alessi, N. E., & Colfer, M. V. (1989). Treatment of adolescents with major depression: Implications of the DST and the melancholic clinical subtype. *Journal of Affective Disorders, 17*, 99–104.

Robbins, D. R., Alessi, N. E., Colfer, M. V., Yanchyshyn, G. W. (1985). Use of the Hamilton Rating Scale for Depression and the Carroll Self-Rating Scale in adolescents. *Psychiatry Research, 14*(2), 123–129.

Rounsaville, B. J., Chevron, E. S., Weissman, M. M., Prusoff, B. A., & Frank, E. (1986). Training therapists to perform interpersonal psychotherapy in clinical trials. *Comparative Psychiatry, 27*, 364–371.

Rounsaville, B. J., Gawin, F., & Kleber, H. (1985). Interpersonal psychotherapy adapted for ambulatory cocaine abusers. *American Journal of Drug and Alcohol Abuse, 11*(3–4), 171–191.

Rounsaville, B. J., Glazer, W., Wilber, C. H., Weissman, M. M., & Kleber, H. D. (1983). Short-term interpersonal psychotherapy in methadone-maintained opiate addicts. *Archives of General Psychiatry, 40*, 629–636.

Rounsaville, B. J., & Kleber, H. D. (1985). Psychotherapy/counseling for opiate addicts: Strategies for use in different treatment settings. *International Journal of Addictions, 20*(6–7), 869–896.

Rounsaville, B. J., O'Malley, S., Foley, S., & Weissman, M. M. (1988). Role of manual-guided training in the conduct and efficacy of interpersonal psychotherapy for depression. *Journal of Consulting and Clinical Psychology, 56*, 681–688.

Rounsaville, B. J., Prusoff, B. A., & Weissman, M. M. (1980). The course of marital disputes in depressed women: A 48-month follow-up study. *Comparative Psychiatry, 21*, 111–118.

Rounsaville, B. J., Weissman, M. M., Prusoff, B. A., & Herceg-Baron, R. L. (1979). Marital disputes and treatment outcome in depressed women. *Comparative Psychiatry, 20*, 483–490.

Rush, A. J., Beck, A. T., Kovacs, M., & Hollon, S. (1977). Comparative efficacy of cognitive therapy and imipramine in the treatment of depressed outpatients. *Cognitive Therapy and Research, 1,* 17–37.

Rutter, M., (1979). *Changing Youth in a Changing World.* London: Nuffield Publications.

Rutter, M., Graham, P., Chadwick, F. D., & Yule, W. (1976a). Adolescent turmoil: Fact or fiction. *Journal of Child Psychology and Psychiatry, 17,* 35–56.

Rutter, M., Tizard, J., Yule, W., Graham, P., & Whitmore, K. (1976b). Isle of Wight studies 1964–1974. *Psychological Medicine, 6,* 313–332.

Rutter, M., Tuma, A. H., & Lann, I. S. (Eds.). (1988). *Assessment and Diagnosis in Child Psychopathology.* New York: Guilford Press.

Ryan, N. D. (1990). Pharmacotherapy of adolescent major depression: Beyond TCA's. *Psychopharmocology Bulletin, 26*(1), 75–79.

Ryan, N. D., Meyer, V., Cahille, S., Mazzie, D., & Puig-Antich, J. (1988a). Lithium antidepressant augmentation in TCA refractory depression in adolescents. *Journal of the American Academy of Child and Adolescent Psychiatry, 27,* 371–376.

Ryan, N. D., Puig-Antich, J., Ambrosini, P., Rabinovich, H., Robinson, D., Nelson, B., Iyengar, S., & Twomey, J. (1987). The clinical picture of major depression in children and adolescents. *Archives of General Psychiatry, 44,* 854–861.

Ryan, N. D., Puig-Antich, J., Cooper, T., Ambrosini, P., Rabinovich, H., Robinson, D., Nelson, B., Iyengar, S. & Twomey, J. (1986b). Imipramine in adolescent major depression in children and adolescents. *Archives of General Psychiatry, 44,* 854–861.

Ryan, N. D., Puig-Antich, J., Cooper, T., Rabinovich, H., Ambrosini, P., Davies, M., King, J., Torres., & Fried, J. (1986a). Imipramine in adolescent major depression: Plasma level and clinical response. *Acta Psychiatrica Scandinavica, 73,* 275–288.

Ryan, N. D., Puig-Antich, J., Rabinovich, H., Fried, J. Ambrosini, P., Meyer, V., Torres, D., Dachille, S., & Mazzie, D. (1988b). MAOIs in adolescent depression unresponsive to tricyclic antidepressants. *Journal of the American Academy of Child and Adolescent Psychiatry, 27,* 755–758.

Sachar, E. J., Finkelstein, J., & Hellman, L. (1971). Growth hormone response in depressive illness. I. Response to insulin tolerance test. *Archives of General Psychiatry, 25,* 263–269.

Saraf, K. R., Klein, D. F., Gittelman-Klein, R., & Groff, S. (1974). Imipramine side effects in children. *Psychopharmacologia, 37*(3), 265–274.

Schoenbach, V. J., Kaplan, B. H., Wagner, E. H., Grimson, R. C., & Miller, F. T. (1983). Prevalence of self-reported depressive symptoms in young adolescents. *American Journal of Public Health, 73,* 1281–1287.

Schulberg, H. C., Scott, C. P., Madonia, M. J., & Imber, S. D. (1993). Applications of interpersonal psychotherapy to depression in primary care practice. In G. L Klerman & M. M. Weissman (Eds.), *New Applications of Interpersonal Psychotherapy* (pp. 283–310). Washington, DC: American Psychiatric Press.

Schwartzberg, A. Z. (1981). *Divorce And Children.* Chicago: University of Chicago Press.

Seligman, M., & Maier, S. (1967). Failure to escape traumatic shock. *Journal of Experimental Psychology, 74,* 1–9.

Shaffer, D. (1988). The epidemiology of teen suicide: An examination of risk factors. *Journal of Clinical Psychiatry, 49*(Suppl. 9), 36–41.

Siegel, L., & Griffin, N. J. (1984). Correlates of depressive symptoms in adolescents. *Journal of Youth and Adolescence, 13*(6), 475–487.

Simeon, J. G. (1989). Depressive disorders in children and adolescents. *Psychiatry Journal of the University of Ottawa, 14*(2), 356–361.

Simeon, J. G., Dinicola, V. F., Ferguson, B. H., & Copping, W. (1990). Adolescent depression: A placebo-controlled fluoxetine study and follow-up. *Progress in Neuro-Psychopharmacology and Biological Psychiatry, 14*, 791–795.

Sklar, F., & Hartley, S. F. (1990). Close friends as survivors: Bereavement patterns in a "hidden population." *Omega, 21*(2), 103–112.

Sloane, R. B., Stapes, F. R., & Schneider, L. S. (1985). Interpersonal therapy versus nortriptyline for depression in the elderly. In G. D. Burrows, T. R. Norman, & L. Dennerstein (Eds.), *Clinical and Pharmacological Studies in Psychiatric Disorders* (pp. 344–346). London: John Libbey.

Smollar, J, & Youniss, J. (1985). Parent–adolescent relationship in adolescents whose parents are divorced. *Journal of Early Adolescence, 5*(1), 129–144.

Southard, M. J., & Gross, B. H. (1982). Making clinical decisions after *Tarasoff. New Directions for Mental Health Services, 16*, 93–101.

Spanier, G. B. (1976). Measuring dyadic adjustment: New scales for assessing the quality of marriage and similar dyads. *Journal of Marriage and Family Living, 38*, 15–25.

Spitzer, T., Endicott, J., & Robins, F. (1978). Research diagnostic criteria: Rationale and reliability. *Archives of General Psychiatry, 35*, 773–782.

Strober, M. (1985). Depressive illness in adolescence. *Psychiatric Annals, 15*(6), 375–378.

Strober, M., Freeman, R., & Rigali, J. (1990). The pharmacotherapy of depressive illness in adolescence: I. An open label trial of imipramine. *Psychopharmocology Bulletin, 26*(1), 80–84.

Strober, M., Green, J., & Carlson, G. (1981). Utility of the Beck Depression Inventory with psychiatrically hospitalized adolescents. *Journal of Consulting and Clinical Psychiatry, 49*(3), 482–483.

Sullivan, H. S. (1953). *The Interpersonal Theory of Psychiatry.* New York: W. W. Norton.

Sullivan, W. O., & Engin, A. W. (1986). Adolescent depression: Its prevalence in high school students. *Journal of School Psychology, 24*, 103–109.

Swift, W. J., Andrews, D., & Barklage, N. E. (1986). The relationship between addiction disorder and eating disorder: A review of the literature. *American Journal of Psychiatry, 143*(3), 290–299.

Targum, S. D., Clarkson, L. L., Magac-Harris, K., Marshal, L. E., & Skewerer, R. G. (1990). Measurement of cortisol and lymphocyte subpopulations in depressed and conduct disordered adolescents. *Journal of Affective Disorders, 18*, 91–96.

Teri, L. (1982a). The use of the Beck Depression Inventory with adolescents. *Journal of Abnormal Child Psychology, 10*(2), 277–284.

Teri, L. (1982b). Depression in adolescence: Its relationship to assertion and various aspects of self-image. *Journal of Clinical Child Psychology, 11*(2), 101–106.

Torgerson, S. (1986). Genetic factors in moderately severe and mild affective disorder. *Archives of General Psychiatry, 43,* 222–226.

Velez, C., & Cohen, P. (1988). Suicidal behavior and ideation in a community sample of children: Maternal and youth reports. *Journal of the American Academy of Child and Adolescent Psychiatry, 27,* 349–356.

Vogel, G. W., Vogel, F., McAbeen, R. S., & Thurmond, A. J. (1980). Improvement of depression by REM sleep deprivation: New findings and a theory. *Archives of General Psychiatry, 37,* 247–253.

Walker, M., Moreau, D., & Weissman, M. M. (1989). Parents' awareness of children's suicide attempts. *American Journal of Psychiatry, 147*(190), 1364–1366.

Wallerstein, J. S. (1983). Children of divorce. In N. Garmezy & M. Rutter (Eds.), *Stress, Coping, and Development in Children* (pp. 265–302). New York: McGraw-Hill.

Wallerstein, J. S., & Kelly, J. B. (1980). Effects of divorce on the visiting father–child relationship. *American Journal of Psychiatry, 137*(12), 1534–1539.

Weinberg, W. A., & Emslie, G. J. (1988). Weinberg Screening Affective Scales (WSAS and WSAS-SF). *Journal of Child Neurology, 3*(4), 294–296.

Weissman, M. M. (1987). Advances in psychiatric epidemiology: Rates and risks for major depression. *American Journal of Public Health, 77,* 445–451.

Weissman, M. M., Gammon, D., John, K., Merikangas, K. R., Warner, V., Prusoff, B. A., & Sholomskas, D. (1987a). Children of depressed parents: Increased psychopathology and early onset of major depression. *Archives of General Psychiatry, 44,* 847–853.

Weissman, M. M., Jarrett, R. B., & Rush, A. J. (1987b). Psychotherapy and its relevance to the pharmacotherapy of major depression: A decade later (1976–1985). In H. Meltzer (Ed.), *Psychopharmacology: The Third Generation of Progress* (pp. 1059–1070). New York: Raven Press.

Weissman, M. M., & Klerman, G. L. (1988). *Interpersonal Counseling (IPC) for Stress and Distress in Primary Care Settings.* New York: College of Physicians & Surgeons, Columbia University, and Cornell Medical School.

Weissman, M. M., Klerman, G. L., Paykel, E. S., Prusoff, B., & Hanson, B. (1974). Treatment effects on the social adjustment of depressed patients. *Archives of General Psychiatry, 30,* 771–778.

Weissman, M. M., Klerman, G. L., Prusoff, B. A., Shlomoskas, D., & Padian, N. (1981). Depressed outpatients: Results one year after treatment with drugs and/or interpersonal psychotherapy. *Archives of General Psychiatry, 38,* 52–55.

Weissman, M. M., Leckman, J. F., Merikangas, K. R., Gammon, D., & Prusoff, B. A. (1984a). Depression and anxiety disorders in parents and children. *Archives of General Psychiatry, 41,* 845–851.

Weissman, M. M., Prusoff, B. A., DiMascio, A., Neu, C., Goklaney, M., & Klerman, G. L. (1979). The efficacy of drugs and psychotherapy in the treatment of acute depressive episodes. *American Journal of Psychiatry, 136,* 555–558.

Weissman, M. M., Prusoff, B. A., Gammon, G. D., Merikangas, K. R., Leckman, J. F., & Kidd, K. K. (1984b). Psychopathology in the children (ages 6–18) of depressed and normal parents. *Journal of the American Academy of Child and Adolescent Psychiatry, 23,* 78–84.

Weissman, M. M., Rounsaville, B. J., & Chevron, E. S. (1982). Training psychotherapists to participate in psychotherapy outcome studies: Identifying and dealing with the research requirement. *American Journal of Psychiatry, 139,* 1442–1446.

Weissman, M. M., Warner, V., Wickramaratne, P., & Prusoff, B. A. (1988). Early onset major depression in parents and their children. *Journal of Affective Disorders, 15*(3), 269–278.

Weissman, M. M., Wickramaratne, P., Warner, V., John, K., Prusoff, B. A., Merikangas, K. R., & Gammon, G. D. (1987c). Assessing psychiatric disorders in children: Discrepancies between mothers' and children's reports. *Archives of General Psychiatry, 44,* 747–753.

Wells, V. E., Deykin, E. Y., & Klerman G. L. (1985). Risk factors for depression in adolescence. *Psychiatric Development, 3,* 83–108.

Wells, V., Klerman, G. L., & Deykin, E. Y. (1987). The prevalence of depressive symptoms in college students. *Social Psychology, 22,* 20–28.

Welner, A., Welner, Z., & Fishman, R. (1979). Psychiatric adolescent inpatients: Eight- to ten-year follow-up. *Archives of General Psychiatry, 36*(6), 698–700.

Wilkes, T. C. R., & Rush, A. J. (1988). Adaptations of cognitive therapy for depressed adolescents. *Journal of the American Academy of Child and Adolescent Psychiatry, 27*(33), 381–386.

Index

Acting out behavior, 73, 88, 95, 105
Adaptation, to environment, 4
Adolescence
    grief in, 90–100
    late, 30, 33
    pregnancy in, 178
    primary task of, 128
    psychiatric illness in, 21
    psychosocial problems in, 26, 27
    role transitions in, 115–117
    sexuality in, 168, 169
    significant relationships in, 101
    vulnerabilities in, 45
Adolescent depression, 20, 23–25, 64,
        193
    differences from adult depression, 25,
        26
    and family relationships, 29, 30, 35;
        see also Families
    longitudinal studies of, 34
    periodic nature of, 26, 34
    pharmacotherapy for, 36–40, 183–187
    psychosocial treatment for, 40–47
    recurrence of, 155, 157
    risk factors for, 28–31, 35
    suicidal feelings in, 23, 25, 27, 30, 88;
        see also Suicidal feelings
    treatment rate for, 47
Adolescent turmoil, 20, 21
Affective disorders, 21, 30; see also De-
        pression
Age
    and comorbidity, 33
    of depression onset, 30, 33

    as risk factor, 28, 32
AIDS, 16
Alienation, parent–child, 21
Amitriptyline, 10, 11, 37–39
Anger, 86, 109, 110, 113
    diffusing, 164
    and loss, 91, 21
    as symptom, 54
Anniversary reaction, 93; see also Grief
Antianxiety agents, 183, 184
Antidepressants, 5, 36–40, 183–187
    administration of, 184, 185
    in adolescents, 25, 36–40, 182, 185
    augmented with lithium carbonate,
        39
    decision to treat with, 182, 183
    dosage, 185
    overdose, 185, 186
    serotonergic, 183
    side effects, 185
    trials of, 37–39
    tricyclic, 36–39, 182, 183, 185
    withdrawal/tapering off from, 186
Antisocial behavior, 33, 105, 179
Anxiety, 14, 33, 91, 121, 122
Assaultive behavior, 163, 164
Assessment methods, 52–57; see also
        Symptom review
    discrepancies in, 53, 54
Attachment bonds, 4, 8
Attachment theory, 29
Attention deficit disorder, 33
Attribution style, 42
Autonomy/independence, 8